The Politics of Envy

Anne Hendershott

THE
POLITICS
of
ENVY

CRISIS
PUBLICATIONS

Manchester, New Hampshire

Crisis Publications
Box 5284, Manchester, NH 03108
1-800-888-9344

www.CrisisMagazine.com

Paperback ISBN 978-1-64413-223-4
eBook ISBN 978-1-64413-224-1
Library of Congress Control Number: 2020943128

First printing

Contents

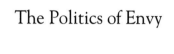

The Politics of Envy

Introduction

One of the seven deadly sins, envy is a painful reminder that people we know are enjoying something that we are not. Sometimes we hate them for the pleasure they seem to be getting from that something. Other times we may not even want what they have, but we know that we don't want them to have it. In its most virulent form, envy is characterized by a desire to take away the coveted object or advantage from the other—even when depriving them means losing something ourselves. For the truly resentful, it is a small price to pay. In his short treatise, *Envy*, Joseph Epstein writes that "of the deadly sins, only envy is no fun at all." Most of us refuse to acknowledge our envy—even to ourselves.[1]

In some ways, envy is the worst of the deadly sins because it leads to so many of the others. Greed begins with envy and wanting more, and envy plays an important role in lustful longings and gluttonous urges. The envious want the unattainable—and they want it all. The resentment that accompanies envy often erupts in anger and resentful rage; and it is inextricably intertwined with pride. Often called the "sin of sins," the sin of pride is—like the sin

[1] Joseph Epstein, *Envy* (New York: Oxford University Press, 2003), 1.

The Politics of Envy

of envy — a narcissistic preoccupation with self. The truly envious are the truly prideful who believe that no one is more deserving of advantages and rewards than they. Saint Augustine of Hippo (354–430) wrote that "pride is the commencement of all sin because it was this which overthrew the devil, from whom arose the origin of sin; and afterwards, when his malice and envy pursued man, it subverted him in the same way in which he fell ... when he said 'Ye shall be as gods.' "[2]

Envy derives from the Latin *invidia*, which means "non sight." This etymology suggests that envy arises from, and creates, a form of blindness or lack of perspective. In *Purgatorio*, Dante Alighieri had the envious punished by having to wear penitential gray cloaks, their eyes sewn shut with iron wire because the truly envious are blind to the goodness, truth, and beauty around them — warning that the envious are blind to reason and love, spending their days tormented by resentment toward those who possess that which they covet. It is an enforced blindness, so that the once-envious souls can no longer look at others with envy and hatred. Still, they can hear those who are envied. Dante spoke of Florence, placed in the second terrace of Hell, in *Inferno* 6, as a city so filled with envy that it overflowed, warning, "Your city, so stuffed full with envy that the sack's mouth spews it up, once held me in the calm and sunlit life."[3] Comparing those who envy to dogs turned into wolves, Dante wrote that the savage nature of the envious can be tamed only through blindness, and once

---

2   Philip Schaff, ed., *A Select Library of the Nicene and Post-Nicene Fathers of the Christian Church*, vol. 5, *St. Augustine: Anti-Pelagian Writings* (New York: Christian Literature Company, 1887), chap. 33.

3   Dante Alighieri, *Inferno*, trans. Anthony Esolen, canto 6:49 (New York: Random House, 1996), 59.

4

humbled, the afflicted finally learn to rely on each other in their suffering.[4] Envy is proscribed in the Ten Commandments as a warning against covetousness. In the book of Wisdom, we are told that it is "through the devil's envy death entered the world" (Wisd. 2:24). In Genesis, envy is portrayed as a destroyer of happiness and contentment. From the story of Eve's envious desire to have the wisdom of God, to the story of Joseph and his envious brothers, we see the destruction of lives through envious acts. John Milton's *Paradise Lost* (1668) presents envy as the serpent in the garden. Consumed with envy toward the Son of God and His creation, Milton's Satan experienced God's love itself as envy. Envious of the awesome power of the Creator, the sight of the Garden and the happiness and love of God's creation fills the devil with hateful envy—and a desire to destroy that creation. In his envious rage, Satan begins to believe that God created all of that in order to inspire envy. It was Satan's envy—his hatred for the good, the true, and the beautiful, that moved him to corrupt Adam's and Eve's love for God and for each other. We are often taught that it was Eve's pride—her wish to be as wise as God—that was the original sin. Yet in book 9 of *Paradise Lost*, Milton reminds us that it was Satan's envy of "this new Favorite of Heaven, this Man of Clay, Son of despite, Whom us the more to spite his Maker rais'd from dust: spite then with spite is best repaid." It was envy that set off a battle in which "spite then with spite is best repaid."[5] It was Satan's envy of the love that God had for His new creation, and that Adam and Eve had for each

4 Dante Alighieri, *Purgatorio* 13:2–3, Digital Dante, https://digitaldante.columbia.edu/dante/divine-comedy/purgatorio/purgatorio-13/.
5 John Milton, *Paradise Lost*, bk. 9, John Milton Reading Room, https://www.dartmouth.edu/~milton/reading_room/pl/book_9/text.shtml.

other that led him to destroy the innocence in the Garden—an envy that was predicted as Adam sadly admits: "that malicious foe, envying our happiness, and of his own despairing, seeks to work our woe and shame by sly assault." Motivated also by envy, the resentful Cain, the son of Adam, was driven to murder Able, his more favored brother, because he became convinced that his brother's sacrifices were more pleasing to God. Cursing God and his brother, Cain lashed out at the source of his envy.

The following chapters will demonstrate that there is much to learn from Dante's warnings. Though most will try to avoid the life-killing envy that has plagued the poor souls in Dante's *Purgatorio*, all must acknowledge having experienced envy. It is part of our human nature to envy and to be envied. In fact, some social scientists suggest that social forces could not operate without envy because the fear of arousing envy acts as a force for social control. The earliest sociologists—including Émile Durkheim (1858–1917)—suggested that envy helps us keep our behavior in check. In his *Envy: A Theory of Social Behaviour*, Helmut Schoeck (1922–1993) suggests that envy "lies at the core of man's life as a social being ... an urge to compare oneself invidiously with others." Like Durkheim, Schoeck maintains that the awareness of the potential envy of others helps us to keep within certain limits—preventing us from deviating too far from the center of consensus.[6] But this idea of the value of envy is challenged in the following chapters.

Envy continues to inspire the creation of dysfunctional political systems designed to remove privilege and honor from the few—disbursing it to the many. Marxism, the pernicious theory that still motivates many within academia and beyond, is based

6   Helmut Schoeck, *Envy: A Theory of Social Behavior* (Indianapolis: Liberty Fund, 1966), 3.

entirely on envy. The Marxist promise of "fairness" to the proletariat was a promise of a utopian world in which all conditions that produce envy will disappear. The Marxist assures us that an egalitarian world would remove all targets of envy so that the envious will have nothing to envy. But, as the following pages will demonstrate, envy creates its own targets, regardless of how equal people may appear to be. In the aftermath of the revolutions to overthrow capitalist systems — whether in Cuba or Nicaragua or Venezuela — the spoils are never evenly divided. In the final days of the Nicaraguan Revolution in 1979, when the Sandinistas marched into Managua, the first thing the revolutionary leaders did was to grab for themselves the luxurious homes left behind by the Somoza regime.

The fact that throughout history there has never been a socialist society that brought about the promised utopian classless conditions is dismissed by today's "democratic socialists." The new socialists claim that such examples of the failure of socialism have not gone far enough in redistributing the wealth equally. In 2019, as Venezuela's socialist regime collapsed amid the starvation of the people in the once-rich nation, the apologists for socialism blamed corruption, cronyism, populism, authoritarianism, and even the corrupt capitalism of the United States and its punitive sanctions on the oil-rich country. In a fawning obituary published in 2013 for Hugo Chavez, the Venezuelan dictator-president, Greg Grandin of the *Nation* wrote that "the biggest problem Venezuela faced during his rule was not that Chavez was authoritarian, but that he wasn't authoritarian enough. It wasn't too much control that was the problem but too little."[7]

---

[7] Greg Grandin, "On the Legacy of Hugo Chavez," *Nation* (March 6, 2013), https://www.thenation.com/article/archive/legacy-hugo-chavez/.

The Politics of Envy

The writers for the *Nation* know, as Marx predicted, that even after the overthrow of the capitalist system in Venezuela and elsewhere, a dictatorship of the proletariat is necessary to tamp down envy, as residues of capitalist thought and envious desires would permeate the new socialist society in the early days. There was always the danger that self-interest, personal gain, and an envious desire for ownership of property could still seep into the socialist system. Therefore, under new socialist systems—including the democratic socialist system proposed here in the United States by some of the Democratic Party candidates for president in the 2020 presidential primary—a revolutionary vanguard of dedicated socialists would usher in the bright future of the new economic order. What Marx called the dictatorship of the proletariat would be appointed to re-educate and monitor how the masses would think, act, and associate in the new socialist order. The dictatorship of the political elite is necessary to suppress any attempt even to speak of the private property of the past. These political elites would be charged with indoctrinating the masses to accept that true freedom and happiness involve ensuring that there is nothing left to envy.

Even in a socialist system, there will always be something to envy. History has shown that envy increases in communist countries because the stakes become so small that even the slightest advantages are envied. No one understood that better than Russian philosopher and historian Aleksandr Solzhenitsyn, a longtime political prisoner in the gulags of the Soviet Union, who wrote, "Our envy of others devours us most of all." In *The Gulag Archipelago*, Solzhenitsyn described the malign envy among those in the dehumanizing conditions of the work camp when "the quantity of bread issued is such that one or two people have to die for each who survives.... Your mind is absorbed in vain calculations.... You are reduced to a frazzle by intense envy and alarm lest somewhere behind your back, others are right now dividing up the bread which could be yours, that somewhere on the other side of that wall, a tiny potato is being ladled out of the pot which could have ended up in your own bowl."[8] Solzhenitsyn knew that even in a society in which all rewards are routinized and scrupulously administered to ensure equality there are still going to be those with more—and those who can acquire more through violence.

As the following chapters will demonstrate, there are deadly consequences when the sin of envy is unchecked. René Girard, a twentieth-century theorist and disciple of Sigmund Freud, argued that envy or what he called "mimetic desire," is the major driver of all violence.[9] For Girard, all social discord originates in mimetic rivalries—competitions in which the envied object becomes secondary to the rivalry itself. In *Not in God's Name: Confronting Religious Violence*, Jonathan Sacks, the former chief rabbi of the United Kingdom, draws from Girard's theory of mimetic desire and argues that envy lies at the root of present-day religious violence and ethnic extremism.[10] We have seen envy as a contributor to the World War II genocide of European Jewry in the Holocaust, and in the Rwandan genocide, when more than one million Tutsi were slaughtered during the Rwandan Civil War of 1994.

There are no easy ways to correct the violent culture of envy. Religion once stood as a check on our envy, but with the declines in organized religion, envy has been allowed to grow, creating a

---

8   Aleksandr Solzhenitsyn, *The Gulag Archipelago: An Experiment in Literary Investigation* (New York: Harper Perennial Modern Classics, 2007), 315.

9   René Girard, *Violence and the Sacred* (Baltimore: Johns Hopkins University Press, 1972).

10 Jonathan Sacks, *Not in God's Name: Confronting Religious Violence* (New York: Knopf, 2017).

The Politics of Envy

kind of anti-religion of its own. The following pages will show that envy can be controlled but it can never be eradicated because envious desire is a universal phenomenon—a part of the human condition—and potentially, the most destructive emotion of all.

1

The Origins of Envy

Although faithful Christians maintain that it is our fallen nature that leads us to the sin of envy, one of the basic tenets of contemporary sociology is that emotions such as envy and jealousy are socially constructed. According to most sociologists, emotions are created and constantly reshaped by the beliefs, attitudes, and values that individuals acquire in the course of their socialization. We learn what to feel and how to feel through our interactions with our families, our peers, our schools, our churches, our politics, and most importantly, the media. This is not to diminish the role that faith traditions and biblical warnings about envy play in the socialization process, but as San Diego State University sociology professor Gordon Clanton suggests:

> Private experiences of emotion are embedded in history, culture, and social structure. Not only our feelings, but also our feelings about our feelings are shaped by psychological, philosophical, and theological frameworks that are institutionalized in social life. Thus, patterns of emotional experience change in response to changes in society and culture.[11]

---

[11] Gordon Clanton, "Jealousy and Envy" in *Handbook of the Sociology of Emotions*, ed. Jan Stets and Jonathan H. Turner (New York: Springer Science Media, 2007), 410.

The Politics of Envy

"Envy" and "jealousy" are often used interchangeably—even by social scientists—so it is sometimes difficult to discern the differences even in social science research. But there is a difference. Envy is hostility or a negative feeling toward someone who has an advantage or something that one does not have and cannot seem to acquire. Jealousy, on the other hand, typically involves an attempt to protect a valued relationship (especially marriage) from a perceived threat (especially adultery). In some ways, jealousy can be a useful emotion—it is the desire to hold on to a loved one—especially when one feels the relationship may be threatened by outside forces. Feelings of jealousy can be a "natural" sign that a loving relationship is vulnerable to attack from the outside. In the *Nicomachean Ethics*, Aristotle (384–322 B.C.) says, "Jealousy is both reasonable and belongs to reasonable men, while envy is base and belongs to the base, for the one makes himself get good things by jealousy, while the other does not allow his neighbor to have them through envy."

Most sociologists point to the fact that levels of envy vary by gender, age, ethnicity, and social class as evidence that envy is socially constructed. According to a University of California–San Diego study published in the journal *Basic and Applied Social Psychology*, more than three-fourths of the nine hundred participants reported experiencing envy during the year previous to the study, with slightly more women (79.4 percent) than men (74.1 percent) reporting having felt envious of another. Of those who reported envy, the vast majority of men (86.2 percent) and women (85.6 percent) reported envying a person of the same gender. There was no research support for the idea that women particularly envy the privileges of men: "Overwhelmingly, people envied others of their own gender. . . . Men envied other men, and women, women. Even in domains like financial and occupational success, where you can imagine that a woman might envy a man his better pay or status, that wasn't usually the case."[12] Forty-one percent of all men admit to envying occupational success, while only 24.5 percent of women envy such success. In contrast, women (23.8 percent) are much more likely than men (13.5 percent) to envy physical attractiveness.

Envy is most likely to be felt when comparisons are made in domains that are especially important to how we define ourselves. Beautiful women are envious of other (more) beautiful women. Successful men are envious of other (more) successful men. We truly care about our performance in a limited number of life domains and therefore are envious only when comparing ourselves in a domain that is especially important to us. For example, writers envy other writers who are more talented and get more lucrative publishing contracts. Business executives envy other executives who have attained higher positions than they; actors envy actors who get the role they think they should have gotten. Studies show that married women envy other women who have husbands who are richer than theirs—just as men envy other men who have wives who are more beautiful than theirs.

Envy also varies by age. While 40 percent of participants in the San Diego study who were under thirty years old said they envied others for their success in romance, fewer than 15 percent of those over fifty claimed such envious feelings. Overall, young people reported more frequently feeling envious over physical attractiveness or romance as well as achievements at school and social success. In contrast, older people—especially men in their forties and fifties—envy monetary success and occupational success in others.

The nature of the relationship between the envier and the envied person differs by gender and age. In older adults, envy was

<hr>

[12]   Inga Kiderra, "Who's the Enviest of Them All?" *UC San Diego News Center*, November 4, 2015, https://ucsdnews.ucsd.edu/pressrelease/whos_the_enviest_of_them_all.

a source of anger toward friends but rarely toward close relatives. But, in younger adults, envy occurred most strongly toward siblings. This is understandable, as they vie for parental favor. Across the life span, envy appears to occur more frequently in friendships than in family relationships. In the limited number of previous studies of envy that have assessed relationship closeness, the results are mixed. One hypothesis is that people respond with envy toward distant successful people, and with pride toward close successful people. However, a rival hypothesis is that "closeness functions like similarity — any increase in relatedness with a person who is superior in a self-relevant domain may create a greater threat to self-evaluation."[13] This would predict that most of the envious responses would occur in close relationships, often within familial relationships.

Additional support for the social constructionist view of the origin of envy can be found in the dramatic cross-cultural differences in levels of envy. In simple societies, the fear of envy is very high. Tribal people believe that they will be envied by their neighbors for any advantage they may gain, and they are likely to believe that the hostile wishes of their neighbors can harm them, bring bad health to their families, and cause their gardens to wither and their goats to die. Compliments are largely absent in tribal and peasant societies.[14] In industrialized societies, such as the United States, fear of envy is low. We are much less likely to refuse an opportunity in order to prevent the envy of others. Russia is well known for having a "culture of envy" that continues even

[13] Nicole E. Henniger and Christine R. Harris, "Envy across Adulthood: The What and the Who," *Basic and Applied Social Psychology* 37, no. 6 (2015): 1–16, https://www.researchgate.net/publication/283619161_ Envy_Across_Adulthood_The_What_and_the_Who/link /564617ca08ae54697fb9d377/download.

[14] Clanton, "Jealousy and Envy," 428.

today. Compared with other industrial societies, Russia is often described as a "high envy" society. Clanton cites the journalist Hedrick Smith, reporting from the Soviet Union during its last days: "In this culture, corrosive animosity took root under the czars in the deep-seated collectivism in Russian life and then was cultivated by Leninist ideology. Now it has turned rancid under the misery of everyday living."[15]

Clanton cites a number of sociological researchers who have noted the "pervasive emotional violence of Russian society, characterized by anger, self-hatred, and emotional overloading akin to posttraumatic stress syndrome." Most believe that envy in Russian society today was exacerbated by the market reforms introduced by Mikhail Gorbachev. The envy of the rank and file is aimed at anyone who rises above the crowd, anyone who gets ahead, even if the gains are honestly earned. As one journalist writes: "In America it is a sin to be a loser, but if there's one sin in Soviet society, it's being a winner."[16] This affects all Russians—including children and teenagers. An internationally known Russian model disclosed that more than a decade earlier, when she won a modeling competition in her country, and the prize was a modeling contract to work in the United States, she was immediately shunned in her high school and beyond. She recalled that even her teachers treated her with disdain. Her parents were shunned also. They still suffer from the envy of their neighbors today, nearly a decade after their daughter was chosen, even as she continues to achieve success in the United States. Despite the fact—or more likely, because of the fact—that she has achieved international fame, she is never acknowledged by her extended family of grandparents or aunts, uncles, and cousins in Russia

[15] Ibid., 436.
[16] Ibid., 437.

as having achieved any success at all when she returns home to Moscow to visit her parents. She no longer sees old friends or even most relatives when she returns home, and she says they are "not happy" for her.[17]

The "historical roots" of Russian envy culture run deep. Russia was among the last European nations to industrialize, so many lived in rural peasant communities throughout much of the twentieth century. And, since medieval times, Russian peasants lived in a world of collective rather than private enterprise. In the 1400s, the Tatar conquest resulted in the establishment of a bureaucracy to collect taxes and supervise the drafting of Russian recruits. The Tatars deputized a Muscovite grand duke to administer the payment of tribute — what Clanton suggests was "an important step in making Moscow a central and dominating power." When the Tatars were defeated in 1522, the czars turned the system to their own purposes, while strengthening it with the addition of a secret-police apparatus. In czarist times, most lived in small clusters of homes, close to one another, not in single homesteads scattered independently across the plains. After serfdom was abolished in 1861, peasants banded together and worked the land together. In 1917, communism forced further collectivization and taught that individual profit was immoral. The communist rulers used terror toward opponents of the regime. In 1990, Gorbachev warned that the culture of envy would "snuff out initiative, deter new entrepreneurs, and cripple the hopes of real economic progress." By the time of the fall of the Soviet Union in 1991, the Russian people had lived under increasingly despotic bureaucratic regimes for more than seven hundred years. All of this contributed to the culture of envy that remains in Russia today.

---

[17] Personal communication with the author in 2017.

The Evolutionary Origins of Envy

While social constructionist theory offers the best explanation of the current culture of envy in Russia, it cannot really explain the true origins of the emotion of envy. Today, there is an increasing interest in attempting to understand the evolution of these emotions. In the 1990s, sociologists began to explore the role of evolution in emotion, but only insofar as "evolution sets the stage at the beginning of the play and moves off stage once the play is in motion."[18] There was a belief that evolution sparked the envy, but then historical, cultural, and social factors become central. Still, sociologists Michael Hammond and Jonathan Turner have argued that it is important to understand the evolutionary origin of emotions and to recognize how the early development of emotions continue to impact social change throughout history.[19] In a chapter in Jan Stets and Jonathan H. Turner's *Handbook of the Sociology of Emotions*, Hammond writes that it is our evolutionary past that sets the stage for the social construction of emotions such as envy. Emotions serve as a bridge between motivational systems based on hardwired instructions for social behavior to systems based on learning and flexibility. Hammond suggests that "We did not evolve from instinctually driven beings to rational cognitive beings. We evolved into emotional beings with amazing cognitive capacities, but nonetheless, our deep sociality is emotional at the core.... We may be rational in our pursuit of certain goals or values, but those

[18] Michael Hammond, "Evolutionary Theory and Emotions," in *Handbook of the Sociology of Emotions*, ed. Jan E. Stets and Jonathan H. Turner (New York: Springer, 2007), 368.

[19] Michael Hammond, "The Enhancement Imperative: The Evolutionary Neurophysiology of Durkheimian Solidarity," *Sociological Theory* 21, no. 4 (2003): 359–374; Jonathan H. Turner, *On the Origins of Human Emotions* (Stanford, CA: Stanford University Press, 2000).

ends only have an impact because of the emotional release associated with them."[20] Hammond notes that Darwin began the investigation into the relationship between emotions and evolution with *The Expression of Emotions in Man and Animals* in 1872. Unlike most of Darwin's other work, however, the study of the origins of emotions such as envy lay dormant for almost a hundred years.[21]

Over the past few decades, the study of the evolution of emotions such as anger, resentment, jealousy, and envy has achieved greater prominence. Sociologist Jonathan Turner argues that the evolution of emotions led to a situation in which we have two competing sets of emotionally loaded activity patterns rooted in our context of origin, and these competing sets of patterns are still shaping behavior today. Working within his acceptance of the framework of Darwinian evolution, Hammond suggests: "Reflecting our general origins among the great apes and our own specific context or origin, we are a compromise species, craving strong emotional attachments and, at the same time, bridling against the constraints in closed social circles laid out by these strong interpersonal ties." For Turner, "this two-sidedness is rooted deeply in our biology and it is not just the product of historically specific ideologies and social structures." Turner argues that "it is illusory to try to detach human biology from the modern sociocultural world because our world is made possible by our hominoid neuroanatomy and is constrained by this biological legacy."[22] What neurologically differentiates humans from the great apes, according to Hammond, was a key adaptation to "rewire" the hominid brain to make emotions increasingly central to social life. With such a rewiring, humans could form stronger bonds than the more loose-knit bonds of apes and, with such bonds, could increase the complexity of social organization. As

[20] Hammond, "Evolutionary Theory and Emotions," 369.
[21] Ibid., 368.
[22] Ibid., 371.

evidence of this "rewiring," Hammond points to data on changes in the relative size of parts of the brain related to cognition and emotion in apes and humans when adjusted for general body size. The neocortex shows the greatest change in the evolution of humans, but there are also striking changes in the subcortical areas tied to emotion. For humans, the subcortical areas are at least two times as large as those in apes. The result was a species with the tools to solve some of the social organization problems inherent in our origin as a low-sociality primate. Such an adaptation was necessary for us to develop a moral code. There can be no morality without emotion. As Hammond writes: "Adherence to moral codes and support for sanctions against breaking those codes are directly related to the emotional weight of these codes. This impact involves both positive and negative emotions [such as envy] and mixes of the two. Without a brain tuned to complex and subtle emotions, moral codes rooted in emotions could not approach the complexity of social organization required by humans in even the smallest populations."[23] Regardless of one's stance on Darwinian evolutionary biology, it is useful to note the relationship between humanity's neurological development and emotions and its subsequent impact on social life.

Some sociologists even go so far as to maintain that evolution and emotions played an important role in the emergence of religion—arguing that the attraction we have to religion is emotional. From this perspective, we are drawn to religion because it provides an emotionally satisfying "arousal release," or what Hammond calls a "common arouser package," which draws individuals to a larger social group, expanding the network of trustworthy exchanges.[24]

[23] Ibid., 371.
[24] Michael Hammond, "The Enhancement Imperative and Group Dynamics in the Emergence of Religion and Ascriptive Inequality" in *Advances in Group Processes* 21 (July 2004): 167–188.

The Politics of Envy

Much of our history involves an increasing tension between our biological heritage and our social constructions. Most evolutionary theorists maintain that pride, guilt, envy, embarrassment, and love are all examples of emotions that have evolved uniquely in humans or at a minimum have uniquely human design features.[25]

One area that has received additional attention from evolutionary psychologists is the role that envy may play in providing a "necessary alert" to individuals being outperformed in areas related to survival and successful reproduction. While most sociological analysis has paid little attention to the evolutionary origins of envy, recent research in evolutionary psychology has focused on the role of emotions such as envy in sex differentiation — especially related to male-female mating behavior. Evolutionary psychologists view sex-evolved dispositions as psychological tendencies that have been built in genetically. And, although radical feminists would have us believe that there is no difference between men and women, we must acknowledge that environmental and reproductive demands can create sex-typed responses. Younger women were particularly likely to envy and be envied for their physical attractiveness, whereas men of all ages were particularly likely to envy and be envied for their occupational success (peaking in envy in their forties). Although these differences are significant, envy in these domains was not exclusive to one gender. Nearly one in four women envied occupational success, and nearly one in five young men envied physical attractiveness in other men.

Much of the research has shown that because differential reproductive success is the engine that drives the process of selection,

[25] Laith Al-Shawaf, Daniel Conroy-Beam, Kelly Asao, and David M. Buss, "Human Emotions: An Evolutionary Psychological Perspective," *Emotion Review* 8, no. 2 (2016): 177.

men and women within their most fruitful reproductive years will most frequently report envying others who possess qualities that increase their desirability to prospective romantic partners.[26] Contemporary research on envy reveals that both men and women tend to envy someone of the same gender and are more likely to envy someone who is approximately their own age. This may be because we have much in common with those we envy—we share the same values, aspirations, and goals. Our closeness allows for recurrent social comparisons—opportunities to understand the advantages of the other. For evolutionary psychologists and sociologists, sex differences are "hardwired." We view those of the same gender as competitors in mating behavior. From an evolutionary perspective, physical attractiveness (an indicator of fertility) is particularly important to men when selecting female mates, whereas a man's status and financial resources are particularly important for attracting women. As a result, women have evolved a specific female innate envy trigger that focuses on other women's looks, whereas men may have evolved a specific male innate envy trigger that focuses on other men's economic resources.[27]

Other researchers dismiss this, claiming that men are no more likely than women to report being envious of someone else's monetary success. In fact, in the youngest age group, 26 percent of men and 30 percent of women envied those with more money than they. This age group is the most likely to be directly involved in competition for mates and therefore would be expected to show the greatest sex difference if the sex-specific innate-trigger hypothesis were correct.[28] The fact that young women are more likely to envy

[26] Danielle J. DelPriore, Sarah E. Hill, and David M. Buss, "Envy, Functional Specificity, and Sex Differentiated Design Features," *Personality and Individual Differences* 53, no. 3 (2012): 317–322.

[27] Ibid.

[28] Henniger and Harris, "Envy across Adulthood."

The Politics of Envy

those with financial resources would still support the evolutionary-psychology perspective in that women would seek out the best providers to ensure survival for their future offspring and would "naturally" choose men who are most able to take care of them and their children. As a result, these women would be most envious of women who appear to have won the competition for the men with most resources.

From an evolutionary perspective, human sex differences reflect the pressure of differing physical and social-environmental demands between females and males in primeval times. As Rochester Institute of Technology psychologist Jennifer Denisiuk writes: "It is believed that each sex faced different pressures and that the differing reproductive status was the key feature in life at that time. This resulted in sex-differentiated behavior. The two sexes developed different strategies to ensure their survival and reproductive success."[29] The emotions of jealousy and envy have always played an important role in mating behavior, and they will continue to play the most important role in the future, no matter how gender neutral we become as a society. Since women invest greatly in the reproduction of offspring, they have developed traits to look for in a mate that help improve the chances that each offspring will survive. That is why women are so very choosy about mates. Men are less choosy about mates, and some attempt to impregnate as many women as possible in order to ensure the continuation of their genetic line.[30] In contrast, women seek mates who have the

[29] Jennifer S. Denisiuk, "Evolutionary Versus Social Structural Explanations for Sex Differences in Mate Preferences, Jealousy, and Aggression," Personality Research Papers (November 2004), http://www.personalityresearch.org/papers/denisiuk.html.
[30] W. Wood and A. H. Eagly, "A Cross-Cultural Analysis of the Behavior of Women and Men: Implications for the Origins of Sex Difference," Psychological Bulletin 128 (2002): 699–727.

resources to support their efforts to give birth and nurture a child; they are strongly motivated to ensure that the children they bear will have the physical and psychological traits necessary to survive and to continue the line. As a result, women prefer intelligent men with high social status and resources to support their offspring. On the other hand, from an evolutionary perspective, men are interested in impregnating a mate in order to have as many offspring as possible. Therefore, men seek young women who are physically fit and attractive because this is an indication that these women will be more likely to give birth to a child successfully. While women focus on the financial resources of a potential mate, men have historically been less concerned about the social status of their chosen mate and more concerned about her physical attractiveness as a sign of health and fecundity.

Although many believe that jealousy and envy are the same emotion, the truth is that jealousy involves an attempt to protect a valued relationship, whereas envy is hostility or a negative feeling toward someone who has an advantage or something that one does not have and cannot seem to acquire. Any quality or achievement that provokes admiration can also provoke envy. Wealth, status, power, fame, success, talent, good health, good grades, good looks, and popularity can all inspire envy.[31] This is not to say that envy is the wish for the object or the advantage that provoked the envy. Rather, envy is, as Gordon Clanton points out, the much darker wish that the person with the object or advantage should lose it. Envy is the pleasure, the malicious joy that is felt when the object of one's envy falls, fails, or suffers.

Many biologists and psychologists see jealousy and envy as "universal instincts" that require the invention of marriage rules — prohibitions against adultery. But sociologists maintain that society

---

[31] Clanton, "Jealousy and Envy," 412.

shapes jealousy and envy—it constructs the emotions—by defining "what constitutes a marriage, what constitutes a threat to marriage, and how to protect a marriage that is threatened by a third party." As Clanton writes: "Sociological analysis reveals that without marriage rules, individuals would not know when to be jealous."[32] According to this claim, it is not jealousy or envy that produces marriage rules; rather, from a sociological perspective, marriage rules create jealousy. From the social-constructionist perspective, jealousy and envy are universal only because every society values marriage and prohibits extramarital sex. These emotions are useful to individuals, couples, and society as a whole because they protect marriage from the betrayal of adultery. Jealousy may preserve social order, but envy can still destroy it.

In contrast to this social-constructionist view, University of Texas psychology professor David Buss maintains that we are "hardwired" to feel emotions of jealousy and envy. Buss points out that there are no cultures in which men are not sexually jealous. In his research, he found that in every supposedly nonjealous culture previously thought to contain no barriers to sexual conduct beyond the incest taboo, evidence for sexual jealousy has been found. The Marquesas Islanders, for example, were once thought to impose no formal or informal prohibitions on adultery. This notion was contradicted by ethnographic reports that stated that "when a woman undertook to live with a man, she placed herself under his authority. If she cohabited with another man without his permission, she was beaten or, if her husband's jealous was sufficiently aroused, killed."[33]

[32] "The New Sexual Revolution: Polyamory on the Rise," NPR, February 18, 2019, https://www.npr.org/2019/02/18/695731314/the-new-sexual-revolution-polyamory-on-the-rise-listen.

[33] David M. Buss, *The Evolution of Desire: Strategies of Human Mating* (New York: Basic Books, 2016), 215.

Beyond the Marquesas Islanders, who are erroneously assumed to be without jealousy, the Inuit culture is famous for its practice of wife sharing—supposedly without jealousy. In many sociology textbooks, undergraduate students are introduced to this culture as an example of the social construction of marriage rules and the absence of jealousy and envy in some cultures. Sociology students learn that wives of Inuit men are thought to be generously shared with strangers and that this practice is not defined as adultery. Therefore, jealousy and envy, both socially constructed emotions, are not present in the Inuit culture. Students are also taught that the Inuit wives who are shared are happy to participate. The reality is, as David Buss writes from an evolutionary perspective: "Contrary to popular myth, male sexual jealousy is the leading cause of spousal homicide among the Inuit, and these homicides occur at an alarmingly high rate. Inuit men share their wives only under highly circumscribed conditions, such as when there is a reciprocal expectation that the favor will be returned in kind.... All of these findings demonstrate that there is no paradise populated with sexually liberated people who share mates freely and do not get jealous."[34]

Even in our own culture, in states such as Texas, the infidelity of a wife was viewed as so extreme a provocation that a husband was legally allowed to kill his wife and her lover if he did so while the adulterers were engaging in the act of intercourse. "Old Roman law granted the husband the right to kill only if the adultery occurred in his own house. Laws exonerating men from killing adulterous wives are found worldwide and throughout human history."[35]

The current trend toward an increasing acceptance of polyamorous relationships may be a futile attempt to change the marriage rules by demanding that couples engaging in polyamorous sexual

[34] Ibid., 215–216.
[35] Ibid., 217.

relationships suspend what is currently viewed as a "socially constructed" emotion of jealousy in order to participate. In an article published in the *Atlantic*, titled "Multiple Lovers, without Jealousy," couples involved in polyamorous relationships were interviewed and claimed that there was "no jealousy" in their open relationships.[36] This is doubtful. Polyamorous relationships are not even a "new phenomenon," as the *Atlantic* might want us to think. As far back as the mid-1880s, the Oneida community practiced a form of Christianity that viewed monogamy as impure. The Oneida taught that God demanded variety in sexual relationships—creating what they called "complex marriage," which called for the continual change of partners. Since there were elaborate prohibitions against procreation, paternity was not an issue. But a society in which members are not allowed to procreate is a society in decline, and the Oneida eventually disbanded after thirty years of complex marriage.

In yet another attempt at ending monogamy by eliminating jealousy and envy, the 1970s ushered in the era of swingers, or those engaging in sexual relationships with multiple partners while married or in a long-term sexual relationship. A subculture with much more permissive marriage rules, swingers did not view sexual exclusiveness as a necessary condition for a happy marriage and purportedly engaged in these open relationships without jealousy. In their 1972 best-selling marriage manual, *Open Marriage: A New Life Style for Couples*, Nena O'Neill and her husband George encouraged couples to strip marriage of its antiquated ideals and romantic tinsel and find ways to make it truly contemporary. Promising a new definition of marriage without jealousy and envy, the book created a scandal but spent more than forty weeks on the *New York*

36 Olga Khazan, "Multiple Lovers, without Jealousy," *Atlantic*, July 21, 2014, https://www.theatlantic.com/health/archive/2014/07/multiple-lovers-no-jealousy/374697/.

Times best-seller list. With statements such as "Sexual fidelity is the false god of closed marriage," the book became a sensation. It was short-lived, though, and by 1977, Nena O'Neill published *The Marriage Premise*, which was described by the *New York Times* as arguing that "fidelity was perhaps not such a bad thing after all."[37]

The truth is that despite the best-selling status of the book on open marriage, swinging was never a popular lifestyle—and there were many marital casualties that accompanied what can be described only as a deviant lifestyle—counter to our biological needs.[38] Helen Fisher, a biological anthropologist whose book *Anatomy of Love: A Natural History of Mating, Marriage and Why We Stray* suggests that open marriages never end up working long-term. The reason for this is biological: "The parts of the brain involved in romantic love are next to areas that help orchestrate thirst and hunger.... Thirst and hunger aren't going to change anytime soon, and neither is the pair-bonding instinct we recognize as romantic love. It evolved so our forebears could focus on one person and begin the mating process." Fisher believes that couples in open marriages are people who "want it all ... to preserve their deep attachment to one partner and have romance with others. They want to be honest about it. But what they don't tell you is that our brains don't do that very well."[39] Fisher understands that romantic attachments

---

[37] Margalit Fox, "Nena O'Neill 82, an Author of Open Marriage, is Dead," *New York Times*, March 26, 2006, https://www.nytimes.com/2006/03/26/books/nena-oneill-82-an-author-of-open-marriage-is-dead.html.

[38] "Swinging Was Great, But Now Hubby Is Jealous," *Sun* (London), July 19, 2013, https://www.thesun.co.uk/archives/news/883924/swinging-was-great-but-now-hubby-is-jealous/.

[39] Dan Savage, "Helen Fisher on Open Marriages," *Stranger*, March 11, 2016, https://www.thestranger.com/slog/2016/03/11/23697459/helen-fisher-on-open-marriages-they-never-end-up-working-long-term.

The Politics of Envy

are "hardwired" and that the norms surrounding marriage cannot be changed as easily as the sexually adventurous swingers might think they can.

In contrast, research on same-sex couples has shown that many of them have indeed successfully negotiated polyamorous relationships. Even couples involved in same-sex "marriages" report multiple partners outside the "marriage." In his popular nationally syndicated advice column, Dan Savage ridicules Helen Fisher's denunciations of open marriages, claiming that he and his partner recently celebrated their twenty-first anniversary and their marriage has been open for seventeen of those years: "We're 1/10 of the way through our third decade together. I'm happy, Terry's happy, and I'd like to think we qualify as a long-term success. Or, hey, maybe Terry and I need Helen Fisher to swing by the house and explain to us how we're really secretly miserable."[40] Or it is likely that, from an evolutionary perspective, gay "marriages" are really something entirely different from heterosexual marriages, with very different marriage rules. Dan Savage calls his same-sex relationship "monogamish."[41] Once the possibility of male-female pair binding and procreation is removed, sexual exclusivity loses its salience. But, for heterosexual marriages among those of childbearing age, it is more difficult to change marriage rules to alleviate jealousy and envy than "changing trends" surrounding polyamorous relationships would suggest. Jealousy and envy have protected heterosexual monogamous relationships throughout history—and in every culture—and any attempts to change those rules dramatically through the "open marriages" of the 1970s, or

[40] Ibid.
[41] Dan Savage, "Dan Savage on Being Monogamish," The Relationship School, June 20, 2018, https://relationshipschool.com/podcast/dan-savage-on-being-monogamish-sc-201/.

28

the polyamorous relationships of today, have failed because people do not feel good about these relationships.

From an evolutionary perspective, bad feelings exist for good reasons. As Randolph Nesse, associate professor of psychiatry at the University of Michigan Medical Center, published in *Human Nature*, "Painful states of mind are not abnormalities themselves, they are parts of evolved defensive patterns.... An evolutionary perspective compels respect for the value of painful feelings. It forces us to acknowledge that many states we might like to see as disorders are not disorders at all, but potentially useful responses to a threat or a loss."[42] From the evolutionary perspective, emotions such as jealousy and envy can be useful. Sometimes we have bad feelings for good reasons.

Envy and a Biblical View of Our Fallen Nature

Rejecting the social-construction theory of the origins of envy, and skeptical of the Darwinian theories of the evolution of envy, many faithful Christians maintain that it is our fallen nature that leads us to the sin of envy. For evidence, they point to the book of Genesis—an account of the devastation that envy leaves in its wake. Beginning with the Fall of Adam and Eve because of their prideful—and envious—desire for the fruit of the tree of the knowledge of good and evil, the first book of the Bible presents the story of Cain and Abel, whose sibling rivalry results in the death of one brother at the hands of another. We are introduced to Abraham as the first to recognize envy for the destructive force it can

[42] Randolph Nesse, "Evolutionary Explanations of Emotions," *Human Nature* 1, no. 3 (September 199-): 262–289, https://www.researchgate.net/publication/225485926_Evolutionary_explanations_of_emotions.

be. In fact, when Abraham and his wife, Sarah, travel to Egypt, Abraham takes precautions because he believes he may be killed by envious men because of their covetousness toward his beautiful wife; and, when he and his nephew, Lot, begin to compete over land, he sees the danger and tries to find a compromise that will remove the potential for envy.

Abraham understood clearly the destruction caused by envy, yet even he did not predict the envy his wife, Sarah, would have for Hagar, her Egyptian slave girl. Because she has been unable to give Abraham a son, Sarah gives Hagar to Abraham as a wife who would bear his child. But when Hagar conceives, Sarah becomes filled with resentful envy toward her and abuses her. Later, when God sends Abraham and Sarah a son, Isaac, Sarah sends Hagar and her son, Ishmael, away, lest Ishmael become heir with Isaac (Gen. 16:5–6; 21:10).

The cycle of envy continues into another generation when Isaac marries Rebekah, who bears twin sons. Rebekah later helps the younger twin, Jacob, to trick Isaac into giving him the firstborn blessing that should have gone to the older twin, Esau. Jacob must then flee from his enraged brother (Gen. 27).

When Jacob later marries two sisters (having been deceived into marrying the older one), the younger one, Rachel, who is barren, becomes envious of her sister Leah, who is able to bear children (Gen. 29). Later, Jacob blesses two of his own sons, Ephraim and Manasseh, giving what should have been the firstborn blessing intentionally to the younger boy — creating another cycle of sibling envy.

Envy continued to haunt the family of Abraham when Jacob's sons become so envious of their father's favorite son, Joseph, that they sell him into slavery in Egypt. Potiphar, a wealthy Egyptian who was one of Pharaoh's officials, the captain of the guard, bought Joseph from the Ishmaelites — eventually making him head of the household and entrusting him with the care of all things owned by Potiphar. Unfortunately, Potiphar's wife tried to seduce Joseph, but when rebuffed by him, she lied and said Joseph had tried to sexually assault her. Potiphar then had Joseph imprisoned. The cycle of envy begun in the garden continues through each generation of parents and grandparents and siblings throughout the entire book of Genesis — and beyond.

In Proverbs 24:17–18, we are warned: "Do not rejoice when your enemy falls, and let not your heart be glad when he stumbles; lest the LORD see it, and be displeased, and turn away his anger from him." In Mark 15:10, we learn that "it was out of envy" that the chief priests had handed Jesus over. Mark concludes that Pilate perceived Jesus' growing fame and reputation as inspiring the envy of the chief priests who had Him arrested and "delivered up" to Pilate.

The early Church Fathers, including Saint Cyprian, the bishop of Carthage in the early part of the third century, who was first to warn that "envy is the root of all evil, the foundation of disasters, the nursery of crimes, the material of transgressions," saw Jesus' exhortation to lowliness as an attempt to keep envy at bay. Cyprian warns that envy was a "gnawing worm of the soul ... when we hate our neighbor for his prosperity, when we make other people's glory our penalty, when we allow envy to be the executioner of our soul." For Cyprian, when we are consumed with envy "no food is joyous, no drink is cheerful," as our envy torments us day and night. Writing in the fourth century, Saint Basil suggested that the reference to envy in Mark 15:10 referred to the respect and love Jesus had earned through His goodness, His kindness, and His miracles. Basil also warned that the chief priests resented that they were losing the privileged position they had enjoyed before Jesus began His healing ministry and pointed to the gossip and slander that was used to attack His reputation. The early Church Fathers make it clear that the envy of the bitterly resentful chief priests sealed the fate of the Savior.

Saint Augustine of Hippo referred to a more theological view of emotions such as envy as "movements of the soul."[43] Augustine saw envy as "one of the seven capital sins ... a root sin that produces a number of poisonous offshoots." He called envy the "diabolical sin" not only because he saw it as seeking to minimize, end, or destroy what is good but also because it leads to other sins: "From envy, are born hatred, detraction, calumny, joy caused by the misfortune of a neighbor, and displeasure caused by prosperity."[44] According to Gerard O'Daly's *Augustine's Philosophy of Mind*, Augustine adopted the physiological descriptions promoted by the Stoics, claiming that bodily changes such as paleness, blushing, and trembling can have psychological causes (fear, shame, anger, envy, love) even if they may also be caused by physical factors. Yet Augustine disagreed with the Stoics in their refusal to believe that passions such as envy can befall all of us—including the sage. Augustine believed that some feelings are beyond the control of reason, occurring spontaneously, unable to be controlled by reason alone. Augustine saw the source of envy and other negative emotions as something "internal" to our fallen nature: our free will. Some philosophers believe that Saint Augustine may have been the first thinker to treat free will as a distinct faculty as an essential part of the mind—one that can also oppose its reason. Still, he believed that it is within our power to consent to these sensations. He proposed that we can refuse to become a slave to envious feelings.[45]

---

[43] Gerard J. P. O'Daly, *Augustine's Philosophy of Mind* (Berkeley and Los Angeles: University of California Press, 1987), 20, 27–28.

[44] *De catechizandis rudibus*, 8: PL 40, 315–316.

[45] Augustine, *The Three Ways of the Spiritual Life*, chap. 1.

The Origins of Envy

In the thirteenth century, Saint Thomas Aquinas attempted to synthesize classic Aristotelian philosophy with principles of Christianity. Aristotle was the first philosopher to record the danger of envy, identifying that we tend to envy those who are close to us in terms of time, space, age, and reputation. Writing that "envy is pain at the good fortune of others," Aristotle warned that envy could destroy the individual and the society. And in the first century A.D., Seneca described all emotions—including envy—as comprising two movements: the first, a reflex-like automatic and involuntary response; and the second, a conscious consideration of how to act upon the automatic response.[46]

In his *Summa Theologica*, Aquinas echoed this view, writing that emotions such as envy corresponded to "movements of appetites."[47] His views on these emotions appear primarily in the *Summa Theologica*, part I-II, questions 22–48, where he speaks of the "passions of the soul" as the emotions caused by external forces. Like Aristotle, Aquinas believed that moderate passions can be functional, but he knew that the passions need to be controlled by reason. Aquinas did not believe that we have to be controlled by these passions. And, like Augustine, Aquinas acknowledged that we have some control over whether we choose to engage with emotions of envy, believing that reason—or what he called a "rational appetite"—can keep emotions such as envy at bay. From this perspective, envy is

---

[46] K. Oatley, *A Brief History of Emotion* (Oxford: Blackwell Publishing, 2004).

[47] Thomas Aquinas, *Summa Theologica*, I-II, q. 59, art. 1. Cited by Timothy Ketelaar "Evolutionary Psychology and Emotion: A Brief History," in V. Zeigler-Hill et al., eds., *Evolutionary Perspectives on Social Psychology, Evolutionary Psychology* (Switzerland: Springer International Publishing, 2015), 56, https://www.researchgate.net/publication/300896653_Evolutionary_Psychology_and_Emotion_A_Brief_History.

a natural response in a fallen world. But it is also an emotion that can and must be controlled.

Envy as Mimetic Desire and Darwinian Theory

There are many who believe that the biblical view of envy as the result of our fallen nature can indeed be compatible with Darwin's evolutionary approach. In fact, René Girard's theory of mimetic desire can be viewed as an evolutionary theory itself because it advances a generative theory of cultural origins. We already know that imitative behavior is common to all forms of animal life. Humans are known as "hypermimetic" because of the increasing brain size in higher-order mammals. An anthropologist as well as a philosopher and historian, Girard appreciates this Darwinian perspective and begins each chapter of a series of his interviews published in his *Evolution and Conversion* with a quote from Darwin's writings. On the occasion of Girard's induction into the Académie Française in 2005, French philosopher of science Michael Serres described Girard as "the new Darwin of the human sciences" for the understanding he brings to the "process of becoming human."[48]

For Girard, mimetic desire is what makes us human. It is what makes it possible for us to break out from routinely animalistic appetites and construct our own identities. Girard knows that when envious desires — competition for the object or target of envy — create chaos and begin to threaten the very survival of a society by inciting violence, society has created a kind of "escape" mechanism in the form of a scapegoat. This scapegoat

---

[48] Andrew McKenna, "Darwin and Girard: Natural and Human Science," Raven Foundation Online (2015), Loyola eCommons, Modern Languages and Literatures: Faculty Publications, and Other Works, https://ecommons.luc.edu/cgi/viewcontent.cgi?article=1005&context=modernlang_facpubs.

is identified by the community or the society and is chosen to "take on" the sins of that society. Girard's anthropological research — building upon the idea of the "totem" in the writing of Émile Durkheim — identified the role of the scapegoat in even the most primitive of societies. He noted that when mimetic desire threatens to erupt in a violent struggle, the earliest communities enlisted a scapegoat to be sacrificed. The scapegoat was chosen to "stand in" for the rival but was "different" in some way from the rivals in the competition. The scapegoat had to be different enough to be identified as being the "other" in what was becoming a violent struggle emerging from envious desires. As the scapegoat is sacrificed, taking on the violence and the sins of that society, there is peace and unity as all rise up against the scapegoat as the "cause" of the problems. The society can "survive" because of the role of the scapegoat.

In a published paper titled, "Darwin and Girard: Natural and Human Science," Loyola University of Chicago professor Andrew J. McKenna applies Darwin's theory of natural selection to Girard's discovery of the scapegoat mechanism that is applied by every society as a solution to violence, which no community can survive.[49] Applying what Darwin says of natural selection to Girard's discovery of the scapegoat mechanism, we can see that Girard's research has the same end as Darwin's: to explain the societal mechanisms we need to employ to survive. The scapegoat is necessary for the society to survive, just as the adaptation and natural selection is necessary for the individual to survive. For Girard — like Darwin — the motive for all life is survival, and Girard has identified the need for a scapegoat to help human beings channel violence away from the community onto an "other." The scapegoat offers the means of survival.

[49] Ibid., 4.

The Politics of Envy

Still, this does not mean that humans are subject to biological determinism. In fact, McKenna points out that it is our hypermimetic desire that frees us from the determinism of natural selection:

> Only mimetic desire can be *free*, can be *genuine*, human desire because it *must* choose a model more than the object itself.... Mimetic desire is what makes us human, what makes it possible for us to break out from routinely animalistic appetites, and construct our own, albeit inevitably unstable identities. It is this very mobility of desire, its mimetic nature, and this very insatiability of our identities, that makes us capable of *adaptation* that gives us the possibility to learn and to *evolve*.... Mimesis is to cultural evolution what natural selection is to biological evolution. What our earliest ancestors learned over thousands, perhaps hundreds of thousands of ritual and sacrificial practices is how to control violence, how to streamline and channel it against a single victim or group of victims as a means to restore unanimity, cooperation, collaboration to their communities.[50]

Neither Girard nor McKenna see why God could not be compatible with Darwinian science. If one believes in God, one also believes in objectivity. Likewise, Pope Emeritus Benedict XVI viewed the evolutionary and creationist views as "complementary" realities:

> The story of the dust of the earth and breath of God does not in fact explain how human persons come to be but rather what they are. It explains their innermost origin and casts light on the project that they are. And, vice versa, the theory of evolution seeks to understand and describe biological

---

[50] Ibid., emphasis in the original.

developments. But, in so doing, it cannot explain where the "project of human persons" comes from, nor their inner origin, nor their particular nature. To that extent we are faced here with two complementary — rather than mutually exclusive — realities.[51]

Pope Francis added support to these thoughts on evolution by noting that "the evolution of nature does not contrast with the notion of creation, as evolution presupposes the creation of beings that evolve.... The scientist must be motivated by the confidence that nature hides, in her evolutionary mechanisms, potentialities for intelligence and the freedom to discover and realize, to achieve the development that is in the plan of the creator."[52]

It is this freedom that is key to understanding the origins of envy from a Christian perspective. Evolutionary theory has been attractive to many because it seems to simplify things. If all life forms descend from a common ancestor, and we are who we are because of random events and natural selection, our lives would be so much simpler. But even many hardcore Darwinists are rethinking this theory. In an essay in the *Claremont Review of Books* titled "Giving Up Darwin," Yale University computer science professor David Gelernter acknowledges that "there is no reason to doubt that Darwin successfully explained the small adjustments by which an organism adapts to local circumstances: changes to fur density, or wing style or beak shape." Even the evolution of emotional responses — including envy — can be added to that list of adaptations or natural selection. Yet "there are many reasons to doubt

---

[51] Pope Benedict XVI, *In the Beginning: A Catholic Understanding of the Story of Creation and the Fall* (Grand Rapids: Eerdmans, 1995), 50.

[52] "Francis Inaugurates Bust of Benedict," Catholic News Agency, October 27, 2014, https://www.catholicnewsagency.com/news/francis-inaugurates-bust-of-benedict-emphasizes-stewardship-43494.

whether Darwin can answer the hard questions and explain the big picture—not the fine-tuning of existing species but the emergence of new ones. The origin of species is exactly what Darwin cannot explain."[53]

And although Gelernter rejects what he calls a "childish" or primitive reading of Scripture, he acknowledges that "biblical religion forces its way into the discussion." Hardly a proponent of a primitive reading of Scripture, Girard also believes that the Bible has the best explanation of the universality of mimetic desire and the need for the scapegoat. For faithful Christians—including René Girard—we can never get beyond what we see as the fact that God created the universe and put man there for a reason. Our task, then, as Christians is to find meaning in our lives and figure out how we are supposed to live. Our emotions—including the emotion of envy—play an important role in all of this.

---

[53] David Gelernter, "Giving Up Darwin," *Claremont Review of Books* (Spring 2019): 104.

2

Narratives of Envy

In 2015, in an attempt to depict the deadly consequences of the sin of envy, the Hudson River Museum in New York filled its galleries with several installations, including fifty-eight large-scale digital color prints depicting characters and scenarios from classic fairy tales whose plots are driven by envious desire. Titled *Envy: One Sin, Seven Stories*, the exhibit was designed to warn of the death and destruction that envy brings. Bartholomew Bland, the deputy director of the museum, told a reporter for the *New York Times* that he was enthused about doing the show because, for him, "envy is the subtlest and the most corrosive of the sins.... It is often expressed under the cloak of something else.... Envy is the hidden sin. In many ways, it is the least visual."[54]

To their credit, the leaders of the Hudson River Museum rose to the challenge by commissioning Brooklyn-based artist Adrien Broom to create the stories, the staging, and the photography for the exhibit. Broom described herself to the *New York Times* reporter as a "storyteller," suggesting that she understands that

[54] Susan Hodara, "Imagining Envy: One of the Seven Deadly Sins," *New York Times*, July 31, 2015, https://www.nytimes.com/2015/08/02/nyregion/imagining-envy-one-of-the-seven-deadly-sins.html.

the concept of envy is best revealed through narratives. The fairy tales, featuring images of elaborately costumed models, brought the impact of envy to life in ways that words alone could not have conveyed. Broom used original renditions of the fairy tales — most of them from the Brothers Grimm — which are far darker and much more frightening and violent than the revisionist Disney stories. Headlining the show was the no-longer-fairest-in-the-land envious queen in "Snow White," whose evil visage is reflected in her infamous mirror. Vain, bitter, and envious of the beauty that Snow White possesses, the evil queen personifies envy in one installation as she is shown holding the poisoned apple, and in another, as she prepares to eat the bloody heart she believes once belonged to the fair Snow White.

In addition to "Snow White," the poisonous effects of envy are highlighted in six additional stories in the show, including "Cinderella," "Beauty and the Beast," "The Singing Bone," "Sprightly Water, Talking Bird, Singing Tree," "The Black Bride and the White One," and "The Goose Girl." The installation portraying "Cinderella" is especially gruesome because, in the original Brothers Grimm version of the story, the ugly and envious stepsisters cut off their toes and heels so they can fit into the glass slipper. Titled "A Good Fit," one of the stepsisters is shown trying to squeeze the tiny shoe onto her bloody foot.

Though archetypes of envy in fairy tales are most often presented as women, including evil stepmothers and stepsisters, the Broom exhibit includes several images of male envy also. In "The Singing Bone" we are introduced to two sons of a poor farmer who set out to win the hand of a fair princess and the riches of the kingdom by killing a giant boar that had been terrorizing the countryside. We are told that the older brother, "a cunning and smart fellow, was doing it out of pride, while the younger, innocent and naïve, was doing it out of the goodness of his heart" to help the people of the land.[55] To accomplish his task, the younger brother is given a magical spear from a magical "little man" he meets in the forest who tells him, "I am giving you this spear because you have a good and pure heart. You can attack the wild boar, and you won't have to worry about him harming you." When the good-hearted younger brother succeeds in killing the boar, envy drives the older brother to murder him. The scenario is depicted in a photograph in the Hudson River exhibit called "The Price of Her Hand": one brother stands over his slain sibling in a portrayal that calls to mind the biblical rivalry between Cain and Abel.

The exhibit was an important one because it showed, as the museum curator pointed out in the *Times* interview, that "envy is personal. . . . It's not the stranger in the woods who grabs you. It's a family member who turns on you."[56] The exhibit also shows that although the good-hearted and the innocent may suffer at the hands of those who envy them, the sin of envy can never be concealed for long—the truth always comes out—and God often plays a role in bringing the hidden sin to light. As the Brothers Grimm warn in their story of the murderous sibling rivalry in "The Singing Bone," "nothing remains hidden from God, and this evil deed was bound to come to light." And so it does. Many years later, the bones of the young brother are discovered when one of the bones magically sings out that his brother had murdered him. The wicked older brother is revealed to be the murderer—and for his crime, the envious evil brother is sewn up in a sack and drowned in the river. The bones of his innocent and pure-hearted brother are laid to rest in a beautiful grave in the churchyard.[57]

---

55 Brothers Grimm, *The Complete Fairy Tales of the Brothers Grimm*, 3rd ed., trans. Jack Zipes (New York: Bantam Books, 2003), 100.

56 Hodara, "Imagining Envy."

57 Brothers Grimm, *The Complete Fairy Tales*, 99.

The Politics of Envy

The original fairy tales by the Brothers Grimm always have a moral ending with good overcoming evil. Like Aristotle, these fairy tales warn us that envy always involves propinquity: we are always envied by those who are closest to us. "Cinderella" is one such story. Of course, most know the happy ending to this story, as the handsome prince recognizes the true beauty of Cinderella—beyond the rags and dirty cinders. Cinderella's tiny foot fits perfectly into the glass slipper, and the prince makes her his wife. But, although the Disney version of the story does not punish the evil and envious stepsisters—allowing them to attend Cinderella's wedding and celebrate with the new princess—the Brothers Grimm version of the story punishes the sisters appropriately and most violently:

> On the day that the wedding with the prince was to take place, the two false sisters came to ingratiate themselves and to share in Cinderella's good fortune. When the bridal couple set out for the church, the oldest sister was on the right, the younger on the left. Suddenly the pigeons pecked out one eye from each of them. And, as they came back from the church, the oldest sister was on the left and the youngest on the right, and the pigeons pecked out the other eye from each sister. Thus, they were punished with blindness for the rest of their lives due to their wickedness and malice.[58]

Envy is often punished with blindness in fairy tales. And although the blindness is often able to be "cured" with repentance, love, and forgiveness, as in "Rapunzel," the blindness can be permanent for those who are hard-hearted. This recalls Dante's *Inferno*, in which the once-envious souls can no longer envy what they cannot see. For Dante, the envious must be tamed because, as Anthony Esolen

[58] Ibid., 84.

writes, "there is something savage in envy, something a social order must overcome." To be "tamed," the envious have their eyes sealed shut, "as hunters seal the wild hawk's eyes to train him to be tame and rest unruffled."[59] The ugly stepsisters needed to be civilized and their envious natures tamed because it is only through blindness that the truly envious can see the error of their wicked ways and truly become civilized.

Fairy Tales Reveal the Terrible Truth about Envy

For the child—and the adult who knows there is still a child in each of us—fairy tales reveal truths about ourselves and the world. Recognizing and avoiding envy is an important part of this truth. As psychologist Bruno Bettelheim wrote in his 1976 book, *The Uses of Enchantment,* "The fantastical, sometimes cruel, but always deeply significant narrative strands of the classic fairy tales can aid in the greatest human task, that of finding meaning for one's life." Children who are familiar with fairy tales understand that these stories speak to them in the language of symbols—not the reality of everyday life. Children know that fairy tales are not real, yet the real events in their lives become important through the symbolic meaning that is attached to such tales. Children know that the events described in these stories happened "once upon a time," in a world far from here. The old castles, the magical fairies, and the enchanted forests housing magical birds and friendly animals existed in a unique fairy-tale time—a time described in the opening lines of the Brothers Grimm's "Frog King" as a time that was long, long ago, "when wishing still helped."

---

[59] Anthony Esolen, "What Dante Can Teach Us About Envy," *Catholic Answers,* November 1, 2009, https://www.catholic.com/magazine/print-edition/what-dante-can-teach-us-about-envy.

The Politics of Envy

These stories are still important today. In fact, they are probably more important than ever as we try to find meaning in our increasingly bereft lives. Increasing numbers of children are no longer raised within a loving community in which the church provides a source of meaning. Fairy tales speak directly to the child at a time when the child's major challenge is to bring some order to the inner chaos of his or her mind. The fairy tales about envy help children understand their own sibling rivalries—a necessary condition for achieving some congruence between their perceptions and the external world. Confirming their inner experiences and thoughts about their envious feelings, fairy tales about envy, and about overcoming envy, help children feel more confident in their ability to overcome these negative emotions. In this way, fairy tales are "fully moral" because their listeners understand that true happiness and peace rely on certain moral precepts or conditions. When these are broken, there can be neither peace nor happiness. As one writer has said: "The condition may vary according to the tale, but the tales mimic the great understanding of Genesis when it declares th⋅· God Himself predicated all future happiness on one and only one condition: from all other trees thou may eat, but from this one thou may not." When Eve defied the condition, death entered the world. The best fairy tales—like all the best stories—"document the moral imperative that there exists a condition, and that if the condition is broken, then all hell may well break loose."[60]

In *Orthodoxy*, G.K. Chesterton writes: "My first and last philosophy, that which I believe in with unbroken certainty, I learned in the nursery.... The things I believed most in then, the things

---

[60] Fr. Ernesto, "G.K. Chesterton on Fairy Tales," *OrthoCuban* (blog), December 30, 2009, https://www.orthocuban.com/2009/12/g-k-chesterton-on-fairy-tales/.

I believe most now, are the things called fairy tales." Chesterton is speaking of the morality of fairy tales: "There is the lesson of 'Cinderella,' which is the same as that of the Magnificat, *exaltivit humiles*, He lifted up the humble.... There is the great lesson of 'Beauty and the Beast' that a thing must be loved before it is loveable."[61] When Chesterton says that fairy tales are "entirely reasonable things," he is speaking of them as experiences, as "mirrors of inner experience, not of reality; and it is as such that the child understands them." The message of the fairy tale operates in the unconscious, offering children solutions to problems they cannot even acknowledge to themselves. The best ones—including the classic ones by the Brothers Grimm and Hans Christian Anderson—address the existential predicament.

In *The Uses of Enchantment*, Bettleheim suggests that the fairy tale reassures, gives hope for the future and holds out the promise of a happy ending for the good, the true, and the beautiful. That is why Lewis Carroll called the fairy tale a "love gift" to a child. The classic fairy tale gave the child an intuitive, subconscious understanding of his own nature and of what his future may hold if he is able to control his envy, and his willfulness, and develop his positive potential. The child senses from fairy tales that to be a human being in this world means having to accept difficult challenges, but also encountering wondrous adventures and triumphing over adversity. As Chesterton suggests, children already know there are dragons (and evil) in this world. The task of the fairy tale is to help children realize that the dragons can be conquered.[62]

---

[61] Bruno Bettelheim, *The Uses of Enchantment* (New York: Vintage Books, 2010), 64.

[62] Ibid., 280.

The Politics of Envy

The Earliest Narratives of Envy

The price to be paid for the sin of envy has always been best told through stories and allegory. And, although most credit Pope Saint Gregory the Great as the first to list and describe in the sixth century what we now know as the seven deadly sins, it is likely that the allegorical stories about virtue and vices of the previous centuries had already influenced the faithful. Themes of envy dominated both the tragic and the comedic plays of classical Athens, with Aristophanes's comedic writing of *phthonos* (envy) directed toward the politicians of the time. Designed to appeal to the audience's latent envy over the financial profit that some corrupt politicians were making even in the "perfect" democratic system in classical Athens, Aristophanes used satire to mock greedy politicians—using envy to hold the lifestyle and practices of politicians up to public scrutiny and, according to Birkbeck College classicist Ed Sanders, "reminding them that they were permanently on display, and militating against egregious misbehavior."[63] Tragedy also drew from themes of envy to drive the narrative in some of the most well-known plays, including Sophocles's *Ajax* and Euripedes's *Hippolytos*. Ajax's behavior is clearly motivated by envy toward Odysseus, and although Ajax wants to kill his rival, "he first wants to humiliate him by tying him to a pillar and whipping him until his back is crimson before he dies."[64] Likewise, writes Sanders, in *Hippolytos*, "there is a trail of evidence that Phaedra also feels *phthonos* for Hippolytos, from her first appearance on stage, and that this *phthonos* contributes to the reasons for leaving her suicide note....

---

[63] Edward Mark Sanders, "Envy and Jealousy in Classical Athens" (doctoral dissertation, University College of London, 2010), 133. See also the published edition: Ed Sanders, *Envy and Jealousy in Classical Athens: A Socio-Psychological Approach* (Oxford, UK: Oxford University Press, 2014).

[64] Sanders, "Envy and Jealousy in Classical Athens," 152.

Even at the earliest stage, while she appears to be in love with Hippolytos, Phaedra envies Hippolytos his carefree lifestyle."[65] After his rejection of her, Phaedra succeeds in depriving Hippolytos of his happy life by using slander and gossip to punish Hippolytos: "An important element of *phthonos* is the desire to level down … the 'if I can't have it, no one will' urge." So Phaedra's gossip serves these twin purposes—punishment and leveling down—of the begrudging envy she directs at Hippolytos.[66]

Beyond these early literary works, theologians devoted much of their writing to warning against vices that would destroy people's souls. Pope Gregory was likely influenced by the Greek monastic theologian Evagrius of Pontus, who first drew up a list of eight "wicked human passions" in the fourth century.[67] Later, the monk Saint John Cassian provided instructions on avoiding what he called the eight vices: envy, gluttony, lust, greed, hubris, wrath, listlessness, and boasting. Saint John Cassian wrote two major spiritual works: *The Institutes*, which provides specific guidelines for those living the "common life" as monks, and *The Conferences*, which is devoted to the training of the "inner man and the perfection of the heart."[68] Saint Cassian gave directions on how to treat what he called the "corrupted will," encouraging us to cure willfulness by subordinating ourselves to the will of God.

Cassian and Evagrius provided the inspiration for asceticism among the monks living in community. And, although their

---

[65] Ibid., 153.

[66] Ibid., 155.

[67] "Seven Deadly Sins," History Department website, University of Leicester, December 12, 2001, https://www.le.ac.uk/arthistory/seedcorn/faq-sds.html.

[68] "Feb 29—St John Cassian (360–435)," Catholic Ireland, February 29, 2012, https://www.catholicireland.net/saintoftheday/st-john-cassian-360-435/.

The Politics of Envy

writings had great influence, it took the earliest poets and play-wrights to "popularize" the warnings about the wicked passions. No one had more influence than the fifth-century Latin poet Au-relius Prudentius, whose one-thousand-line allegorical poem the *Psychomachia* depicted the battles between the Seven Virtues and the Seven Vices. Describing the conflict as a battle in the style of Virgil's *Aeneid*, the *Psychomachia* (Battle of Spirits or Soul War) became the most popular poem of the time.[69] Using female personi-fications of the virtues of Hope, Sobriety, Chastity, and Humility, as well as the personified vices of Envy, Pride, Wrath, and Lust, the poem depicts the war between good and evil, providing a graphic depiction of each of the battles between virtue and vice:

> The next person to step out on the grassy field is Chas-tity, the virgin, shining in armor. Lust, who has come from Sodom, is armed with torches. The vice thrusts a burning pine knot dipped in Sulphur and tar into the maiden's eyes. But, without fear she strikes the hand with a stone and the blazing torch is knocked away. With only one thrust of her sword, she pierces the throat of the whore and stinking fumes with clots of blood are spat out; the foul breath poisons the near-by air.[70]

Throughout the poem, each vice is utterly decimated by virtue. For example, when the sin of Lust is defeated, she is forced "to lie there

[69] Aparajita Nanda, "The Battles Rages On: The Psychomachia and The Faerie Queene, Book I" in S. Chaudhuri, ed., *Renaissance Essays* (Oxford University Press, 1995), https://scholarcommons. scu.edu/cgi/viewcontent.cgi?article=1129&context=engl.

[70] Aurelius Prudentius Clemens, *Psychomachia* or "The Battle for the Soul of Man," Wayback Machine, https://web.archive.org/web/20020429135514/http://www.richmond.edu/~wstevens/gr-valtexts/psychomachia.html.

defeated in the dirt ... the way of death ... the gateway to ruin. You stain our flesh and you plunge our spirits into the pit of Hell. Bury your head in the abyss of grief, you are a pestilence without power, you are frozen. Die, whore; go down to the damned."[71]
Pride meets a similar fate as she "spurs her horse into a fierce gallop, flying along with the reins slack hoping to stun her foe with her shield's weight and then trample Lowliness. But, her horse stumbles, and Pride is thrown into a pit that Deceit has already dug across the field." Although the *Psychomachia* does not personify envy in such graphic terms, the sin of envy makes an appearance toward the end of the poem in reference to the need for Love without Envy and without Pride: "Without peace, nothing pleases God, He will not take your gift at the altar if you hate your brother, if you should die for Christ by leaping in the fire and letting its tresses envelop you but still ... if you kept some unkindly desire, your sacrifice would mean nothing." The Christian virtues led by Faith ultimately triumph over the vices in a series of battles—moving on to build a holy city (in man's soul) in which will stand a temple dedicated to Wisdom. The moral was clear: "human beings' earthly activity was useless unless it related to higher spiritual goals."[72]
Although C. S. Lewis has been critical of the *Psychomachia* because he believed that the type of battles described are not appropriate activities for most of the virtues, he acknowledges that "possibly Courage would be able to fight or that maybe we can make a shift with Faith." Lewis could not understand how Patience, Mercy, or Humility would ever have been able to fight

71 Clemens, *Psychomachia* or "The Battle for the Soul of Man," Wayback Machine, https://web.archive.org/web/20020429135514/ http://www.richmond.edu/~wstevens/grvaltexts/psychomachia. html.
72 Malcolm Barber, *The Two Cities: Medieval Europe 1050–1320* (London: Routledge, 1992), 406.

in a battle. Still, even he understood the power of the narrative in teaching about the deadly sins—and drew from this narrative himself in his own creative works. Some critics believe that Lewis may have "missed the complexity inherent in the Prudentian allegory ... suggesting that the allegory participates in the history of human salvation.... It is a sophisticated version of Christian history operative in several moral senses."[73] Whether it misses the mark for Lewis, it must be acknowledged that the *Psychomachia* has had a tremendous impact on the allegorical writing of the Middle Ages and the Renaissance. Poets, playwrights, artists, and novelists have drawn inspiration for their art by writing about the impact of these seven deadly sins. In fact, the thirteenth century's *Summa Seu Tractatus de Viciis* by Guilielmus Peraldus (1190–1271) became the most influential treatise on the seven deadly sins and is said to have inspired Medieval and Renaissance writers such as Malory, Chaucer, Dante, Spenser, Marlowe, and of course, Shakespeare.

Historians suggest that Pope Gregory was influenced by the works of these early writers—including the *Psychomachia*.[74] Ranking the sins' seriousness based on how much they offended against love, Pope Gregory portrayed pride as the most serious sin, with envy next. Anger, sloth, avarice, gluttony, and lust completed his list. And, although Saint Thomas Aquinas contradicted the notion that the seriousness of the sins could be ranked in this way, the Church has maintained the list of the sins ever since. Paragraph 1866 of the most recent edition of the *Catechism of the Catholic Church* contains an explanation of the vices classified according to the virtues they oppose. The *Catechism* explains that these sins "are called 'capital' because they engender other sins,

---

[73] Nanda, "The Battles Rages On."
[74] Barber, *The Two Cities*, 406.

other vices." The seven deadly sins of pride, envy, covetousness, lust, gluttony, anger, and sloth are such shameful transgressions against God and society that they cause the death of the body as well as the soul.

Although envy was not added to the list of the deadly sins until Pope Saint Gregory the Great catalogued his list in the sixth century, many writers after him have focused in some way on envy as an especially despicable sin — one that brings death and destruction to the envier. Edmund Spenser's *The Faerie Queene* portrays envy "wearing a cloak embroidered with eyes and chewing a venomous toad, hating above all the love that binds all social classes together."[75] Some authors have suggested that in writing *The Faerie Queene*, Spenser must have been influenced by the *Psychomachia*. In fact, one of the contributors to Oxford University's 1995 publication *Renaissance Essays* suggests that Prudentius's work had an impact on much of the allegorical writing of the Middle Ages and the Renaissance. In her essay "The Faerie Queene," Aparajita Nanda writes, "A Prudentius-like battle between the virtues and the vices abounds in the dramatic as well as the poetic literature of the Middle Ages and is carried well into the Renaissance." She points out several parallels between the battles of the *Psychomachia* and the battles waged by Spenser's Red Cross Knight, and she concludes that just as the battles of the *Psychomachia* have vanquished evil, so the Red Cross has triumphed over evil. Moreover, evil has been rendered ineffectual and is dead for all intents and purposes. Still, in *The Faerie Queene*, as in the *Psychomachia*, there is an unanswered question that "makes us rethink the other possibility ... that despite the horrifying deaths meted out to the Vices in both the *Psychomachia* and *The Faerie Queene*, the unwritten message cannot be ignored, a message that

---

[75] Esolen, "What Dante Can Teach Us."

says that the battle between the virtues and the vices rages on, only at a different place and a different time."[76]

Likewise, Chaucer's "Parson's Tale" declares that envy is the worst of sins because "envy takes sorrow in all the blessings of his neighbor."[77] And, although readers have long been horrified by Dante's searing description of the punishment in Purgatory endured by those who envied others—having their eyes sutured shut with iron wire—no one can help us understand the sin of envy better than Shakespeare. Drawing more from the ideas of the European Middle Ages, which was characterized by a belief in an omniscient God with control over our lives, than from the Renaissance writers, Shakespeare viewed envy as a part of our fallen human nature. The idea of the sin of envy, "the green-eyed monster which doth mock the meat it feeds on," drives the narrative in much of Shakespeare's work. In fact, envy motivates some of the most vicious characters in Shakespeare's tragedies, including the villainous Iago.

Envy as Mimetic Desire in Shakespeare

Othello is often called a "tragedy of character" play because it focuses on the passions and sinfulness of its major figures. The title character, Othello, is a Moorish prince who is living in Venice, having been appointed to be a general in the Venetian Army. He is very much in love with his beautiful wife, Desdemona, who married him against her family's wishes. The villainous Iago is the battle-weary resentful ensign and aide to Othello who has been passed over for promotion in favor of Othello's lieutenant, Michael Cassio. Iago is envious of Cassio for receiving the promotion that

[76] Nanda, "The Battles Rages On."
[77] Geoffrey Chaucer, "Parson's Tale," in *The Canterbury Tales*.

he felt was owed to him and is resentful toward Othello for failing to recognize his own true gifts. At one point in the story, Iago
describes Cassio as "one who hath a daily beauty in his life that
makes me ugly."

When Othello is called away to battle against the Ottomites in
Cyprus, Iago plots his revenge, as he is left to arrange Desdemona's
travel to Cyprus to join her husband. Taking this opportunity to
implicate falsely Othello's favored lieutenant, Iago tells Othello
that Desdemona has been unfaithful to him with Cassio. In a blind
rage, Othello murders the innocent Desdemona for what he believes
is her unfaithfulness, only to discover too late that she had been
faithful all along. When he realizes he has been deceived by Iago,
Othello's grief drives him to suicide. Now that Cassio is in charge,
he condemns Iago to be imprisoned and tortured as punishment
for his crimes. Iago never repents and never acknowledges what
drove him to cause such misery.

It is clear to those who study the subtle and not-so-subtle ways in
which envy operates, Othello is perhaps the most poignant depiction of the devastation that is left in the wake of this sin. Yet there
is some disagreement among critics on whether envy was indeed the
motivation for Iago's manipulations. Some have pointed to the fact
that when he is caught, Iago refuses to provide any explanation for
his crimes, providing no clue to his motivation. Concluding that
Iago is a psychopath whose only motivation is "an immature surge
toward instant pleasure," that he is "unable to form lasting bonds of
affection" and has "no real loyalties, but serves only his own ends,
using people ruthlessly with no concern for their feelings," many
attempt to avoid blaming envy for the violence.[78] For evidence of
Iago's psychopathology, one writer points to the fact that Iago has

---

[78] Fred West, "Iago the Psychopath," *South Atlantic Bulletin*, 43, no.
2 (May 1978): 27–35, https://www.jstor.org/stable/3198785.

an "absolute lack of remorse … viewing with equanimity all the hideous results of his manipulations…. All the horror is in just this—that there is no horror."[79]

Iago may have had no remorse, but that is hardly proof that envy was not the motivation for his evil actions. Shakespeare knew—as we all know—that few will admit to envious feelings, even to oneself. Throughout the narrative, Iago exhibits several signs of his resentment and envy. Describing Cassio's "daily beauty" that "makes me ugly" is an indicator of envy. One need not be a psychopath to become blinded by envy. In his character study of Iago, Harold Bloom wrote, "Iago is a pyromaniac who wants to set fire to everything and everyone."[80] Iago's motivation can be nothing other than envy; his lack of remorse supports the idea that he believed that his revengeful actions were justified. The resentment that emerges when envy grows can cause murderous acts so horrible that we can hardly imagine them. Shakespeare is unique in his ability not only to imagine these acts but also to depict them in the most moving ways.

In *Theater of Envy: William Shakespeare*, René Girard argues that the key to understanding Shakespeare is to understand "mimetic desire" or envy. Girard's mimetic theory holds that people desire objects and experiences not for their intrinsic value but because they are desired by someone else. We mime, or imitate, their desires. For Girard—and most likely, for Shakespeare—it is original sin: "With mimetic desire, envy subordinates a desired something to the someone who enjoys a privileged relationship with it. Envy covets the superior being that neither the someone nor something

[79] Hervey Cleckley, *The Mask of Sanity*, 2nd ed. (Saint Louis: C. V. Mosby, 1950), 155.
[80] Harold Bloom, *Iago: The Strategies of Evil* (New York: Scribner, 2018), 4.

alone, but the conjunction of the two, seems to possess."[81] Quite simply, Girard suggests that we all borrow our envious desires from others. Our desire for an object or an experience is always provoked by the desire of another person for the same object or experience. This means that the relationship between the individual and the desired object or experience is not direct. Rather, there is always a triangular relationship: the individual, the model we aspire to be, and the object or experience. Attracted to the object, we see the model as a "mediator" in our desires. It is, in fact, the model who is sought—a desire to "become" the model in some way. Girard calls this type of envious desire "metaphysical" because, for him, all desire is a desire to be.

Girard explains that he used the word "envy" rather than "mimetic desire" in the title of his book on Shakespeare because envy is the traditional "provocative word, the astringent and unpopular word, the word used by Shakespeare himself."[82] Girard suggests that "envy" is the only word that continues to scandalize us:

> Our supposedly insatiable appetite for the forbidden stops short of envy. Primitive cultures fear and repress envy so much that they have no word for it; we hardly use the one we have, and this fact must be significant. We no longer prohibit many actions that generate envy, but silently ostracize whatever can remind us of its presence in our midst.[83]

For Girard, "all envy is mimetic."[84] And, more importantly, Girard contends that mimetic desire, or envy, is the major driver of all violence—including our own contemporary religious extremism

---

[81] René Girard, *A Theater of Envy: William Shakespeare* (South Bend, IN: St. Augustine's Press, 2004), 4–5.

[82] Ibid., 4.

[83] Ibid.

[84] Ibid., 5.

and terror. Expanding on this in his *Violence and the Sacred*, Girard suggests the following:

> It is the rival who should be accorded the dominant role.... The rival desires the same object as the subject, and to assert the primacy of the rival can lead to only one conclusion. Rivalry does not arise because of the fortuitous convergence of two desires on a single object; rather, the subject desires the object because the rival desires it. In desiring an object, the rival alerts the subject to the desirability of the object. The rival, then, serves as a model for the subject, not only regarding such secondary matters as style and opinions but also, and more essentially, regarding desires.[85]

With mimetic desire, the subject desires to "become" the rival —transforming himself into the other as a way of being. Girard points out that in some ways, Othello is envious of Cassio: "Cassio is everything that Othello is not: white, young, handsome, elegant, and above all, a true Venetian aristocrat. A real man of the world, always at ease among the likes of Desdemona. Othello admires Cassio so much that he selects him rather than Iago as his lieutenant."[86] Shakespeare's Iago shares the same mimetic desire, and by creating the character Iago as envious both of Cassio, his professional rival, and of Othello, Girard suggests:

> Shakespeare gives his villain mimetic consistency and thus successfully deflects toward him a great deal of ugliness that should belong to Othello. A whole landscape of infernal jealousy and envy appears in broad daylight that remained hidden in *Much Ado About Nothing*—a hiddenness that

[85] René Girard, *Violence and the Sacred*, trans. Patrick Gregory (Baltimore: Johns Hopkins University Press, 1979), 145.
[86] Girard, *A Theater of Envy*, 290.

makes the comedy seem enigmatic at times to the point of unintelligibility.[87]

Still, it is in his comedies that Shakespeare makes mimetic desire most visible. Referring to it as "the love by another's eye," or "love by hearsay," in Sonnet 42, Shakespeare refers to envy as mimetic desire when his character says: "Thou dost love her, because thou know I love her." In *The Two Gentlemen of Verona*, Shakespeare makes mimetic envy explicit when he chooses the name of Proteus, the Greek god of transformation, for a character who literally personifies mimetic desire in his envious desire to "become" his friend Valentine. At the beginning of the story, Proteus visits his old friend Valentine and hears Valentine talk about his newest love interest. Using glowing praise to describe Silvia, his new paramour, Valentine invites his friend to admire Silvia also; Valentine needs the validation from his friend. But when Proteus finally meets Silvia, he falls "instantly" and passionately in love with her. There are, of course, disastrous consequences, yet the mimetic dilemma is never really resolved. Near the end of the play, just after Proteus attempts to rape Silvia, Valentine rescues Silvia from the rape, but then appears to offer her to his friend when he says: "All that was mine in Silvia, I give thee." In this way, as Girard writes, "Valentine appears to let his rival, Proteus, have the disputed object, Silvia, declaring himself ready, like Abraham, to sacrifice his lover on the altar of friendship."[88]

This scenario points to what Girard calls the "double bind" of mimetic desire: "Valentine and Proteus can be friends only by desiring alike and when they both desire the same object, they become enemies. Neither one can sacrifice friendship to love or love to

[87] Ibid., 293.
[88] Ibid., 16.

friendship without sacrificing what he wants to retain and retaining what he wants to sacrifice."[89] Likewise, in the tragic poem *The Rape of Lucrece*, Shakespeare's Collatine unwisely praises his beautiful and virtuous wife in front of his friend Tarquin, with violent results similar to those in *The Two Gentlemen of Verona*. As Girard points out:

> The proudest men want to possess the most desirable objects; they cannot be certain that they have done so as long as empty flattery alone glorifies their choice; they need more tangible proof, the desire of other men, as numerous and prestigious as possible. They must recklessly expose their richest treasure to these desires. If too securely possessed, even the greatest and rarest possessions—wife, mistress, fortune, kingdom, superior knowledge, everything—lose their appeal.... Tarquin's desire is envious, but so is Collatine's. His envy of Tarquin's envy makes him just as mimetic as this rival, identical with him. The difference between hero and villain is undermined.[90]

Envy, Not Revenge, Drives the Narrative in Hamlet

Those who have studied Shakespeare's tragedies may have been taught that *Hamlet* is a story of revenge. Most of us were introduced to the fatally flawed Prince Hamlet, who returns from school to his home in Elsinore as a grief-stricken young man, mourning the recent death of his father, the king, yet, appearing to be unable to muster the strength—or the will—to take revenge for that murder. And, although it is true that on its surface, the play appears to focus on the long and dreary delay by the young prince to avenge the murder of his father by Claudius, his father's brother, it

---

[89] Ibid., 18.
[90] Ibid., 23.

is clear that a close reading of the play reveals that the real driver of the narrative is envy.

Indeed, as Rhodri Lewis's *Hamlet and the Vision of Darkness* points out, "life in Elsinore is measured not by virtue but by the deceptions and grim brutality of the hunt."[91] Themes of envy are woven throughout the earliest scenes of the play, when the ghost of the recently murdered King Hamlet appears to the young prince to warn him that Claudius was his murderer, and that his murder needed to be avenged. Claudius is presented as a man driven by mimetic desires to "become" King Hamlet in every way, possessing all that his brother had possessed—including the king's wife, Queen Gertrude. The young Hamlet is thoroughly disgusted by all of this—especially when he learns that his recently widowed mother has consented to marry Claudius, her husband's brother (and murderer) in order to maintain her envied status as queen. And, although Freud and his followers point to what they believe is the Oedipal desire in Hamlet's despair over his mother's marriage to Claudius, other critics—including Girard—have ridiculed what they see as "Freud's delightfully arrogant assertion" about Hamlet's Oedipal motivation.[92]

When Hamlet begs his mother to end her marriage to Claudius, Girard suggests that it is not for Oedipal reasons, or "the tons of Freud that have been poured over the passage," but, rather, because Hamlet believes that his mother "feels indifferent" to her marriage to Claudius. Girard suggests Hamlet believes that Gertrude perceives no difference between the two brothers: "The reason she could marry the two brothers in rapid succession is that they are so

[91] Rhodri Lewis, *Hamlet and the Vision of Darkness* (Princeton: Princeton University Press, 2017), front flap of book jacket.
[92] Joshua Rothman, "Hamlet: A Love Story," *New Yorker*, August 14, 2013, https://www.newyorker.com/books/page-turner/hamlet-a-love-story.

much alike and she feels the same indifference to the one as to the other. It is this overwhelming indifference that Hamlet perceives, and he resents it because he is trying to fight it in himself. Like so many other queens of Shakespeare, Gertrude moves in a world where prestige and power count more than passion."[93] Hamlet has contempt for his mother in part because he perceives that she was unfaithful to his father before his death. But, as Girard points out, in order to embrace the goal of revenge, the young prince must first "enter the circle of mimetic desire and rivalry."[94]

Hamlet finally gains the strength he needs to do the murderous act of revenge when Ophelia dies and he witnesses Laertes, Ophelia's grieving brother, leap into his sister's grave in his sorrow. The anguish of Laertes has a profound mimetic effect on the young prince. Girard suggests that it is as if Hamlet needed a model, or what Girard calls a "mimetic incitement," for how to feel about her death and his father's betrayal by Gertrude and Claudius. In act 5, Hamlet appears to acknowledge this by saying, "The bravery of his grief did put me into a towering passion."

Yet, the towering passion of Laertes takes a great toll — inciting violent revenge in Hamlet — creating chaos throughout Elsinore. Girard suggests that Shakespeare intended *Hamlet* to be a play that is against revenge by attempting to show the death and destruction that follows it. In some ways, Girard suggests that the young Hamlet is the only moral man in the play because he is willing to delay his passion for revenge — questioning the instruction of a ghost about avenging the murder of his father. Girard's thesis is that "Hamlet is far from the clumsy revenge artist defined by a tragic flaw of indecision.... Hamlet is Shakespeare's annihilation of the revenge tragedy genre so popular in his day; it is the bold

---

[93] Girard, *A Theater of Envy*, 276.
[94] Ibid., 278.

statement that the cycle of revenge is wrong, uninteresting, and insufficiently motivated."[95] In some ways, "the tragedy of Hamlet is not that he is flawed, but that his audience expects him to commit murder when he feels no moral imperative to do so."[96] It is through this framework of envy as mimetic desire that Shakespeare could write a revenge tragedy while still criticizing the genre—and the revenge itself. Girard suggests that Shakespeare attempted to teach us that there is wisdom in hesitation when we are called to violence.

One of the benefits of studying Shakespeare's narratives of envy is that we can gain a better understanding of all that continues to inspire us in our contemporary narratives. *Hamlet* has probably influenced the creation of more novels and screenplays than any other play in the canon of English literature. Even children have benefitted from the inspiration *Hamlet* has provided to the creators of the Disney animated movie *The Lion King*, the story of Mufasa, the benevolent king of the lions living on Pride Rock, who is killed by an envious scheming brother named Scar. And, like the young Prince Hamlet, Simba, the lion prince, son of Mufasa, delays acting against his father's murderer until he is forced to do so. Simba—like Hamlet—is visited by his father's ghost and learns that it was his uncle who caused the death of his father. The evil Scar—whose bright green eyes and menacing countenance signal his envious nature even to children—is determined to destroy all who threaten his reign, including Simba.

Although the creators of Disney's *The Lion King* will not acknowledge that their animated film was based on Shakespeare's *Hamlet*, they admit that the thematic similarities between the

95   Daniel R. Kim, "René Girard, Hamlet and the Tragedy of Mimesis," Daniel R. Kim, May 30, 2019, https://danielrk.com/general/2019/05/30/hamlet.html.
96   Ibid.

two are undeniable. In a 2011 interview with Blu-Ray.com, Rob Minkoff, codirector of the original film, said that because the film was considered an "original story" there was always the need to anchor it to something familiar:

> When we first pitched the revised outline of the movie to Michael Eisner, Jeffrey Katzenberg, Peter Schneider and Tom Schumacher, someone in the room announced that its themes and relationships were similar to *Hamlet*. Everyone responded favorably to the idea that we were doing something Shakespearean so we continued to look for ways to model our film on that all-time classic.... I'd be happy if we had even unconsciously channeled the old Bard.[97]

The obvious difference between *Hamlet* and *The Lion King* is that there is a happy ending for Simba and the rest of the lions on Pride Rock as Simba becomes the new king and Scar is killed. Yet that was not the original intent. Earlier versions of Disney's *The Lion King* included a tragic ending in which the envious Scar murders the young Simba by pushing him off a cliff. In fact, in the original storyboards (available online) the villainous Scar murmurs, "Goodnight, sweet prince" to Simba as the young lion falls to his death. The line is taken directly from the closing scene of Shakespeare's tragic play when Hamlet's friend Horatio whispers it to the dying prince.[98]

[97] Samantha Vincenty, "The Lion King's Surprising Connections to Hamlet," *Oprah Magazine*, July 12, 2019, https://www.oprah-mag.com/entertainment/tv-movies/a28376309/the-lion-king-hamlet-comparison/.
[98] Ibid.

3

Envy and the Other-Directed Man

The 1950s is often viewed as a period of stability and solidity—a peaceful time after the trauma of World War II—when most Americans just wanted to build good lives for themselves and their families. It was a time when the majority of people attended Church services, filled traditional gender roles, and generally did what was expected of them. But all was not quite what it seemed. And, in 1950, when sociologists David Riesman, Nathan Glazer, and Reuel Denney published *The Lonely Crowd: A Study in the Changing American Character*, it was an unexpected best seller because it documented what people knew intuitively—that the character of the country was beginning to change. Riesman and his coauthors recognized that the definition of the "good life" had begun to change as America evolved from a manufacturing and producing society "governed by the imperative of production, to a society governed by the imperative of consumption."[99]

Although the authors may not have recognized it in 1950, in some important ways, the emerging culture of conspicuous

---

[99] David Riesman, Nathan Glazer, and Reuel Denney, *The Lonely Crowd: A Study in the Changing American Character* (New Haven: Yale University Press, 1950), xii.

The Politics of Envy

consumption described in *The Lonely Crowd* paved the way for the culture of envy we are currently experiencing. What Riesman called an "other direction" in the national character took hold as concerns about how other people were living became more important than the tradition-directed or inner-directed way of life of the past. And, as people began to look outward to others for guidance on what constituted a good life, the potential for feelings of envy emerged.

At the time *The Lonely Crowd* was published, the country was in the midst of a baby boom and still appeared to be inner-directed and tradition-oriented, yet Riesman realized that the other-directed type would continue to expand until it dominated the nation's character. Riesman understood that the norms of consumer culture and domesticity that had begun to emerge in the late '40s would flourish in the '50s with the expanding advertising industry. New norms and values of innovation and novelty began to emerge and become disseminated through movies and women's magazines. The new norms affected every area of life — including homemaking, as the *Joy of Cooking* arrived to introduce adventurous new ways to prepare family meals, replacing the staid old reliable *Boston Cookbook* of the past decades. The new outer-directed American no longer cared as much about adult authority but was hypersensitive to peers and the mass media.

Changes in entertainment arrived in the 1950s with the creation of television and soon became an important source of socialization — a way to learn about the changing norms and values of society and family life. While this process began a decade earlier with radio programs, the culture portrayed on television contrasted sharply with radio. There began to be dramatic changes in the ways in which characters and families were presented and portrayed. For example, the popular '50s-era television sitcom *Father Knows Best* began as an NBC radio series in 1949 and ran until March 1954. Starring Robert Young, the radio series in 1949 portrayed the character of General Insurance salesman Jim Anderson as a traditional authority figure of the father who "rules" his family with love, sarcasm, and a droll sense of humor. But all of this changed in the mid-1950s with the move to television: Jim Anderson's television character was softened from the stern authoritarian to what *The Complete Directory to Prime Time Network and Cable TV Shows* has called "a thoughtful milquetoast father who offered sage advice whenever one or more of his children had a problem." Typical of other family-oriented television programming that emerged during that time, the *Directory* observed, the Andersons were "truly an idealized family, the sort that viewers could relate to and emulate."[100] And emulate they did.

As the years passed, people began to define themselves in reference to the ways in which others—including fictionalized television families—lived their lives. Without any idea of what social media was to become nearly half a century later, Riesman predicted that the coming "other-directed society" would leave every aspect of our lives open and vulnerable to being judged by others. People had no idea how prescient he had been. Powerful social forces—including, most importantly, reality-television shows and social media—have pulled us in ways that Riesman could not have imagined. But although Riesman could never have predicted how intrusive social media would become in our lives, he knew that other-directed Americans would be especially vulnerable to such transparency. He warned about what he called the "continual sniffing out" of other people's tastes, and as a result of the escalation of this consumerism, many people would begin to define themselves in terms of having tastes that are viewed as

[100] Tim Brooks and Earle F. Marsh, *The Complete Directory to Prime Time Network and Cable TV Shows: 1946–Present* (New York: Ballantine Books, 1979), 207.

The Politics of Envy

"acceptable" or even "enviable" to others on social media. Riesman likely anticipated that other-directed individuals would become increasingly concerned with how they were perceived by others, but he could never have known how far we would go to create the perfect persona, or what sociologist Erving Goffman (1922–1982) called our "presentation of self." As Riesman writes, "The other-directed person wants to be loved rather than esteemed," in order to relate to others. Just as Jim Anderson of *Father Knows Best* had to give up his stern patriarchal role in the transition from radio to television, becoming the "kinder and gentler" prototype of the TV dad in order to be acceptable to changing audience expectations, the other-directed man began to change his character to meet changing expectations in real life as approval from others became ever more salient.

Still, it is unlikely that Riesman could have imagined that so many would become so obsessed with the need for approval from others. Today's other-directed individuals need assurance that they are emotionally in tune with others. Anxious for signs of approval from Instagram or Facebook friends, they tally up their "likes" to demonstrate their success in choosing books to read or cooking skills to showcase. They post pictures of extravagant vacations to exotic locales or of elaborate house renovations. But, more importantly, they post proof of their successes in relationships. In an other-directed world, it is the experiences of others that provide the benchmarks by which people evaluate their own self-worth. And, when approval seekers are disappointed with their responses, they become anxious and depressed. A direct contributor to the current "age of envy," the other-directed American finds himself anxiously measuring himself against those he believes may be living happier and more fulfilling lives than he.

Although all generations have been vulnerable to the anxiety caused by the movement to an other-directed society, millennials, the first generation raised on the Internet and social media, have been the most affected by the shift. As the generation that came of age in the wake of one of the worst recessions in history — still dealing with economic uncertainty, student debt, and diminishing financial prospects — millennials are experiencing anxiety like no previous generation. On top of facing economic uncertainty, millennials have been our most insulted generation — labeled as the "most narcissistic generation" of all time in the book *Generation Me,* "lazy and *entitled*" in a *Time* magazine cover story, and the "trophy generation" because of the medals they are awarded merely for participation in events.

The media's favorite label for millennials is the "snowflake generation" because they are viewed as overly sensitive and easily offended and thus vulnerable to "melting" from criticism. Sometimes the criticisms are especially harsh, as in 2009, when Emory University English professor Mark Bauerlein published a book calling millennials the "dumbest generation." He cited as evidence the fact that SAT reading scores are at their lowest in forty years, and writing scores have fallen nearly every year since the writing section was added to the SAT in 2005. Blaming the parents of the "trophy generation," Bauerlein believes that "millennials are a cohort supremely self-congratulatory" with little substance to back it up.[101] An article in the *Harvard Business Review* suggests that millennials enter the workplace with high expectations but not the kind that pleases bosses: "Millennials strive for a work-life

---

[101] Mark Bauerlein, *The Dumbest Generation: How the Digital Age Stupifies Young Americans and Jeopardizes Our Future* (New York: Tarcher/Penguin, 2009). See also Mark Bauerlein, "Emory's Mark Bauerlein Doubles Down on The Dumbest Generation," *Atlanta,* February 1, 2016, https://www.atlantamagazine.com/news-culture-articles/emorys-mark-bauerlein-doubles-down-on-the-dumbest-generation/.

balance, but this tends to mean work-me balance, not work-family balance.... They want time for themselves and space for their own self-expression. Overall, the dominant definition was 'enough leisure time for my private life' (57 percent), followed by 'flexible work hours' (45 percent) and 'recognition and respect for employees' (45 percent)."[102]

Like all stereotypes about every rising generation throughout history, the negative descriptors of millennials and the new generation of college students, Generation Z, are overstated. Still, there is one truth about the current group of college students and young adults that cannot be denied. The new generation is more anxious than previous generations. Anxiety about grades, relationships, family pressures, and excelling at sports or other extracurricular activities is higher than in any previous generation. There is a growing body of research that confirms this. Longitudinal data collected by the University of California, Los Angeles Higher Education Research Institute (HERI) provides valuable insights into the beliefs, values, goals, and opinions of today's first-year students.[103] Based on responses from 137,456 full-time first-year students at 184 U.S. colleges and universities, the HERI study concludes that "political polarization on campuses is the most extreme it has been in the study's 51-year history." The student respondents to the survey were born in the late 1990s and came of age in the aftermath of 9/11. In some ways, they have been shaped by that pivotal event, just

[102] Henrik Bresman, "What Millennials Want from Work," *Harvard Business Review*, February 23, 2015, https://hbr.org/2015/02/what-millennials-want-from-work-charted-across-the-world.

[103] Kevin Egan et al., *The American Freshman: National Norms Fall 2016* (Los Angeles: Higher Education Research Institute, 2016), https://www.heri.ucla.edu/monographs/TheAmericanFreshman2016.pdf.

as the boomers were shaped by the Vietnam War and the sexual revolution. It has all had an effect.

The 2016 HERI survey measured for the first time how frequently respondents felt anxious in the past year, and more than one-third (34.5 percent) of full-time first-year college students indicated that they "frequently felt anxious." Tightly scheduled like children, with more hours of homework and fewer hours of free time than any of the previous generations, the current generation feels pressured to succeed. Today's other-directed young people are incredibly anxious and constantly worried about disappointing their parents, their teachers, their peers, and most importantly, themselves. A recent survey of more than five hundred university counseling-center directors revealed that for the seventh year in a row, anxiety has been the most predominant concern among the current cohort of college students.[104] Anxiety overtook depression as the number-one concern on college campuses in 2009. In 2017, 51 percent of students who visited a counseling center presented with concerns about anxiety, followed by depression (41.2 percent), relationship concerns (34.4 percent), suicidal ideation (20.5 percent), self-injury (14.2 percent), and alcohol abuse (9.5 percent). On average, 26.5 percent of students seeking services take psychotropic medications.

Sociologist Frank Furedi has suggested that the anxiety and emotional fragility expressed by so many undergraduates is the outcome of the prevailing ethos of socialization that infantilizes them. He believes that the socialization of young people has become

[104] David R. Rietz, Carolyn Bershad, Peter LaViniss, and Monica Whitlock, "The Association for University and College Counseling Center Directors Annual Survey," reporting period: September 1, 2015, through August 31, 2016, https://www.aucccd.org/assets/documents/aucccdpercent202016percent20monographpercent20-percent20public.pdf.

reliant on therapeutic techniques that encourage them to "interpret existential problems as psychological ones." Furedi suggests that "they find it difficult to acquire the habit of independence and make the transition into forms of behavior associated with the exercise of autonomy." He concludes that "there has been a perceptible shift from instilling values to the provision of validation."[105] Riesman would concur, since the other-directed identify themselves only through references to what others earn, consume, and believe in; they are becoming unable to know themselves. The value of autonomy is compromised in the other-directed individuals, and they are unable even to understand why finding meaning in life could be important. Data from the HERI study corroborates this, as only 47 percent of millennials view "developing a meaningful philosophy of life" as "very important" or "essential" today. This is compared with 68 percent of the 1975 cohort of respondents, who believed that it was "very important" or "essential" to develop a meaningful philosophy of life. Still, 75 percent of the millennials in the 2016 survey believe helping others who are in difficulty is "very important" or "essential," as compared with only 68 percent of respondents in 1975 and only 63 percent of Gen X respondents in 1995.

Millennials and Gen Z are far more pragmatic generations. When asked about their life goals, 82 percent of the respondents replied that "being very well off financially" was "very important" or "essential," compared with only 47 percent of the 1975 respondents. In contrast, 72 percent of millennials claim that "raising a family" is a "very important" or "essential" life goal. And despite their civic-minded attitudes, organized religion continues to decline

---

[105] Frank Furedi, "Why Millennials Are So Fragile," *Minding the Campus*, January 2, 2017, https://www.mindingthecampus.org/2017/01/02/why-millennials-are-so-fragile/.

in importance for millennials. The 2016 HERI survey was the first one that gave students the option to select agnostic or atheist as religious affiliations, and nearly 30 percent of incoming freshmen indicated that they were agnostic, atheist, or had no religious affiliation. In some important ways, social media has become like a religion for many millennials. The HERI survey has been studying students' use of online social networks since 2007. And from 2007 through 2015, about 25 percent of students consistently reported spending six or more hours per week on social media. But, in 2016, the proportion of students using social media for at least six hours per week jumped to 40.9 percent, nearly 14 percentage points higher than the previous high of 27.2 percent reached in both 2011 and 2014.

The Incels as the Ultimate Other-Directed Individuals

Social media continues to shape the behavior of millennials and Generation Z, sometimes in negative ways. On April 23, 2018, twenty-five-year-old Alek Minassian killed ten people and injured sixteen in Toronto, Canada, by intentionally driving a white Ryder rental van into a group of innocent pedestrians. Shortly before the attack, he posted a message on Facebook stating: "The Incel Revolution has begun!"[106] The term "Incel" was first used in a Reddit online group by young men to describe their unsuccessful ability to initiate sexual relations with women. Mostly millennials, Incels ("involuntary celibates") have found support and encouragement online from other men in similar circumstances. Minassian's

[106] Anna Mehler Paperny and Nichola Saminather, "Toronto Police Eye Deadly Van Attack Suspect's Cryptic Message," Reuters, April 24, 2018, https://www.reuters.com/article/us-canada-van/toronto-police-eye-deadly-van-attack-suspects-cryptic-message-idUSKBN 1HV1AY?feedType=RSS&feedName=worldNews.

The Politics of Envy

Facebook post praised the value and the courage of Incels and called on the Incel community to "overthrow all the Chads and Stacys." Minassian then paid homage to notorious Incel Elliot Rodger by posting "All hail Supreme Gentleman Elliot Rodger!" Elliot Rodger is a hero to some Incels because he had killed six people in a May 2014 rampage in Isla Vista, California, before shooting himself. Rodger had referred to men who are success-ful with women as "Chads" and to the unattainable women who rejected him as "Stacys."

In the 1990s — the early days of the Incel community — the online groups for the involuntary celibate functioned more as a self-help community. One of the founders of the earliest Incel communities in the 1990s, who now uses the handle "Reformed Incel" spoke with a *Vox* reporter and recalled that in the early days, the Incel community was "a welcoming place, one where men who didn't know how to talk to women could ask the com-munity's female members for advice." But, as the years went on, the community's goals became much darker. Reformed Incel told the reporter that women are no longer part of the Incel community and that "Rage has completely taken over."[107] In November 2017, Reddit banned a community dedicated to In-cels that had forty thousand members and had included posts advocating violence.

While the original Incel community was closed by Reddit, there are currently online sites like r/BrainCels, and r/ForeverAlone at Reddit where lonely young men who feel rejected and inadequate can find others to help them through the pain. *Vox* reports that over the past two decades, the Incel community, which numbers

---

[107] Zack Beauchamp, "Our Incel Problem," *Vox*, April 23, 2019, https://www.vox.com/the-highlight/2019/4/16/18287446/Incel -definition-reddit.

somewhere in the tens of thousands, has fallen under the sway of a profoundly sexist ideology that they call the "blackpill." It amounts to a fundamental rejection of women's sexual emancipation, labeling women shallow, cruel creatures who will choose only the most attractive men if given an option. An informal *Vox* poll of 1,267 BrainCels users found that 90 percent of the forum participants were under the age of thirty. Despite drawing users largely from majority-white countries, BrainCels has an ethnically diverse set of contributors; 55 percent of the site's user base is white, with significant percentages of posters who identify as East Asian, South Asian, black, and Latino.

All of these young, involuntarily celibate men are drawn to the Incel sites because they believe that their looks or other personal traits have "ruined their romantic chances." They often share stories of personal trauma and rejection.[108] John, one of the Incels interviewed for the *Vox* article, said he was drawn to the site because he felt that the users of the site were the only people who understood his experience as an unattractive man unable to find a woman to love. Forum users were people he could commiserate with, virtual friends who swapped jokes and memes that helped everyone get through the day: "Most people will not be in my situation, so they can't relate. They can't comprehend someone being so ugly that they can't get a girlfriend. What I noticed was how similar my situation was to the other guys. I thought I was the only one in the world so inept at dating."[109]

In some ways, John would have benefited from the earlier iteration of the Incel community of the 1990s because it offered support as well as suggestions on how to meet women—holding out hope for a future for Incels. But, according to the *Vox* research, "things

[108] Ibid.
[109] Ibid.

changed in the 2000s.... The nascent Incel community became divided between two online forums: one called IncelSupport and another called LoveShy." IncelSupport was more in keeping with the original mission, open to men and women. Moderators banned misogynistic posts. In contrast, LoveShy had a less stringent moderation policy and users were free to vent about the "Chads and Stacys"—blaming them instead of their own inadequacies for their lack of success with women. One of its administrators openly praised mass killers. Then, in 2014, Elliot Rodger went on his killing spree in Isla Vista, California. He began his attack by stabbing two male roommates and a visiting friend. He then drove to a sorority house near the University of California, Santa Barbara (UCSB) campus, where he killed two female students and one male, wounding fourteen more before turning his gun on himself. All of those who died were UCSB students. Rodger identified himself online as an Incel, and according to *Vox*, "that devastated the original Incel community."

It is clear that envy toward "the Chads" as well as resentment toward the women who rejected him drove Elliot Rodger. Incels have an elaborate social stratification system based on one's desirability and ability to attract women. For the Incels, the dating and mating scene is a kind of sexual class system. At the top of the hierarchy are the most attractive men—the Chads. Incels believe that roughly 20 percent of the population is made up of Chads but about 80 percent of women are interested only in men of this class. "Stacy," the Incel term for the most attractive women will consent to sex only with "Chad." The bottom 20 percent of women will consent to sex with the vast majority of men who fall somewhere in the middle of the attractiveness tier, alternatively called "betas" or "normies." And at the bottom are Incels: men who are so innately unappealing that they can never convince women to date them.

Incels appear to some — including the author of the *Vox* essay on Incels — to be misogynistic because of their ongoing rants about women. But their envious hatred toward other men, especially attractive and desirable men, is, as Girard and Riesman would have predicted, the true driver of their rage. Support for this can be found in a major research study, published online, by university-based scholars here and abroad that investigated the vernacular used by Incels in their online interactions. The goal of the research was to assess whether the Incels.me forum fostered radicalization. Using a Deep Learning system of research that is able automatically to detect and quantify hateful rhetoric, the study investigated more than sixty-five thousand messages (about 1.5 million words) from the Reddit website Incels.me during a six-month period between November 2017 and May 2018. In order to quantify the types of messages sent by the Incels they were studying, the researchers compared fifty thousand Incels.me messages to fifty thousand neutral texts composed of forty thousand paragraphs from random English *Wikipedia* articles and ten thousand random English tweets to account for Internet slang.[110]

The research revealed that a recurring concept in Incel jargon is that of the "black pill." This concept emerged from a scene in the film *The Matrix*, when the protagonist, Keanu Reeves's character, is offered a choice between a red pill, which reveals the true, and often unpleasant, nature of reality, and a blue pill, which would allow him to live in comfortable ignorance. Worse than the red pill, whose users believe they are oppressed, is the black pill: black-pill takers are under the hopeless belief that unattractive men will never be

[110] Sylvia Jaki et al., "Online Hatred of Women in the Incels.me Forum: Linguistic Analysis and Automatic Detection," *Journal of Language Aggression and Conflict* 7, no. 2 (November 2019): 240–268, https://www.jbe-platform.com/content/journals/10.1075/jlac.00026.jak.

able to participate in the mating marketplace because man's sexual success is almost entirely determined by unalterable biological traits: things such as his jawline, cheekbones, or eye-socket shape. In the Incel community, this means that a minority of attractive men have access to the majority of all women, while the other men are left to compete over a minority of women. The analysis of the top keywords reveals reference to gender, physical traits, and swear words. Some words constituted coded language. For example, "Chad" and "Tyrone" are derogatory denominations for attractive and successful young men (alpha males, bad boys, bros, jocks), and "Stacy" denotes an attractive "roastie," a promiscuous young woman. Many of the online posts focused on negations ("nothing," "never").

Although the authors titled their research study "Online Hatred of Women in the Incels.me Forum," their research findings do not entirely support the title. Their own research demonstrates that the Incels do not "hate" all women as much as they seem to hate the attractive men who have been successful with women. This is envy. When the authors presented a psychological profiling of the subjects of their study, they found that "isolation" was a strong issue for them. The pain of being alone without a female partner was palpable in the study results, as was the craving for female contact: "I've never touched a non-related female even for a handshake or something." Another said: "I wish I could be friend-zoned but girls are too repulsed by me to even consider me a friend." Incel communication was also characterized by negativity. Although there were a few positive users in the forum who addressed their situation, for example, by going to the gym (gymcel), this is often experienced as a strain because of the high number of "Chads" in the gym ("gym-celing is literally torture"). Anger at the "Chads" often surfaced in their posts, as one Incel forum user wrote: "I hope one day I get the confidence or the opportunity to seriously injure a Chad at my High School."

Although misogyny, or fear or hatred of women, emerged in the findings, the study authors had to acknowledge that "not all users hate all women." A discussion thread designed as a poll asked whether the forum users hate all women and found that about 55 percent answered positively, while about 45 percent answered negatively. One user wrote: "I don't hate all women. And I believe that most brothers here in the Forum also don't hate them. We hate the situation we are in." Many of the Incels resent women, though, as well as women's freedom to choose partners. *Vox* author Zack Beauchamp writes, "In their view, there would not be Incels if women weren't given the freedom to choose who they want to have sex with." The logical conclusion of the black pill to those in the Incel community is, as Beauchamp points out, that women should never have been given any rights: "The blackpill bundles the Incel sense of personal failure with a sense of social entitlement: the notion that the world owes them sex, and that there is something wrong with a society in which women don't have to give it to them."[111]

New York Times columnist Ross Douthat wrote about this sense of loss in the Incels in a 2018 op-ed, suggesting that "the sexual revolution created new winners and losers, new hierarchies to replace the old ones, privileging the beautiful and socially adept in new ways and relegating others to new forms of loneliness and frustration. Our widespread isolation and unhappiness and sterility might be dealt with by reviving or adapting older ideas about the virtues of monogamy and chastity and permanence and the special respect owed to the celibate."[112] Douthat cites Professor Robin Hanson, a George Mason economist whose comments on Alek Minassian, the

---

[111] Beauchamp, "Our Incel Problem."

[112] Ross Douthat, "The Redistribution of Sex," *New York Times*, May 2, 2018, https://www.nytimes.com/2018/05/02/opinion/Incels-sex-robots-redistribution.html.

The Politics of Envy

Toronto Incel, were disturbing to many. Suggesting a kind of sexual redistribution system, Hanson writes: "If we are concerned about the just distribution of property and money, why do we assume that the desire for some sort of sexual redistribution is inherently ridiculous? After all, one might plausibly argue that those with much less access to sex suffer to a similar degree as those with low income, and might similarly hope to gain from organizing around this identity to lobby for redistribution along this axis and to at least implicitly threaten violence if their demands are not met." Hanson's musings were met with derision by many—especially *Slate* author Jordan Weissmann, who asked, "Is Robin Hanson the Creepiest Economist in America?" But even Douthat had to acknowledge that "as offensive or utopian the redistribution of sex might sound, the idea is entirely responsive to the logic of late-modern sexual life, and its pursuit would be entirely characteristic of a recurring pattern in liberal societies."[113] *Vox*'s Beauchamp points out that both the Incels and Douthat share the same sense that something important was lost when women's sexuality became less heavily regulated by social norm and law.

All of this was predicted in the *The Lonely Crowd* in 1950. Riesman anticipated that eventually the other-directed man would seek to consume and savor experiences over "things." A person's drive toward these experiences comes not from within but from watching other people enjoying experiences he does not have as he attempts to match the quality of those experiences, especially in romantic relationships. When he feels that he cannot measure up, he feels envy and anxiety. Eventually, these feelings devolve into anger, and in the case of some radical Incels, rage. As Riesman wrote:

> The consumption of love, despite all the efforts of the mass media, does remain hidden from public view. If someone else

[113] Ibid.

has a new Cadillac, the other-directed person knows what that is, and that he can duplicate the experience. But, if someone has a new lover, he cannot know what that means. Cadillacs have been democratized. So has sexual glamour, to a degree: without the mass production of good looking, well-groomed youth, the American pattern of sexual competition could not exist. But there is a difference between Cadillacs and sexual partners in the degree of mystery. And with the loss or submergence of moral shame and inhibitions, but not completely of a certain unconscious innocence, the other-directed person has no defenses against his own envy.... He does not want to miss, day in and day out, the qualities of experience he tells himself the others are having.... The other-directed person looks to sex not for display but for a test of his or her ability to attract, his or her place in the rating-dating scale—and beyond that, in order to experience life and love.[114]

Riesman acknowledges that the main reason for the change is that women are no longer objects for the "acquisitive consumer" but are peer groupers themselves. As women become "knowing consumers," the anxiety of men, lest they fail to attract and satisfy the women, also grows. But, at the same time, Riesman points out, this is another test that attracts men who, in their (outer-directed) character, want to be judged by others. "The ability of women to respond in a way that only courtesans were supposed to in an earlier age means, moreover, that qualitative differences of sex experience—the impenetrable mystery—can be sought for night after night, and not only in periodic visits to a mistress or brothel."[115]

[114] Riesman, Glazer, and Denney, *The Lonely Crowd*, 147.
[115] Ibid., 148.

The Politics of Envy

The envy-driven, resentful men who are left out of the dating and mating marketplace have become today's most desperate members of *The Lonely Crowd*.

While, Riesman's typology may begin to help us understand how the change from tradition-directed or inner-directed to other-directed has contributed to the dilemma of the Incels, it is not the only explanation for the anxiety and the loneliness these young men are experiencing. The status uncertainty and the status hierarchies that the Incels decry are not an aberration—rather, they are part of our human nature. Hierarchies are the natural order of the world, whether we want to acknowledge them or not. And, although even fewer of us are willing to admit it, women have always been attracted to the highest-status men they can find. They recognize that the higher-status mate is key to the survival of their offspring. Today, as women are achieving parity with men in the workplace, many of them have incomes of their own to trade, and they are demanding higher-status men in the mating marketplace. This makes it even more challenging for the unattractive, uneducated, and socially awkward low-status men who are increasingly left behind.

University of Toronto psychology professor Jordan Peterson understands and articulates the importance of hierarchies, status factors, and envious desire better than most social scientists. Peterson's 2018 book, *12 Rules for Life*, a kind of literary self-help guide that has been helpful to hundreds of thousands of grateful readers, has sold more than one million copies—most to male millennials and Generation Z members hungry for the truth. His YouTube channel and podcasts have made him famous—primarily because he is willing to tell the truth about how our lives can be better if we begin to take responsibility for them. Peterson understands Incel culture better than anyone because he understands what he calls "the crushing force of sexual selection." He acknowledges that "women are choosy maters" (unlike female chimps, their closest animal counterparts). He knows that

> most men do not meet female human standards. It is for this reason that women on dating sites rate 85 percent of men as below average in attractiveness. It is for this reason that we all have twice as many female ancestors as male.... It is Woman as Nature who looks at half of all the men and says, "No ... you don't measure up." For the men, that's a direct encounter with chaos, and it occurs with devastating force every time they enter the mating marketplace and are turned down for a date. Human female choosiness is also why we are very different from the common ancestor we shared with our chimpanzee cousins, while the latter are very much the same.

According to Peterson (and decades of anthropological research), "women's proclivity to say no, more than any other force, has shaped our evolution into the creative, industrious, upright, large-brained (competitive, aggressive, domineering) creatures that we are. It is Nature as Woman who says, 'Well, bucko, you're good enough for a friend, but my experience of you so far has not indicated the suitability of your genetic material for continued propagation.'"[116]

Peterson is a hero to many young males because he understands their anxiety and their dilemma. He understands and articulates the fact that the radical left wants to eliminate hierarchies, even though these hierarchies are the natural order of the world. In his book, Peterson illustrates this idea of the natural order of hierarchies by describing the social behavior of lobsters. Lobsters are invertebrates with serotonin, and they, too, have natural hierarchies. Peterson

[116] Jordan Peterson, *12 Rules for Life* (Canada: Random House, 2018), 41.

suggests that "natural hierarchies" emerge within the lobster population because some lobsters are bigger and better than others. They have more fully evolved. He also suggests that like lobsters, it is possible that men might be "in charge" in a given arena because they are naturally better at the task because of their "nature." This is why most progressives fear and condemn him.

Peterson is correct to acknowledge that young men who are not in monogamous relationships are at a greater risk for violence or self-harm than men who are in monogamous relationships. The criminology research has documented this fact for decades. Recent research published by the Centers for Disease Control in Atlanta, Georgia, reveals that "men who feel the least masculine are three times more likely to commit violent assaults with a weapon or assaults that lead to an injury." About six hundred men between the ages of eighteen and fifty were surveyed on their perception of the male gender, self-image, and behavior in relation to drugs, violence, and crime. Findings suggest that shorter or weaker men with poor self-images are "angrier and more violent" than those with stronger self-images. This is called "male discrepancy stress."[117]

Peterson has indicated that society needs to begin to pay attention to all of this. He knows that men without female partners are at risk, and he suggests that society needs to try to make sure those men find mates. Unfortunately, rather than paying attention to Peterson's warnings, many progressives have attempted to destroy him. In May 2018, Nellie Bowles, a writer for the *New York Times*, spent two days visiting with and interviewing Peterson for a comprehensive story on his phenomenal success. Peterson was

---

[117] Dennis E. Reidy et al., "Masculine Discrepancy Stress, Substance Use, Assault and Injury in a Survey of U.S. Men," *Injury Prevention* 22, no. 5 (October 2016), https://injuryprevention.bmj.com/content/22/5/370.

generous with his time, opening up his home, his office, and his work to Bowles. But rather than presenting an honest overview of Peterson's perspectives on the contributors to "order and chaos" in our society, Bowles distorted much of Peterson's message in his book and in his online lectures, making erroneous assertions that Peterson wants society to "force" women to marry men through "enforced monogamy." Misunderstanding the anthropological term "enforced monogamy," which simply means socially promoted, culturally inculcated monogamy, Bowles blunders through her published interview, showing her unfamiliarity with anthropology and Jungian psychology. Enforced monogamy is an important concept that has driven studies of kinship and marital ties in anthropology for more than a century, and it simply suggests that society should find ways to support male-female pair bonding because it helps keep society functioning well. Oblivious to the anthropological origins of the term, Bowles claims that Peterson's idea of forcing monogamy on individuals is absurd and implies that Peterson longs for a "redistribution of sex," in a kind of "Handmaid's Tale" society in which women are chosen for lustful males. Bowles writes:

> Aside from interventions that would redistribute sex, Peterson is staunchly against what he calls equality of outcomes, or efforts to equalize society. He usually calls them pathological or evil … preventing hordes of single men from violence, he believes is necessary for the stability of society. Enforced monogamy helps neutralize that. In situations where there is too much mate choice, a small percentage of the guys have hyper-access to women and so they don't form relationships with women.[118]

---

[118] Nellie Bowles, "Jordan Peterson, Custodian of the Patriarchy," *New York Times*, May 18, 2018, https://www.nytimes.com/2018/05/18/style/jordan-peterson-12-rules-for-life.html.

The Politics of Envy

While some of this is true, Bowles's unfamiliarity with the anthropological term "enforced monogamy" is typical of many of Dr. Peterson's progressive critics. They simply do not understand the decades of evolutionary and sociological research behind his assertions. It is a long-established fact that any society with large numbers of frustrated men without female partners is a society that is becoming dangerous. It is a fact that men become frustrated when they are not competitive in the sexual marketplace. But, Peterson's critics appear to be unaware of the fact that societies with socially enforced monogamous conventions have been shown to decrease male violence, and they also help provide mothers with comparatively reliable male partners, increasing the probability that stable, father-intact homes will provide optimal shelter and socialization for children. And, as Girard would have predicted, reducing the number of unmarried men reduces the envy-driven competition for female partners and thus reduces the incidence of rape, murder, assault, robbery, and fraud in societies that value pair bonding enough to encourage it.[119] In some ways, the Incels are correct in their assertion that the Chads are capturing the highest-status women—leaving little for the rest. But, as the following chapters will point out, in a chaotic society like ours, most women are not the winners in this competition either.

---

[119] Jordan Peterson, "On the *New York Times* and 'Enforced Monogamy,'" *www.jordanbpeterson.com*, June 8, 2018, https://www.jordanbpeterson.com/media/on-the-new-york-times-and-enforced-monogamy/.

4

Crimes of Envy

Feelings of envy are often accompanied by a sense of injustice — a belief that unfair circumstances or improper actions have given an advantage to one who is undeserving of such a benefit or "prize." A kind of righteous indignation emerges in the envier, justifying feelings of anger and hostility toward the target of the envy. Such envious resentment can produce a readiness to act aggressively toward the target — sometimes with deadly consequences.[120]

This is exactly what occurred a few years ago in New York City in what became known as the "Nanny Murders." In an envious rage over what she believed was the injustice of the conditions of her employment as a nanny, Yoselyn Ortega, age fifty-five, an embittered, resentful family caregiver, fatally stabbed the two beautiful young children in her care. Prosecutors argued — based on statements from Ortega herself — that envy was at the root of the nanny's revengeful act. Ortega told investigators that her employer, the children's mother, Marina Krim, "made her work too hard" while Krim did "nothing." Ortega made statements to the media

---

[120] Richard H. Smith, "Envy and the Sense of Injustice" in *The Psychology of Jealousy and Envy*, ed. Peter Salovey (New York: Guilford Press, 1991).

that she had to do "everything.... I worked as a babysitter, and she wanted me to do everything. She wanted 5 hours of cleaning."[121]

Despite Ortega's hostility, it was clear from media reports and court records that the Krim family had been especially kind to the nanny—providing her with expensive gifts and paid vacation time, as well as the funds to travel to see her extended family at her home in the Dominican Republic. On one such visit, the Krim family was invited to accompany Ortega to the Dominican Republic to spend a few days visiting with Ortega's family. In the court proceedings following the murders, Krim described a friendly, even "close" relationship with Ortega. But, none of that prevented the envy-driven hostility that Ortega harbored toward Krim—which escalated into the revengeful murder of the two Krim children: Lucia, age six, and Leo, age two.

In the court proceedings following Ortega's murderous rampage, Krim said that she had offered Ortega an extra hundred dollars each week for an additional five hours of household work each week because the nanny had complained that she did not have enough money. Krim offered the additional work in an effort to help Ortega, but the request for housework caused Ortega to become enraged—and envious of what the nanny viewed as the "easy life" Krim enjoyed. The envious resentment grew. The case that the prosecution team successfully built focused on the pernicious envy that Ortega held for the mother of the children in her care. In an unusual filing, the prosecutors used the word "envy" in the court documents and made a strong case that Ortega resented the family's Upper West Side apartment. Using her own statements,

[121] Reuven Fenton, Lia Eustachewich, and Emily Saul, "Killer Nanny Complained about Mom Right after Grisly Murders," *New York Post*, March 8, 2018, https://nypost.com/2018/03/08/killer-nanny-complained-about-mom-in-first-statement-after-grisly-murders/.

the prosecutors created a case that suggested that Ortega resented what the family enjoyed; she resented the love and affection the family shared as well as the "toys and clothing and opportunities" that the children had. But, most of all, prosecutors pointed out that Ortega resented what she called the mother's "free time," which enabled her to pursue her personal interests in art. During her initial interrogation, she complained to prosecutors that her own son in the Dominican Republic had nothing but what she was able to send him since she left her country to pursue work in the United States eight years before. Ortega railed against the injustice of it all.

In a heart-wrenching criminal trial that lasted for seven weeks, jurors heard testimony from both the father and the mother of the murdered children. The mother, Marina Krim, described the desperate moments when she returned to her home to discover that Ortega had just murdered her children in the family's home. Krim had been at a swimming class with her three-year-old daughter, Nessie. Ortega was to have dropped off Lucia, Krim's six-year-old daughter, at her dance class, and Krim was to pick her up. But, when Krim arrived at the dance studio, Lucia was not there. Frantic, Krim raced home with Nessie—telling the court about how she walked into what she called an "eerily quiet apartment, darkened but for the light in the back bathroom," where she found Ortega standing over the two lifeless Krim children—their little bodies punctured by dozens of stab wounds.[122]

While Ortega's attorneys attempted to mount an insanity defense—claiming that she believed that Satan himself had forced

---

[122] Associated Press, "New York Nanny Who Killed Two Children Convicted of Murder," *Guardian* (Manchester), April 18, 2018, https://www.theguardian.com/us-news/2018/apr/19/new-york-nanny-who-killed-two-children-convicted-of.

her to kill the children—it was clear that she was very much aware of her actions when she stabbed both children in the family home. In fact, this cruel woman waited until Krim had arrived home so that the mother could witness the murder of her children. Assistant district attorney Stuart Silberg said during his closing arguments that Ortega acted out of what he called "jealous hatred" of the children's mother. "She did it intentionally with a full understanding of exactly what it was she was doing with every stab, every slash." Rejecting the defense attorney's claims that Ortega "snapped" and did not know what she was doing, the prosecutors maintained that Ortega, who had worked for the family for two years, was treated as a member of the family. But Ortega grew to resent the comfortable and loving life the family enjoyed while her own family experienced poverty and dysfunction.

Ortega was found guilty of the murder of the children and was sentenced to life in prison—the maximum penalty. In sentencing Ortega, Judge Gregory Carro borrowed the words of one witness who described the former nanny's actions as "pure evil" and said the jurors were right to reject Ortega's defense that she could not be held responsible because she had suffered from a mental disease or defect and could not understand her actions or know they were wrong. At the sentencing hearing, the children's mother was allowed to address the court about the horror that her family experienced at the murderous hands of Ortega. Pointing to the envious hostility Ortega held for them, Krim told the court that although Ortega had murdered her two much-loved children, the nanny "had not succeeded in her ultimate goal: To destroy what Kevin and I had created and built—an inspired, happy, thriving family. . . . Instead, she destroyed her own family."[123]

---

[123] Jan Ransom, "Yoselyn Ortega, Nanny Who Killed Two Children, Is Sentenced to Life in Prison," *New York Times*, May 14, 2018,

Krim revealed the real motivation behind all mimetic desire —the envy behind Ortega's deadly attack. It was clear to everyone, including the judge and the jurors, that Ortega envied the happiness and the love that the Krim family enjoyed. It was clear that Ortega became angry and resentful toward Mrs. Krim and acted out on the hostility that grew each day that she witnessed that kind of family happiness. While this is certainly an extreme case, it is an illustration that envious feelings are often characterized by a sense of injustice. In his *Theory of Justice*, philosopher John Rawls (1921–2002) suggests that envy can lie "behind the veil of ignorance along with the parties' knowledge of their conception of the good" and warns that when envy masquerades as resentment or righteous indignation, the envious feelings become legitimated—even moral.[124] Ortega's bitterness over her plight in life caused her to attempt to destroy the happy lives of people who were kind to her.

This is not unusual. But Rawls erroneously believes that envy poses a problem primarily because of inequality. He acknowledges that envy can become a problem if the inequality becomes so great that it arouses envy to a "socially dangerous extent.... The envy experienced by the least advantaged towards those better situated is normally general envy in the sense that they envy the more favored for the kinds of goods and not for the particular objects they possess." The upper classes are envied for their greater wealth and opportunity, while those envying them want similar advantages for themselves. The problem is whether the principles of justice, with fair equality of opportunity, is likely to engender in practice

----

https://www.nytimes.com/2018/05/14/nyregion/manhattan-nanny-sentenced-life.html.

[124] John Rawls, *Theory of Envy* (Boston: Harvard University Press, 1999), 464–465.

too much destructive general envy.[125] Still, Rawls believes that when "principles of justice" and equality are adopted and put into practice, they lead to social arrangements in which envy and other destructive feelings are diminished. His conception of justice claims to eliminate the conditions that give rise to what he calls "disruptive emotions" such as envy.

Yet Rawls underestimates the prevalence of envy and erroneously claims that "a rational individual is not subject to envy, at least when the differences between himself and others are not thought to be the result of injustice and do not exceed certain limits." Rawls is much more concerned about resentment, appearing to support feelings of resentment as legitimate "moral feelings" that emerge when there is injustice: "If we resent our having less than others, it must be because we think that their being better off is the result of unjust institutions or wrongful conduct on their part." But how could Rawls's conception of justice have prevented the notorious nanny murders? It was not just the "injustice" of her wages that Ortega was enraged about; rather, it was what she viewed as the injustice of the loving family that she witnessed yet could not enjoy with her own family. There will always be something to envy—even when wealth is evenly distributed.

Envy is pernicious. The individual who envies is prepared to do things that will make both himself and the person he envies worse off, as long as the discrepancy between them is sufficiently reduced. Murdering the beloved Krim children was the price Ortega was willing to pay in order to reduce the discrepancy between herself and her rival, Marina Krim, the children's devoted mother and the true object of the nanny's envy. To Ortega, it was a small price to pay to bring the Krim family down to the level of her own unhappiness. Murder, however, is not the most common outcome

[125] Ibid., 466.

of envious rage. Envy-driven vandalism and arson are much more common—but they, too, can lead to death.

Envy and Vandalism

Vandalism, arson, corporate subterfuge, cyberstalking, and even physical violence can emerge when envious individuals begin to perceive that someone is enjoying something that, in a "more just world," would belong to them. A sense of justifiable rage emerges from the perceived injustice of it all. The psychologist Erich Fromm (1900–1980) saw hostility based on envy as analogous to the aggressive behavior of children who want a toy that another child wants. Young children often have not yet learned to control their angry impulses and will try to take the toy by force through biting or hitting the other child. In these cases, the target for the child's rage is clear.

Still, there are many times when envy cannot find a specific target for rage over the natural inequalities inherent in living in a free society. In these cases, seemingly "senseless" vandalism is often the result, as envious individuals engage in malicious damage to private or public property as a way of expressing rage or frustration over such inequality. More than four decades ago, Stanford psychology professor Philip G. Zimbardo attempted to make sense of apparently "senseless" vandalism, and in a series of controlled experiments, he demonstrated that malicious vandalism—damage done to property as part of a general expression of rage or frustration—is often directed at symbols of middle-class property, public institutions, subways, schools, and automobiles. Such vandalism depends on the prevailing social-political climate, the context of the behavior, and the degree of association between the perpetrator of the act and those in influential positions who assign the labels to these destructive behaviors.

The Politics of Envy

According to Zimbardo's research, malicious vandalism can be seen as a personal acceptance of being rejected by society and being alienated from its institutions. To the perpetrator, such vandalism is justified by his "outsider" status. Zimbardo pointed out that the property destruction that occurred during the 1960s racial disturbances in Watts, Newark, and other American cities were labeled "mindless" until one researcher noted that the targets chosen were not arbitrary. The report of the National Advisory Commission on Civil Disorders (1968) noted that "in at least nine of the cities studied, the damage seems to have been the result of deliberate attacks on white-owned businesses—especially Jewish-owned businesses—characterized in the Negro community as unfair or disrespectful toward Negroes."

Similar patterns of envious rage and frustration were evident in the 1992 riots in Los Angeles, when Korean-owned businesses were targeted for vandalism and destruction through arson.[126] More than 1,700 Korean businesses were destroyed because the African American community opposed the widespread Korean ownership and control of real estate across South Central Los Angeles. African American and Latino rioters believed that they did not have the same entrepreneurial opportunities. A Korean business owner who was interviewed on the local television news decried the fact that no fire trucks were coming to Koreatown to put out the fires: "This is no longer about Rodney King.... This is about the system against us." It was an envy-inspired insurrection against Korean-owned businesses. In the year leading up to the riots, rapper Ice Cube released an album, *Death Certificate*, that predicted that a "revolution" was inevitable. With songs like "A

---

[126] Brentin Mock, "What Was Lost in the Fires of the Los Angeles Riots," *CityLab*, April 25, 2017, https://www.citylab.com/equity/2017/04/what-was-lost-in-the-fires-of-the-la-riots/524145/.

Bird in the Hand," or "Black Korea," the lyrics spoke directly to
the rage and frustration emerging from the envy that permeated
the culture of the South Central Los Angeles community in the
1980s and '90s. Many sociologists believe that this led directly to
the riots. The hateful tension between African American youth
and Korean storeowners is clear in the lyrics to "Black Korea": "So
pay respect to the black fist. Or we'll burn your store right down
to a crisp. And then we'll see ya. Cause can't turn the ghetto into
Black Korea."[127]

In the aftermath of the 1992 riots, some blamed the Koreans themselves for causing African Americans to envy them. An
article in the *Joong Ang Daily*, in Seoul (reprinted in the *Los
Angeles Times*) warned: "The Korean community in the United
States should take a closer look at its lifestyle and engage in self-
reflection. Koreans in the United States have built a community
through diligence and faithfulness. This also has been a subject
of envy from Americans of different minority races. What the
Koreans in America should improve is their measures to deal
with such envious feelings. If we accumulate wealth, we must
also be prepared to share that wealth with other members of the
community."[128] Likewise, the *Jerusalem Post* suggested that "no
democracy can afford to be smug about such explosions. In the
contest with socialism and communism, free-market democracies
have proved their indisputable superiority. But they have not yet

[127] Ice Cube, "Black Korea," *Death Certificate* (Los Angeles: Paramount
Studios, 1991), https://genius.com/Ice-cube-black-korea-lyrics.

[128] Staff of the *Los Angeles Times, Understanding the Riots: Los Angeles Before and After the Rodney King Case* (Los Angeles: Los
Angeles Times, 1992). See also "The Press: The Whole World
Watches—and Reacts—to L.A. Riots," *Los Angeles Times*, May
5, 1992, https://www.latimes.com/archives/la-xpm-1992-05-05-
wr-1498-story.html.

The Politics of Envy

adequately addressed the problems of internal national rivalries, ethnic tensions and socio-economic chasms." And an op-ed in the *Hong Kong Standard* pointed out the inequality that inspires envy: "Of course in a capitalist economy, there are winners and losers. It cannot be otherwise. But any advanced society which allows to develop a huge, under-employed, under-educated, impoverished sub-class living in violence-racked, drug-ridden slums is storing up for itself the sort of trouble the United States is now experiencing."[129]

Sociological theory on relative deprivation points out that none of these "suggestions" would ever have worked to diminish envy. The idea that "sharing their wealth" or "hiding their wealth" would inoculate the Koreans from the hostility that emerged from the adjacent Latino or African American populations would never have worked to ameliorate the problem of envy. Relative deprivation emerges when you believe you are worse off than the people you compare yourself with. And in this case, people began to feel that the Latino and African American residents of South Central Los Angeles were worse off *because* the Koreans themselves were doing better than they were. Therefore, the perception that the Koreans *caused* the Latino and African Americans to be poor emerged in the community, so burning down Korean businesses was viewed as a "rational" way to remove the ability of the Koreans to have anything worth envying. There were subsequently fewer shopping options for the remaining population, leading to higher prices and fewer grocery choices for everyone. But, for the vandals, the fewer purchasing options and higher prices were a small price to pay for the satisfaction of destroying the lives of the Korean targets of their envy.

[129] Ibid.

Crimes of Envy

Envy and Arson

Under the old common law, the crime of arson was defined as the willful and malicious burning of the dwelling of another.[130] Today, we define arson much more broadly to include all kinds of buildings and structures, including personal property, such as cars, clothing, and other possessions. Envy is often a motivating force in cases of arson.

For example, in an envy-driven episode of arson, ten new houses —many of them unoccupied—in a new subdivision twenty-five miles south of Washington, DC, were torched and destroyed in the fall of 2005. Many of them had been purchased by black families living in the upscale Hunters Brooke subdivision in Charles County, Maryland. Sixteen other houses were heavily damaged at a cost of $10 million. Five men—all of them white—were charged with the crime of arson. According to trial records, the five, equipped with flares, accelerant, and a police scanner, went door to door in Hunters Brooke in the drizzly predawn hours, attempting to set fire to thirty-five unoccupied homes. Although some of the owners of the torched homes thought the perpetrators should have been charged with a hate crime because so many of the homes were owned by black families, prosecutors claimed that there was no indication that race was the motivating factor. Searches of the five suspects' homes, computers, and cars turned up no hate-group or white-supremacist materials or other evidence suggesting racial motives. Rather, the prosecution focused on "other motivating factors"—specifically, the envy of people who could afford half-million-dollar homes. Members of the few white families whose homes were also torched suggested that "envy, not racism, motivated the arsonists." Judy

---

[130] William C. Braun, "Legal Aspects of Arson," *Journal of Criminal Law and Criminology* 43, no. 1 (1952): 53, https://scholarlycommons.law. northwestern.edu/cgi/viewcontent.cgi?article=3986&context=jclc.

Manning, a white homeowner in Hunters Brooke told a *New York Times* reporter, "They were jealous that people other than them could afford these houses."[131]

Prosecutors and defense attorneys concluded that the defendants were motivated by several factors. One was ostensibly the desire to make a name for themselves for their car-racing club, the Unseen Cavaliers. Prosecutors also suggested that a major motivating force was that "they felt slighted by life." All were convicted of arson—but none were convicted of hate crimes. Only one of the defendants admitted to racist motives, but it is still likely that an envious racism was a significant factor in the crime these five white arsonists committed against the upwardly mobile black families who were to move into the kinds of upscale homes that were out of the perpetrators' reach.[132]

Beyond racist envy, the *Independent* reported that two grandfathers in the UK were targeted by envious arsonists after winning first and second prizes in the 2013 Bexley in Bloom garden competition. Firefighters were called after their plots and their garden sheds were burned to the ground. One of the prize-winning gardeners told reporters that he suspects that the fire may have been set in retaliation for his unbeaten record at Bexley in Bloom. He followed up a Best Allotment Plot victory the previous October with further success in July: "There could be jealousy going on.... We can't say anything and accuse anyone but that's what we think. We got first and second prize at the Bexley in Bloom competition

---

[131] Gary Gately, "Pall of Racism Remains over Neighborhood Repaired after Arson," *New York Times*, October 6, 2005, https://www.nytimes.com/2005/10/06/us/pall-of-racism-remains-over-neighborhood-repaired-after-arson.html.

[132] Greg Barrett, "Prison Terms Set in Arson," *Baltimore Sun*, December 6, 2006, https://www.baltimoresun.com/maryland/bal-md.arson06dec06-story.html.

in July." According to the *Independent*, "Bexley police confirmed that they are treating the blaze, which broke out during National Allotments Week, as suspicious."[133]

Arson has frequently been prompted by envy and competition among college students—especially those at elite universities. Helmut Schoeck described these types of fires in his book *Envy: A Theory of Social Behaviour*. In 1967, there were three fires set in student housing at Cornell University:

> In the worst fire, on April 5, 1967, eight students and a professor died in the blaze. On May 23, a second fire broke out in a dormitory on campus, and a third occurred on May 31 in a building occupied by some of the same students evacuated from the house burned on April 5. All three fires involved dormitories housing students who were enrolled in a special program for exceptionally brilliant students. It is a program that may lead to a Ph.D. in six years instead of the usual ten or more years of undergraduate and graduate work. Only 45 of Cornell's more than 13,000 students are enrolled in that special program. Four of the eight students who died in the April 5 fire were members of the special Ph.D. group. Most of the students who were threatened by the fire on May 23 were also enrolled in the special program, as were seven of the nine students who were driven out by the fire of May 31. Neither the District Attorney nor the County Coroner believe that it was all due to coincidence. The fires could only have been started by human agency. The Coroner did

---

[133] Adam Sherwin, "Green Eyes and Green Fingers: Did Envy Lead to Arson Attack on Award-Winning Allotments?" *Independent* (London), August 12, 2013, https://www.independent.co.uk/news/uk/crime/green-eyes-and-green-fingers-did-envy-lead-to-arson-attack-on-award-winning-allotments-8758030.html.

not use the word "envy" but spoke of "human malice," a term often used in place of envy.[134]

Since that time, there have been several cases of envious arson on university campuses. In 1983, Pueblo, Colorado, fire chief Robert Drake blamed "envy, jealousy, resentment and hatred" as the cause for several fires in the dormitory at the University of Southern Colorado.[135]

Gender is increasingly playing a role in envious arson. While much less common, arson investigators have found that fires started by women have increased dramatically over the past few decades. According to Dian Williams, the founder and president of the Center for Arson Research in Philadelphia, for women, "most of these fires focus on domestic issues involving jealous rage or revenge." David Kerr Wilcox, a clinical instructor in psychology at Harvard Medical School, echoed this, claiming that "women tend to set fires in the context of some sort of relationship. Revenge fire setting for women generally attaches to a specific target ... usually a reaction to some emotionally charged issue in their lives ... it's the igniting of rage, jealousy and envy."[136] In most reported cases of female-initiated arson, the motivation is more often jealousy involving a romantic rival or a love triangle. The film *Waiting to Exhale*, released in 1995, is viewed as "inspiring" episodes of arson by spurned and jealous women. Angela Bassett, the main character in the movie who has abandoned her career dream of having a

---

[134] Schoeck, *Envy*, 131.

[135] "Arson Caused Fire Spawned by Envy, Jealousy, Revenge and Hatred," UPI Archives, March 11, 1983, https://www.upi.com/Archives/1983/03/11/An-arson-caused-fire-spawned-by-envy-jealousy-revenge-and/7195416206800/.

[136] Patti Rosenberg, "Female Arson Rate Grows," *Daily Press*, November 24, 2004, https://www.dailypress.com/news/dp-xpm-20041124-2004-11-24-0411240233-story.html.

catering business to raise a family and support her husband, is told by her husband that he is leaving her for a white woman he works with. In a rage, the woman takes all her husband's clothes, puts them into his expensive car, and sets the car on fire. A clip of the scene has become a very popular GIF.[137] The rage-filled copycats continue even today. Sometimes things go horribly wrong, as when a woman in Clearwater, Florida, Carmen Chamblee, thought she was setting her ex-boyfriend's car on fire but found out later that the car belonged to a complete stranger. Chamblee was charged with second-degree arson.[138]

There have also been many crimes of envy perpetrated by one female against another. This is not a new phenomenon. Schoeck describes a case in May 1959, when an attractive twenty-year-old college student, Rose Watterson, was brutally attacked in her college dormitory at Warren Wilson College. The assailant, her college roommate, Patricia Dennis, struck Watterson four times in the face with a hatchet. Schoeck notes that "the newspapers carried pictures of the two girls. Before the incident, Rose was undoubtedly pretty, though not exceptionally so, Patricia distinctly less attractive, a bit on the chubby side and, even in the photograph taken before the deed, her expression almost hostile." During the first hearing, she stated her motive was "jealousy" of her prettier roommate.[139]

---

[137] *Waiting to Exhale* Burning Car Scene GIFs, Tenor, https://tenor.com/search/waiting-to-exhale-burning-car-scene-gifs.

[138] Sara DiNatale, "Woman Who Set Clearwater Car on Fire Thought It Was Her Ex-Boyfriend's," *Tampa Bay Times*, September 3, 2016, https://www.tampabay.com/news/publicsafety/crime/woman-who-set-clearwater-car-on-fire-thought-it-was-her-ex-boyfriends/2292178/. See also Gina Mei, "Woman Arrested after Setting a Car on Fire That She Thought Was Her Ex's," *Cosmopolitan*, September 6, 2016, https://www.cosmopolitan.com/lifestyle/news/a63723/woman-arrested-after-she-sets-a-car-on-fire-thinking-its-her-exs/.

[139] Schoeck, *Envy*, 130.

The Politics of Envy

According to *Sky News*, in April 2012, a twelve-year-old girl from China murdered and dismembered her sixth-grade classmate because of what was viewed by the prosecutors in the case as "envious resentment." The murder took place in Guangxi Province in Southwest China. According to press reports, the twelve-year-old became envious of her friend because other children were playing with her. The perpetrator was told she was fat and not as pretty as the classmate. According to her school principal, "both children had high grades" but the perpetrator was "not a confident girl.... She was not an ugly girl, but she is a bit chubby." The victim was "tall and slim."[140] The night of the murder, the two girls were watching television together when the twelve-year-old smashed a stool over the other child's head, knocking her unconscious. She then used a kitchen knife, a beer bottle, a paper knife, and a pair of scissors to dismember the body and put the parts into plastic bags. It was clear that envy of the other girl's physical attractiveness was the motivation for the horrific crime, and it seemed that the court agreed. Yet for some inexplicable reason, the court showed leniency to the perpetrator, causing an outcry from the victim's family.

Envy and the Rwandan Genocide

In his 1999 National Book Critics Circle Award–winning book, *We Wish to Inform You That Tomorrow We Will Be Killed with Our Families*, Philip Gourevitch chronicled the mass killing, within a three-month period, of nearly one million people of Rwanda in a civil war between the Hutu and the Tutsi. Through interviews with

---

[140] Mark Stone, "Jealous Girl Murders and Mutilates Classmate," *Sky News*, May 9, 2013, https://news.sky.com/story/jealous-girl -murders-and-mutilates-classmate-10446303.

survivors, Gourevitch focused on the psychological and political challenges of survival in a country "composed largely of perpetrators and victims."[141] Envy was a common theme throughout his book. In one memorable interview, Eliel Ntakirutimana, a Rwandan heart surgeon in Laredo, Texas, spoke of how his elderly father—formerly a pastor of a Christian congregation in Rwanda—was able to find refuge in the United States but was now being protested and threatened by fellow Rwandans in the United States for what they said was his role in the massacre. Denying that his father had any role in the genocide, Dr. Ntakirutimana blamed what he called "Rwandan envy" for the harassment of his father, saying: "You know Rwandans. Rwandans go crazy with jealousy. Rwandans don't like if you are rich or in good health." The doctor viewed any charges against his father as the result of typical Rwanda "class envy and spite." He added, "They see us as rich and well-educated. They can't take it. . . . Prior to the genocide, the Ntakirutimana family owned five hundred acres in Kibuye—kingly proportions in Rwanda—with coffee and banana plantations, many cattle, and all those good Rwanda things. . . . Of course, everyone resents him and wants to destroy him."[142]

Envy has long been prevalent in a country that Gourevitch describes as "landlocked and dirt-poor. A little larger than Vermont, but a bit less populous than Chicago, a country so dwarfed by neighboring Congo, Uganda, and Tanzania, that for the sake of legibility, its name has to be printed on most maps outside the lines of its frontiers. As far as the political, military, and economic interests of the world's powers go, it might as well be Mars . . . and when Rwanda had a genocide, the world's powers left Rwanda to

---

[141] Philip Gourevitch, *We Wish to Inform You That Tomorrow We Will Be Killed with Our Families* (New York: Picador, 1999), 38.
[142] Ibid., 39–40.

it."[143] Although Gourevitch's book notes the envy that permeated the population, he does not identify envy as the primary cause of the genocide that racked the country in 1994. But in the 2000 book *Sacrifice as Terror*, Christopher Taylor presents compelling evidence that envy may have played the most important part in the Rwandan genocide.[144]

Taylor provides the historical context that contributed to the envy. Colonized in 1890 by Germany, the population was composed of three ethnic groups: the more numerous Hutu, which made up more than 80 percent of the population; the historically dominant Tutsi, which made up almost 20 percent; and the pygmoid Twa, which made up less than 1 percent, a very small, marginalized group.[145] Rather than try to control the country directly, Taylor points out that Germany administered Rwanda indirectly through the Tutsi minority because the Tutsi were politically dominant in the areas with which the German colonizers had the most experience, and because the Tutsi had a strong monarchy with a somewhat centralized administration.[146] After World War I, when the Germans were defeated, Belgium was awarded the territory of Rwanda by the League of Nations. Tutsi continued to be favored and achieved great economic success in the impoverished country—but some racial animosity began to emerge as the economic disparities grew. Gordon Clanton writes that "under Belgian colonial rule, ambiguities about ethnic group membership were settled by an economic criterion: those with ten or more cows were classified as Tutsi, those with fewer as Hutu. Resentment built up among the Hutu. After 1926, the Belgians required Rwandans to carry

[143] Ibid., 149.
[144] Christopher C. Taylor, *Sacrifice as Terror: The Rwandan Genocide of 1994* (Oxford, UK: Berg Publishers, 2001).
[145] Gordon Clanton, "Jealousy and Envy," 438.
[146] Ibid.

an identity card, indicating the person's ancestry."[147] Tutsi power expanded throughout the region and began to be concentrated in the hands of a relatively small number of Tutsi administrators in collaboration with Belgian officials.

Envy grew as economic disparities expanded, with the Hutu at the bottom of the hierarchy. Taylor noted that Hutu envy was exacerbated by the European belief that the Tutsi were more attractive than the Hutu because they were taller and thinner and had a facial shape more attractive to Europeans. Clanton points out that many European men married Tutsi women, further strengthening the control of Tutsi over Hutu and adding to the Hutu envy of the Tutsi: "Many upper-class Tutsi understood that it was to their advantage to reinforce European perceptions of their natural superiority and they obliged with pseudohistorical fabrications extolling their intellectual, cultural, and military achievements."[148]

The balance of power and influence between the Tutsi, the Hutu, and the Belgians in Rwanda began to change quickly in the mid-1950s as Belgian administrators shifted support away from the Tutsi. According to *Season of Blood: A Rwandan Journey*: "The Tutsis who had served their purpose well in the heyday of colonial power began to look very unpromising as potential rulers of a future independent Rwanda. Anything like a free vote would mean the end of Tutsi rule and the influence of the Belgians.... The Belgians came to recognize the inevitability of Hutu rule, promptly switched sides and began to support the PARMEHUTU (the Party for the Emancipation of the Hutus).[149] Violence began to break out between Hutu and Tutsi in 1959, and many Tutsi fled

[147] Ibid.

[148] Ibid.

[149] Fergal Keane, *Season of Blood: A Rwandan Journey*, quoted in "Independence: A Messy Power Shift," Rwandan Stories, http://www.rwandanstories.org/origins/power_shift.html.

the country, leaving a strong Hutu majority, which took control of the government in a United Nations–sponsored election when Rwanda gained its independence in 1962. The Hutu took control and exploited lingering fear of the Tutsi for their own political purposes. By 1993, a multiparty government was established, but it was probably too little, too late, and in 1994, the Hutu president of Rwanda was assassinated. After that, the Tutsi began to be hunted down as "cockroaches or rats to be exterminated ... portrayed as foreign invaders, intent on turning the Hutu into slaves. Radio propaganda encouraged the Hutu to kill their Tutsi neighbors. By the time the Hutu government distributed machetes, telling the Hutu that it was "time to go to work," there was nothing to stop them from murdering their own neighbors.

Clanton suggests that the Catholic Church played a role in stoking divisions when it began to shift its support from the Tutsi elite to the Hutu masses who comprised a majority of the converts. Taylor maintains that the shift for the Church was encouraged by the fact that more and more of the missionary priests were recruited from blue-collar, Flemish-speaking areas of Belgium and fewer from the French-speaking elite. It may simply have been a case of the Church aligning itself with the poor and disenfranchised — the least of the citizens of Rwanda — a practice that the Church has always embraced and still embraces today in its advocacy for immigrant populations. It should be noted that the first voice of authority in the world to say openly in 1994 that what was occurring in Rwanda was *genocide* was Pope Saint John Paul II. Despite this statement from the pope, the *Crux* editors pointed out, "it took time for the United Nations to discuss and agree upon using the term genocide for what was happening in Rwanda."[150]

[150] The Editors, "Church in Rwanda Has 'Never Stopped Weeping' Since Genocide, Archbishop Says," *Crux*, February 13, 2019,

The involvement of individual Catholic priests and nuns as perpetrators in the massacre cannot be denied. In March 2017, Pope Francis met with Rwandan president Paul Kagame to apologize and acknowledge that some Catholic priests and nuns had "succumbed to hatred and violence" by participating in the genocide. The *Guardian* reported that while two hundred priests and nuns—Tutsi and Hutu—were among those murdered, several other priests and nuns were complicit or even participated in the violence. An estimated five thousand people were killed at the Ntarama Catholic church on August 15, 1994. It has been alleged that one priest, Father Athanase Seromba, ordered his church to be bulldozed, killing two thousand Tutsi men, women, and children sheltering inside. Another priest, Father Wenceslas Munyeshyaka, was charged with helping to draw up lists of people to be killed and raped, according to allegations issued by the United Nations International Criminal Tribunal for Rwanda in 2005.[151] There are reports of nuns leading the Hutu extremists to kill the women and children hiding in their convents and garages.[152] According to *Genocide in Rwanda: Complicity of the Churches*, published by Paragon Books, two Rwandan nuns from the Benedictine Monastery of Sovu in Rwanda stood trial in Belgium in April 2001 and were convicted of genocide. Both received prison sentences of fifteen

https://cruxnow.com/church-in-africa/2019/02/church-in-rwanda-has-never-stopped-weeping-since-genocide-archbishop-says/.

[151] Harriet Sherwood, "Pope Francis Asks for Forgiveness for Church's Role in Rwanda Genocide," *Guardian* (Manchester), March 20, 2017, https://www.theguardian.com/world/2017/mar/20/pope-francis-asks-for-forgiveness-for-churchs-role-in-rwanda-genocide.

[152] Ellen Carmody, "The Catholic Church, the Rwandan Genocide, and Reconciliation," curriculum instruction, Avila Institute, https://www.avila.edu/_userfiles/Education/Fulbright-Hays%20Project/Educator%20Microsite/Special%20Topic%20Presentations/The_Catholic_Church_and_the_Rwan.pdf.

years—despite Vatican protests.[153] Eventually four Catholic priests were indicted by the United National tribunal. Among them was the Rwandan priest Seromba, who was sentenced to fifteen years in prison in 2006, later increased to life imprisonment.[154]

Although we may never know the extent of the involvement of individual priests and nuns in the massacres, it cannot be denied that the Catholic Church in Rwanda was compromised by its political ties to the Hutu masses. But the Hutu comprised the majority of the Catholic Church's converts and, after a time, the majority of its priests and bishops. Without Catholic Church support, Tutsi political dominance in Rwanda was doomed, and most traces of it were undone during the revolutionary years of 1959 to 1962. According to the *Guardian*, Archbishop Vincent Nsengiyumva sat on the Hutu party's central committee for nearly fifteen years, even as it implemented policies that discriminated against Tutsis. There was discrimination within the Church itself, including quotas for seminarians, so that 96 percent of the men studying to become priests were Hutu.[155] Witnesses claim that when the massacres began, the archbishop stood by as Tutsi priests, monks, and nuns were taken to be murdered, but those allegations were never verified. Likewise, there have been allegations that after the genocide, a Catholic network allegedly helped priests and nuns who had been complicit in the violence to reach Europe and evade justice.

---

[153] Martin Neyt, "Two Convicted Rwandan Nuns" in *Genocide in Rwanda: Complicity of the Churches*, ed. Carol Rittner (New York: Paragon Books, 2004), 251.

[154] Deborah Bloom and Briana Duggan, "Rwanda's Catholic Church Says Sorry for Its Role in 1994 Genocide," CNN, November 21, 2016, https://www.cnn.com/2016/11/21/africa/rwanda-catholic-church-apology/index.html.

[155] Carmody, "The Catholic Church, the Rwandan Genocide, and Reconciliation," 3.

The chief prosecutor of the International Criminal Tribunal at the United Nations accused the Vatican of obstructing perpetrators' extradition to face trial.[156]

As Samantha Power's 2002 Pulitzer Prize–winning book, *A Problem from Hell: America and the Age of Genocide*, pointed out, despite Pope Saint John Paul II's warnings, the United States and the United Nations did little to intervene during the genocide—even though it was clear to many government officials that the genocide was occurring.[157] By the end of the three-month period of Rwandan genocide in 1994, nearly one million people were killed, with 80 percent of the Tutsi population murdered.

The violence that occurred in Rwanda is difficult to understand. Poor people have always envied rich and powerful people, but they have not always reacted by burning, looting, and killing. Rather, it is as Rawls has suggested and as psychologist Roy Baumeister points out in his *Evil: Inside Human Violence and Cruelty*: it is injustice, not inequality, that breeds this kind of murderous violence.[158] It is mainly when poor people come to think that their poverty or their unequal treatment is unfair that they burst into violence. For decades, the Tutsi had an unfair advantage, and they treated the Hutu people as second-class citizens because they had become second-class citizens. While this can never justify the evil committed in Rwanda, the hostility and hatred the Hutu felt for the Tutsi can be understood. As Baumeister writes, "Evil usually enters the world unrecognized by the people who open the door and let it in. Most people who perpetrate evil do not see what they are doing as

[156] Sherwood, "Pope Francis Asks for Forgiveness."
[157] Samantha Power, *A Problem from Hell: America and the Age of Genocide* (New York: Basic Books, 2002), xx.
[158] Roy F. Baumeister, *Evil: Inside Human Violence and Cruelty* (New York: Holt, 1997), 50.

evil."[159] In the *Summa Theologica*, St. Thomas Aquinas wrote that the existence of evil in the world is the single greatest obstacle to Christian faith and doctrine. Evil strikes at people's fundamental beliefs. Episodes of genocide like this test one's faith. But if these events are looked at through the lens of the malevolent sin of envy, we can begin to understand and try to reduce the envious resentment that leads to such evil.

[159] Baumeister, *Evil*, 2.

5

Envy and Anti-Semitism

Although the industrialized Germany of the 1930s may appear to be a world away from the agrarian society of Rwanda in the 1990s, both countries experienced mass killings, accompanied by ideological and military preparation prior to each and the systematic use of conspiracy theories and myths to justify the covert plans for slaughter. In both cases, scapegoating emerged during periods of severe economic and social stress.

In Germany, the debt from World War I, and the humiliation of the Treaty of Versailles, which further indebted the already economically stressed country, contributed to the "need" for someone to blame. In Rwanda, the decline in coffee prices in the mid-1980s set off a period of political extremism and a scapegoating of the Tutsi population. This scapegoating built on the longstanding resentment toward the Tutsi for what some authors have seen as their "colonizing" of northern Rwanda in the 1920s. After 1929, Belgian authorities systematized indirect rule through Tutsis who had been educated at the Catholic missionary-run administrative school in Nyanza. The early Catholic missionaries educated the Tutsi elite, and some — including Christopher Taylor — have blamed these missionaries for inculcating the Tutsi

The Politics of Envy

with ideas of their own "natural superiority and predisposition to govern."[160]

University of Wales sociologist Helen M. Hintjens points out that by the time democratization was imposed on Rwanda in the early 1990s, Hutu president Juvénal Habyarimanas's regime responded by rallying the majority Hutu against the Tutsi, a purported racial enemy, hoping to prevent regional and class divisions from finding more open political expression. In Rwanda, like Nazi Germany, there emerged a redefinition of national identity along exclusively racial or ethnic lines that built upon prejudices that the Tutsis had engaged in from the 1920s. These developments became the prelude to the later implementation of genocide.[161]

There are many parallels between the genocide in Rwanda and the genocide perpetrated against the Jews in Nazi Germany. In fact, some academics, such as Hintjens, have suggested that many of the mechanisms through which genocide was planned, accomplished, and justified in Rwanda were the same as those used in 1930s Germany.[162] The Tutsi in Rawanda had become, as one social scientist wrote, "much like the Jews in Nazi Germany, socially dead people, whose murder was as acceptable as it became common."[163] There were strict ethnic quotas in Nazi Germany that locked Jews out of civil service and other government-related jobs. Likewise, in the decade before the Rwanda genocide, careers in the army, the priesthood, civil service, and the government were essentially "closed" to Tutsis. The economic crisis in Rwanda was being blamed on a conspiracy of traders, merchants, and

---

[160] Taylor, *Sacrifice as Terror*, 42.

[161] Helen M. Hintjens, "Explaining the 1994 Genocide in Rwanda," *Journal of Modern African Studies* 37, no. 2 (June 1999): 241.

[162] Ibid., 241.

[163] P. Uvin, "Prejudice, Crisis and Genocide in Rwanda," *African Studies Review* 40, no. 2 (1997): 113.

intellectuals—professions in which the Tutsi tended to specialize. Tutsi economic and professional success had already elicited envy from the Hutu elite. In the immediate prelude to the genocide, there was a dramatic increase in malaria, combined with severe food shortages—all of which began to be blamed on the Tutsi. And, as in Nazi Germany, there was a tremendous increase in the size of the army in Rwanda from seven thousand troops in 1989 to more than thirty thousand by 1994 as financial assistance provided to the government for food and drug imports was report-edly diverted into arms purchases.[164]

Hintjens points out that "religious images of suffering and sac-rifice were often invoked in the propaganda around the time of the genocide." The propaganda was intended to convince the Hutu that the Tutsi had to be removed from society to ensure the survival of the Hutu. Tutsis began to be blamed for all of the evils of the colonial era, and all the problems of the years since independence, including the economic and political crises of the 1980s and 1990s. There were also concerns about the "mixing of the races" of Hutu and Tutsi—another parallel with Hitler's own obsession with the desire of Jewish men and women to marry outside their "race."[165] A key document for Rwandans was the "Ten Commandments of the Hutu," first published in the Rwandan Hutu supremacist magazine *Kanguar* in 1990. The first three Hutu commandments forbade sexual relations between the two "races" and openly accused Tutsi of using their women to enslave elite Hutu men. It became an obligation of Hutu women to "rescue" their husband, brothers, and sons from Tutsi women.

In the same way that Nazi propaganda presented images of Jewish people as rodents and insects, the Hutu press dehumanized

---

[164] Hintjens, "Explaining the 1994 Genocide in Rwanda," 257.
[165] Ibid., 264.

The Politics of Envy

Tutsis as cockroaches. As had been the case in Nazi Germany, anyone expressing any sympathy with the Tutsi was automatically branded a public enemy. During the Rwanda genocide itself, physical features such as a "long nose or long fingers or tall height were considered a sufficient basis for a sentence of death." Identity cards were issued—similar to the gold stars that Jewish residents of Nazi Germany were forced to wear—and needed to be presented at all checkpoints set up throughout the country during the genocide. Mixed Hutu-Tutsi babies and children were killed to prevent them from later seeking revenge for their parents' deaths. Intermarried couples were killed to punish them for marrying the enemy. All of this was foreshadowed in the Holocaust of World War II. As we saw in the last chapter, a growing hateful envy among the Hutu played the most important role in the massacre in Rwanda in 1994—as it had in Nazi Germany. In each case, the scapegoat emerged from the malign envy, causing untold suffering and death.

The Role of Envy in Scapegoating the Jews

René Girard has argued that the major driver of all conflict and violence is mimetic desire—desire that is aroused by the craving of another. For Girard, all envy is mimetic. In his work on Girard's theory of mimetic desire and scapegoating, Gil Bailie, the founder and president of the Cornerstone Forum and a former student and longtime friend of Girard, appears to understand the relationship between mimetic desire and violence better than anyone. He writes:

> If one acquisitive gesture awakens another acquisitive desire, and if the mimetic nature of the rivalry set in motion by these competing desires forces the rivalry it provokes to escalate in intensity, the conflict itself will have two social ramifications. First, the rivals' desire, exaggerated by their

rivalry, will glamorize the object of their desire in the eyes of still others, awakening the desire of onlookers and drawing them in. Secondly, as the conflictual vortex grows wider and more vertiginous, the rivals will grow more obsessed (negatively) with each other than positively with the original object of their mutual conflicting desires.[166]

For Girard, all societal strife can be related back to the mimesis of desire and the contagious nature of the conflict it incites. The very existence of human culture "requires" that the constant threat of violent conflict arising from the mimetic nature of desire or envy be somehow counterbalanced. Unfortunately, throughout history, people have drawn upon what Girard has called the surrogate-victim mechanism—or the scapegoat—in order to make human culture possible or to achieve social order. To do that, people encourage a form of mimetic contagion in which participants become vulnerable to mimetic suggestion and begin to make accusatory gestures toward rivals. As Bailie points out, "The highly contagious nature of the situation makes it inevitable that sooner or later one of these accusatory gestures will attract imitators. The accusatory gesture, when imitated, bonds all those who join in the gesture, lending a moral certitude to the accusation.... Functioning very much like a black hole, the gravitational power of this accusatory consensus becomes irresistible, sucking into its vortex both matter and light, so to speak, both the testimony of the senses and the sentinel of moral judgment."[167]

---

[166] Gil Bailie, "Violence and the Sacred: René Girard's Insights into Christianity," http://www.aislingmagazine.com/aislingmagazine/articles/TAM26/R.Girard.html; first published as "Rene Girard's Contribution to the Church of the 21st Century," *Communio: International Catholic Review* 26, no. 1 (Spring 1999): 134–153.
[167] Ibid.

The Politics of Envy

There is a growing body of evidence that the anti-Semitism that permeated the culture of Nazi Germany in the decade before the Holocaust did not spontaneously originate with racist ideology or religious animosity, as is often supposed. Rather, a growing number of scholars, including, most notably, German historian Götz Aly in his 2011 book, *Why the Germans? Why the Jews?*, suggest that the virulent hatred toward the Jews in Germany in the 1930s and '40s was rooted in a more basic emotion: envy of the advantages enjoyed by the Jews. Some have even suggested that the National Socialist Party itself—the Nazi Party—was itself propelled by envy.[168] Others have suggested the German Jews were targeted because they declared that they are the "chosen ones of God." No theme in the Hebrew Bible is more fundamental than "chosenness" in the Covenant between God and Israel. In Deuteronomy 7:6–8, we are told that the Jews were chosen by God to be His own beloved treasure. In his farewell address to the Children of Israel, Moses said that the Jews were selected not because of their power or numbers but "because God loves them." But it was not "chosenness" that brought the horrors of the Holocaust. The Jews in Germany had rejected their "chosen" status during the latter part of the nineteenth century to assimilate into German culture. Yet this rejection made no difference in preventing the Holocaust.

There is a long and ugly history of anti-Semitism here and abroad. Prior to the nineteenth century, the hatred of Jews in Germany was overwhelmingly religious in nature. During the medieval era, Jews were blamed for plagues and crises and were believed to engage in evil practices such as poisoning wells and sacrificing Christian children. Because of the fear they inspired, Jews faced recurrent and horrific pogroms and were forced to live in ghettos. That

---

[168] Gotz Aly, *Why the Germans? Why the Jews?* (New York: Picador Press, 2011), 5.

situation gradually changed in the nineteenth century with Jewish emancipation and increasing levels of acceptance. But, according to Bavarian Jewish author Siegfried Lichtenstaedter (1865–1942), although virulent anti-Semites regarded Jewish religious tradition as "practically irrelevant" by 1933, "social anti-Semitism" continued.[169] Still, by 1933, Jews in Central and Western Europe occupied relatively high social positions—a fact held against them by Gentiles who had not achieved similar social mobility. Jews were regarded less as adherents of an alien faith and more as members of a secular socioeconomic group that somehow disproportionately profited from modern life.

Lichtenstaedter suggested that the Germans hated the Jews because Jews were competition for "survival, honor, and prestige." In his 1935 book, Lichtenstaedter asked if Jews as a group were perceived as being disproportionately happier than other groups: "Why shouldn't this give rise to jealousy and resentment, worries and concerns about one's own future?" There is a great deal of empirical data presented by Götz Aly to support this belief. To provide evidence for his contention that it was envy that inspired the Holocaust, Aly drew from published sources from nineteenth and early-twentieth century Germany, including polemics, petitions, memoirs, journal articles, and parliamentary protocols—all printed during the years before the Holocaust. Some of the writings promoted the Aryan race or sounded warnings about the impending consequences of the Great Depression and the popular appeal of Hitler and the Nazi Party. But none of the authors cited in Aly's book knew what horrors the German anti-Semites had in store for the Jews between 1933 and 1945. None of the writers who were documenting the norms, values, and beliefs held by German

---

[169] Siegfried Lichtenstaedter, *Zionismus*, 37, cited by Aly, *Why the Germans?*, 4.

citizens during the years leading up to the Holocaust could have known of the genocidal acts that would be perpetrated on the Jews in Germany: "Unlike us today, no one who lived, observed and made judgments back then had to explain a crime that beggars description. That's what makes these sources so valuable."[170]

Sociologist Werner Sombart (1863–1941) was one of the authors who documented the cultural milieu that reigned in the decades before the Holocaust. Aly points out that in a 1912 sociological analysis of academia during the pre-Holocaust period in Germany, Sombart found that, on average, "Jews are quite a lot more clever and industrious than we are," and he used this insight to justify prohibiting Jews, for the most part, from holding academic chairs in universities. Sombart admitted that it was "regrettable" that most of the time, if there were two candidates, the "stupider one," not the Jew, was chosen. Nonetheless, Sombart supported protective restrictions because otherwise, "all university lectureships and professorships would be held by Jews or Jewish converts to Christianity."[171]

Aly points out that "Sombart was not a racist," even though the logic of racial anti-Semitism drove his arguments. Aly adds that Sombart specifically rejected the assumption that Jews had specific racial characteristics, arguing that "the standards of proof of our racial theoreticians ... like all of their opinions, are drawn out of thin air and remain unsullied by any of the usual scientific rigor." Valuing sociological facts over speculation, Sombart concluded that Jewish social influence would grow all the faster "the less adroit and more sluggish and divorced from economic reality the majority population becomes."[172] Still, Sombart—like many German

---

[170] Aly, *Why the Germans?*, 10.
[171] Ibid., 130.
[172] Ibid.

intellectuals—later embraced anti-Semitic ideas. In his 1934 book *German Socialism*, he deemed the Nazi regime a legal form of state, recommending that Jews be stripped of their rights. He warned: "In order to liberate us from the Jewish intellect, which should be a main task of the German people and above all of socialism, it is not enough to shut out all the Jews." Instead, Sombart insisted that the entire "institutional culture should be reconfigured so that it can no longer serve as a bulwark of the Jewish intellect." Philosopher Friedrich Paulsen (1846–1908) advanced similar arguments in a proposal to bar Jews from occupying too many academic chairs: "If the learned careers were subjected to open competition in the same ruthless fashion as other economic careers, they would in time fall overwhelmingly, if not monopolistically, into the hands of the Jewish populace with its superior wealth, energy and persistence."[173]

Aly documents dozens of instances of anti-Semitic writings by Gentile professors during the decades prior to the Holocaust. In 1916, the economist Gustav Schmoller reviewed a work by the private lecturer Hugo Preuss, whom he described as "one of the most gifted new teachers of governmental law." But he introduced Preuss to his readers with the following words: "He has become one of the leaders of the Berlin communal freethinking movement, which, based as it is socially within circles of Semitic millionaires, now more or less dominates our capital city." Schmoller complained that Jews like Preuss were such "orthodox democrats … I cannot escape the notion—as industrious and admirable as they are—that their political outlook and judgment are excessively informed by a single idea.... In their circles there is such superiority of intelligence, character, and talent that they consider it unjust and harmful to state and society that their tightly knit community does not yet dominate the university, the military

[173] Ibid., 131.

and the top echelons of the civil service." Despite their obvious superiority, Schmoller found it proper to admit only small numbers of Jews to the higher ranks of the military or the civil service. Otherwise, Schmoller warned that "they would swiftly develop into an intolerant dictator of the state and its administration.... Once you admit the first Jewish full professor, you'll have five of them or more in ten years' time."[174]

Aly also documents examples of dozens of brilliant scholars who were excluded from academia just because they were Jewish. In 1908, University of Berlin historian Dietrich Schafer wrote a scathing evaluation aimed at preventing Georg Simmel, one of the founders of modern sociology, from being given an academic chair at the University of Heidelberg. The son of Jewish converts, Georg Simmel, whose work is still widely read and respected by sociologists and political philosophers today, was described by Schaefer as "an Israelite through and through, in his external appearance, his demeanor, and the character of his intellect." Envious and resentful descriptions of Simmel's talents were woven throughout Schafer's evaluation of the popular lecturer, who was accused of possessing a "pseudointellectual manner" that is "greatly valued by certain circles of listeners in Berlin." Schafer dismissively wrote that Simmel's "primary audience has an extremely high contingent of women, even by Berlin standards.... The Oriental world too—people who have flooded to and settled in Berlin from the eastern countries semester after semester is also well represented.... There's not a lot that's positive to be gleaned from his lectures, but people do get a momentary prick of excitement and intellectual enjoyment.... Considering how these circles stick together, the Jewish, half-Jewish or philo-Semitic lecturer will always find fertile soil at a university at which thousands of comparable listeners

[174] Ibid., 132.

are available."[175] Obviously, Georg Simmel was not hired at the University of Heidelberg.

The disrespect shown Simmel was replicated at universities throughout Germany—often against the leading lights of social and political thought. Nineteenth-century legal scholar Eduard Gans was described by historian Max Lenz as "the epitome of what was bad about lawyers." Despite the fact that at the age of nineteen, Gans was already publishing brilliant essays, Lenz described how the legal faculty battled to exclude Gans from the faculty when the young scholar had "the presumption to ask for a teaching position" even though, as Lenz pointed out with disgust, he had "neither experience nor official rank nor social position on his side." Lenz praised the Berlin students who had "refused to acknowledge the authority of this beardless boy" and recalled that the University of Heidelberg "had no desire to see a Jew as one of their colleagues." In Berlin, the legal faculty accused Gans of "superficial striving for novel and spectacular discoveries" that were "utterly misguided and without scientific merit." In 1825, Gans converted to Protestantism, and at the age of twenty-seven, he was granted an academic chair.

Jews experienced similar discrimination in the military and civil service. In 1901, the Prussian minister of justice was called before Parliament to explain why he had yielded to pressure and was no longer appointing any Jewish notary publics. He justified himself by claiming that the judicial administration was "the only one that hired Jewish assessors at all.... All other state administrations refuse to take on any Jewish gentlemen." At this time, there was not a single Jewish career officer in the Prussian military, nor had any Jew been promoted to the officer rank of the reserves since 1886.

Yet, once Jews were allowed to participate in education, they outperformed their Christian counterparts. In 1886, 46.5 percent

---

[175] Ibid., 133.

of Jewish pupils in Prussia earned degrees above those of simple trade schools. By 1905, that number rose to 56.3 percent. The comparable figures for Christian pupils in the same period were just 6.3 and 7.3 percent, respectively. Aly concludes that "compared with their Christian peers, Jewish pupils were around eight times more likely to earn a better class of secondary school degrees." Catholics lagged more than 50 percent behind their Protestant peers, and Jews were far ahead of both. In 1910, the vast majority of sixth-grade pupils at the Mommsen Gymnasium in Berlin were of the Jewish faith.[176]

Götz Aly's data reveals that Jewish parents were much more likely to stress the importance of learning to their children and to monitor their progress carefully. Jewish daughters were encouraged as well as sons so that by 1901, 11.5 times as many Jewish girls went on to higher grades as their Christian counterparts. In some districts of Berlin and the provinces, the differences were even greater. Beyond education, the Jewish advantage in health was "one to envy." In 1840, twenty-one of every hundred newborn Christian infants died within a year, compared with only fifteen of every hundred Jewish babies. The Royal Prussian Office of Statistics attributed the discrepancy to the fact that "the Jewish wife does not have to do heavy labor outside her home, better preserves her energy when pregnant and while breast feeding, and can keep a closer eye on her child." Jews also outlived Christians — a fact that statisticians attributed to unhealthy Christian eating habits as well as to "Jewish temperance in the enjoyment of spirits."[177]

All of these advantages in education and health contributed to the growing envy toward what became known as the "Jewish advantage," but the real cause of the anti-Semitic envy was the

[176] Ibid., 23.
[177] Ibid., 29.

economic advantage that Germany's Jews began to enjoy. As Aly points out, "The economic rise of Jews was the main reason that hatred for Jews became part of the culture of the broad masses.... Jews were often pioneers who put their faith in the future. In contrast to the Christian, the Jewish entrepreneur represents progress in the area of social life." Tax records show this difference quite clearly. In Frankfurt in the early twentieth century, the average Jew paid four times as much in taxes as the average Protestant and eight times as much as the average Catholic. In Berlin, Jews accounted for 30 percent of city tax revenues, although Jews constituted only 15 percent of the tax-paying population and only 5 percent of the population as a whole. In 1934, sociologist Jakob Lestschinsky noted that "the golden times of the first blossoming of capitalism had brought to German Jews more advantages than comparable classes in the non-Jewish population."[178] Most studies have concluded that prior to World War I, German Jews earned five times the income of the average Christian.

Despite continued discrimination, the advantages that Jewish families experienced prior to 1933 combined to provide fertile ground for envy to grow. In 1922, a best-selling novel was published that provided a blueprint for beginning to address what became known as the Jewish advantage: *City without Jews: A Novel for the Day after Tomorrow*, a satirical novel that describes a fictional Vienna in the throes of rampant inflation and crisis—and anti-Semitism. The people elect Dr. Karl Schwertfeger, "a political savior from the Christian Social Party." This character is based on Dr. Karl Lueger, the anti-Semitic mayor of Vienna from 1897 to 1910 who forcibly modernized the city and protected the interests of the Christian middle classes while railing against the Jews. The novel begins with a crowd scene in which Vienna citizens gather

[178] Ibid., 32.

to denounce the Jews. There are repeated cries of "Jews out!" as
Schwertfeger arrives and enters the chamber of Parliament, where
he will speak in defense of the long-planned "Law on the Expulsion of Non-Aryans from Austria." The proposed law would give
all Jews six months to get their finances in order and leave the
country. Those who defied the law by secretly remaining in Austria
or taking more than the allowed sums of money would be subject
to the death penalty.

While Hugo Bettauer, the author of the novel, intended his
satire to be a criticism of the growing anti-Semitism in Vienna,
Aly points out that it inflamed passions by bringing up questions
such as these: "Who are the ones who are driving the automobiles?
Who is splurging in nightclubs? Who is filling the coffeehouses and
the expensive restaurants? Who is draping his wife with jewels and
pearls?" The answer: "the Jew!" The fictional character of Schwertfeger suggests that the Jews have gotten so far ahead of the Gentiles
in Austria because of "their catlike flexibility, their instantaneous
intellectual grasp of things, their cosmopolitan sensibility divorced
from tradition.... They have become our masters and have seized
control of our entire economic, intellectual and cultural life."[179] In
the novel, the trains filled with Jews begin pulling out of the stations
ahead of schedule, and there are some "outbreaks of sympathy" from
the onlookers. Schwertfeger responds by ordering trains to depart
only at night and to use the switching yards on the outskirts of the
city. The promise of future advantages once the Jews are removed
helps to ease the qualms. In Vienna, forty thousand apartments
that used to belong to Jews become free. But all is not well once
the Jews are gone. Without the Jews to scapegoat, the ruling party
collapses, and the economic and intellectual life of the city grinds

[179] Ibid., 144.

to a halt. Eventually the expulsion law is repealed, and Jews and Gentiles once again coexist.

Bettauer's story was prophetic: the expropriation of Jewish property, the advantages enjoyed by Gentiles looking for apartments, and the academic chairs given to Gentile professors. Hitler cleared out more than forty thousand apartments that had been rented or owned by Viennese Jews. He also stripped Jews of their worldly goods, drove them abroad, and loaded the remaining ones into cattle cars bound for concentration camps in Eastern Europe. The deportation trains departed from remote switching yards, and a total of 48,593 real people ultimately left Vienna in this fashion. Only 2,098 survived.[180]

Envy and Anti-Semitism Today

In just the past two years, dozens of unprovoked physical assaults on innocent Orthodox Jewish pedestrians have occurred in the middle of the day in the Crown Heights neighborhood of Brooklyn, New York. Most recently, the attacks have become deadly. In December 2019, a shooting rampage in a Jersey City kosher market targeted innocent Jews as they shopped, and a machete attack was perpetrated on a rabbi and his family and friends while they prayed in a Hanukkah celebration in their own home in Rockland County, New York. On October 27, 2018, eleven Jews were gunned down as they prayed in their synagogue in Pittsburgh, Pennsylvania—mirroring a shooting in San Diego, California, the previous year. While incidents took place throughout the country, the states with the highest numbers of hate crimes against Jews are obviously those with the largest Jewish populations: California, New York, New Jersey, and Massachusetts. Combined, these states accounted for more than half of the total incidents in the United States.

[180] Ibid., 146.

The Politics of Envy

New York City's Orthodox Jewish population—especially in Crown Heights—has been the target of repeated attacks. In just the past year, a rock was thrown at a bus carrying Jewish children to school, breaking a window of the bus and injuring some of the children; a thirty-year-old African American woman slapped three Jewish women and yelled profanities at them; and a group of black teenagers assaulted a member of the Hasidic community in Brooklyn—hitting him with a chair. According to an op-ed published in the *New York Post* by Crown Heights resident Malka Groden, when documentary filmmaker Ami Horowitz asked black Crown Heights residents why they thought the attacks on Jews were taking place, the responses clearly reflected feelings of envy coupled with classic anti-Semitic stereotypes of Jews as "domineering exploiters." One resident complained that "it seems like Jewish people own all the buildings out here and they own everything and they're not sharing nothing.... It seems like they own all the property, and we don't. They don't even try to help us." Another echoed this theme of envy: "They own everything down here. They're coming over here and taking over but they're not bringing it back to us."[181] Black-Jewish tensions have been high in the Crown Heights neighborhood for decades. Residents there still cite the murder of Yankel Rosenbaum during the 1991 Crown Heights riots, and the incitement by black leaders such as Al Sharpton and the chanting of "death to the Jews" in the streets.

Anti-Semitism is a recurrent phenomenon in modern history—peaking in some periods and receding in others. Given the ongoing problem of anti-Semitism, it is helpful to review the findings of a 2015 study by José Leopoldo Duarte on "The Role of Envy in Anti-Semitism." The study was designed to test whether anti-Semitism is often

---

[181] Malka Groden, "Fear and Loathing in Crown Heights," *New York Post*, January 17, 2020.

a case of malicious envy: whether perceptions of Jews' extraordinary achievements drive unfavorable implications for both an individual and his group status relative to Jews. Anti-Semitism emerges when people focus on negative attribution and uncharitable explanations for Jewish achievement. The Anti-Defamation League (ADL) has already documented some of these "uncharitable explanations." In an ADL survey administered in 2011, 14 percent of Americans thought Jews "have too much power in the United States today." Sixteen percent believed that Jewish businesspeople are "so shrewd, others don't have a chance," and 19 percent believed that Jews "control Wall Street."[182] Stereotypes such as these extend through the past century. As far back as 1932, researchers reported stereotypes of Jews as "shrewd, ambitious, industrious, intelligent, sly, and grasping." In 1950, another major study found that the most frequent stereotype about Jews was that "money is their god" and that "they control everything" and "use underhanded business methods."[183]

To test his hypothesis that envy drives anti-Semitism, Duarte sorted anti-Semitic beliefs into two types: (1) stereotypes that *undercut* the merit of Jews' achievements by attributing them to unfair advantages, such as power-behind-the-scenes conspiracies, conniving, manipulative business practices, and (2) stereotypes that *offset* Jewish achievements by attaching unfavorable traits or defects to Jews. For example, false physical stereotypes, including "unattractiveness" or genetic deficiencies, or physical weaknesses are often used to diminish their achievements or to offset those achievements by balancing them against negative traits. Duarte believes that people become envious when they witness Jewish

[182] José Leopoldo Duarte. "The Role of Envy in Anti-Semitism" (doctoral dissertation, Arizona State University, 2015), https://repository.asu.edu/attachments/164104/content/Duarte_asu_0010E_15634.pdf.

[183] Cited in ibid., 4.

achievement, and this increases the acceptance of anti-Semitic stereotypes—even when they are false. He predicted that anti-Semitism would compensate for self-esteem threats presented by Jews' greater achievements and accomplishments, and he hypothesized that the greater the achievements of the Jews, the more likely the individual would engage in negative stereotyping. To test his hypotheses, he set up elaborate research situations designed to gauge the relationship between Jewish achievement and the level of anti-Semitic stereotypes. Findings revealed that Jewish achievements increased self-reported envy and endorsement of undercutting stereotypes by participants in the study. Participants explained Jewish achievements using stereotypes such as these: "They're born with lots of advantages"; "Their business people are so shrewd that others don't have a fair chance at competition"; and "They have too much power in the business world."[184]

Envy-driven stereotyping can become dangerous when like-minded people band together in their belief that the envious have not achieved more in their own lives is because the Jews have achieved too much—and achieved it in underhanded or dishonest ways. The envious individuals begin to view the Jews as the embodiment of the desires and possessions that constitute "authentic" being. As Girard would predict, rivals begin to covet not just the common objects but the others' wholeness or being. In mimetic rivalry, the other (Jew) exists simultaneously as model and an obstacle, and eventually the coupling of the two leads to violence, as the rival begins to see the Jew as monstrous. The Ku Klux Klan has had a history of terrorizing minority racial groups as well as ethnic groups such as Jews and Catholics, but its influence has been on the wane for many decades.

White supremacist groups like the Klan have been partially eclipsed by the recent attention drawn to the extremist Black

[184] Ibid., 49.

Hebrew Israelites, a black hate group that believes that black Jews are the true chosen people and that "white" Jews are the descendants of Satan. Followers of this group believe that the twelve tribes of Israel defined in the Old Testament are different ethnic groups, or nations, and that whites are not among them — nor are Jews, who they believe are "imposters." According to Heidi Beirich, director of the Intelligence Project at the Southern Poverty Law Center (SPLC), which tracks hate groups, the SPLC has labeled the Black Hebrew Israelites a hate group because their ideology is informed by bigotry, viewing Jews as "devilish imposters or devils because they [the Black Hebrew Israelites] think of themselves as the true Israelites."[185]

The SPLC has compiled a long list of enemies identified by the Black Hebrew Israelites, including, most importantly, those they call the "fraudulent Jews" and those Jews who attend "the synagogue of Satan." They also list "all white people," who are believed to have been "descended from a race of red, hairy beings, known as Edomites, who were spawned by Esau, the twin brother of Jacob, later known as Israel in the Old Testament." The list of those hated by the Black Hebrew Israelites continues with "Asians, promiscuous black women, abortionists, continental Africans who sold the lost tribes of Israel, who were black, to European slave traders, and gay people, who according to the extremist Hebrew Israelites should all be put to death."[186] Regarding the last group on this list, the SPLC

---

[185] Sarah Maslin Nir, "Black Hebrew Israelites: What We Know about the Fringe Group," *New York Times*, December 11, 2019, https://www.nytimes.com/2019/12/11/nyregion/black-hebrew-israelites-jersey-city-suspects.html.

[186] "Racist Black Hebrew Israelites Becoming More Militant," Southern Poverty Law Center, August 29, 2008, https://www.splcenter.org/fighting-hate/intelligence-report/2008/racist-black-hebrew-israelites-becoming-more-militant.

reports that "in December 2006, three gay men who were violently assaulted inside an Atlanta nightclub identified their attackers as Hebrew Israelites; no arrests were made."[187]

Key to understanding the anti-Semitism of the Black Hebrew Israelite sect is their hatred toward those black Africans who sold the "true chosen people" (blacks) into slavery. Believing that they (the Black Hebrew Israelites) were displaced as the chosen ones by white Jewish imposters, who are devils, they await the coming of the black Jesus who will destroy all whites when he returns. Like the Ku Klux Klan, the Black Hebrew Israelites have broadened their hatred to include Catholics. Many of us were first introduced to the vile tactics of the Black Hebrew Israelites at the January 2019 March for Life on the National Mall in Washington, DC, when a member of the movement began harassing a group of Catholic high school students from Covington Catholic High School in Northern Kentucky. Videos of the confrontation by the black hate group have been viewed by millions of people—confirming peoples' worst fears about the tactics of the deviant religious sect.

The Black Hebrew Israelites have recently escalated their violence against Jews. The two perpetrators in the attack on the kosher market in Jersey City that ended with the death of six people, including a police officer who was responding to the shooting of Jewish shoppers, are both connected to the Black Hebrew Israelites. David N. Anderson, age forty-seven, and his partner, Francine Graham, age fifty, had posted anti-Semitic and anti-police screeds on Internet forums in the past. According to neighbors, Anderson could be heard "shouting at night that his religion was the only true religion, while others—specifically Catholicism and Judaism—were false. Soon, he said, Ms. Graham joined in the chants."[188]

---

[187] Ibid.

[188] Nir, "Black Hebrew Israelites."

Grafton Thomas, another anti-Semitic perpetrator who appears to have been inspired by the Black Hebrew Israelites, stormed a Hanukkah celebration filled with dozens of congregants at a rabbi's home in Rockland County, New York. Announcing, "No one is leaving," the alleged perpetrator started hacking those present with an Ozark Trail machete. He was charged with five counts of "obstructing the free exercise of religion in an attempt to kill." Federal hate crime charges were added to the charges, which can carry a life sentence. According to reports published in the *New York Daily News*, Thomas kept what the newspaper called "an anti-Semitic journal."

The paper also reported that Thomas had googled "Why did Hitler hate the Jews" just two weeks before he committed the hate crime. Grafton Thomas's journal included questions such as "why people mourned for anti-Semitism when there is Semitic genocide," and included references to Adolf Hitler and Nazi culture on the same page as drawings of a Star of David and a swastika. A search of Thomas's cell phone by police revealed that he had searched "German Jewish temples near me," "Zionist temples in Elizabeth, NJ," "Zionist temples of Staten Island," and "Prominent companies founded by Jews in America" in the weeks leading up to the Saturday attack. On the day of the slashing spree, Thomas clicked on an article titled "New York City Increases Police Presence around Synagogues."[189] There were also references in Thomas's journal to the Black Hebrew Israelite movement, and the *New York Post*

---

[189] Stephen Rex Brown, "Accused Monsey Stabber Grafton Thomas Spewed Anti-Semitic Hate in Journal: Feds," *New York Daily News*, December 30, 2019, https://www.nydailynews.com/new-york/nyc-crime/ny-monsey-stabber-charged-hate-crimes-20191230-r3tsypjs-jjei7gkznebu7efshu-story.html.

reported that Thomas had attended the Black Hebrew Israelites' services in East Harlem.[190]

Key to understanding this type of scapegoating is to understand mimetic desire, or envy. Girard's mimetic theory holds that people desire objects and experiences enjoyed by others, not for their intrinsic value but because they are desired by someone else. We mime or imitate their desires. The Jews are viewed by the Black Hebrew Israelites as "having more" than others. The Orthodox Jews who have been targeted have loving families with strong fathers, meaningful lives, and deep faith in God—all of which are likely unconsciously envied by others in their neighborhoods.

In his most recent book, *Not in God's Name*, Rabbi Jonathan Sacks helps us understand the distorted belief system of the hate group, drawing upon Girard's view that the root cause of such hatred and violence is mimetic desire, the wish to have what someone else has.[191] It is not a coincidence that Esau plays a prominent place in the belief system of the Black Hebrew Israelites. Nowhere in all of the biblical literature is mimetic desire more clearly demonstrated than with the biblical story of Jacob and Esau and their sibling rivalry. Jacob longs to "become" Esau: he desires to occupy Esau's place in his father's eyes. He buys Esau's birthright, dresses in Esau's clothes, and takes Esau's blessing deceptively from his father. When the blind Isaac asks Jacob who he is, he replies, "I am Esau, your firstborn." Jacob did all of this because Esau was everything Jacob was not.

[190] Princess Jones, "My Visit to Hate-Linked Sect's World Headquarters," *New York Post*, January 5, 2019, https://nypost.com/2020/01/04/inside-the-secretive-black-hebrew-israelite-sect-of-harlem-linked-to-monsey-stabber/.

[191] Rabbi Jonathan Sacks, *Not in God's Name: Confronting Religious Violence* (New York: Schocken Books, 2015).

In many ways, the Black Hebrew Israelites imitate, or, as Girard would say, mimic many of the practices and external signs of traditional Judaism. Many male Black Hebrew Israelites wear oversized jewel-encrusted necklaces with the Star of David or symbols of the tribe of Judah, sold on the streets of Harlem today, as well as on Etsy and Amazon. In their places of worship, Black Hebrew Israelite women are required to engage in the ritual cleansing practices of the Orthodox Jews — including niddah, the separation of women during their periods of ritual impurity. All Black Hebrew Israelites are blessed with holy oils before they can enter their temples, and women must undergo a ritual cleansing after giving birth. Yet, even as they adopt the clothing, jewelry, and practices of Orthodox Jews, the Black Hebrew Israelites believe that the traditional "white" Jews are the imposters — satanic devils who usurped the birthrights of the blacks and help sell the true black Jews into slavery. As Girard would predict, the envious covet not just the common objects of rituals and advantages of the others, but they also begin to covet the others' wholeness or being — and thus the faithful Jewish man or woman becomes an existential threat to their very being.

6

Envy as the Path to Political Power

Demagogues appeal to envy because they believe that promising to destroy the advantages enjoyed by others will win votes and inspire loyalty. Sometimes it does. As the envy-driven horrors of Rwanda and Nazi Germany demonstrate, pledging to disrupt the envied lives of a despised "other" can be a ticket to victory for a political candidate savvy enough to convince voters that he has their best interests at heart.

More than twenty-five years ago, Doug Bandow, Senior Fellow at the Cato Institute, pronounced in his book *The Politics of Envy: Statism as Theology* that we "live in an age of envy." Pointing out that "people don't so much want more money for themselves as they want to take it away from those with more," Bandow suggested that although "greed is bad enough, eating away at a person's soul, envy is far worse because it destroys not only individuals, but also communities, poisoning relations."[192] A Christian libertarian, Bandow wrote that "those who are greedy may ruin their own lives, but those who are envious contaminate the larger community by letting their covetousness interfere with their relations with others.

[192] Doug Bandow, *The Politics of Envy: Statism as Theology* (Rutgers, NJ: Transaction, 1994), 302.

The Politics of Envy

One can satisfy greed in innocuous, even positive ways—by being brighter, working harder, seeing new opportunities, or meeting the demands of others, for instance." In contrast, envy today is rarely satisfied without the use of the coercive power of the state: "The only way to take what is someone else's is to enlist one or more public officials to seize land, impose taxes, regulate activities, conscript labor, and so on.... Statism has become the basic theology for those committed to using government to coercively create their preferred version of the virtuous society."[193] Bandow views statism—the out-of-control growth of government power to confiscate the property, wealth, and labor of others—as a grave threat to both traditional religion and human liberty. He worries greatly about the growth of government because he believes that much of that growth was built on envy; and he encourages Christians and libertarians to find common cause in the goals of preventing the growth of what he called the "false god" of statism and of returning our society to one in which both virtue and freedom flourish. Politics in Bandow's "age of envy" has resulted in a desire not to produce more for oneself, but to take as much as possible from others.

Bandow was prescient about the growth of government and the envy that has driven it. He would not be surprised that the secular atheist ideology that has grown over the past two decades distorts our understanding of reality. Those distortions work to hide the true goal of politics under atheism, which is, of course, power. Once God is banished, we become creatures not of God but of society politics, and we then have the choice either to rule or to be ruled. The stakes can be no higher because, for the secular atheist, man is the highest thing, and so power among men is the highest good. That is why everything is now political and why

[193] Ibid., xviii.

people lose their minds over elections. Bandow understands that there will always be a significant portion of the population who will vote for the candidate who promises to take away the most wealth — and sometimes the very freedom — from the greatest number of "undeserving" people. But the 2016 election of President Donald Trump disproved the theory that promoting the envy of the rich helps to win elections. Rejecting progressive promises to destroy the rich and the powerful, voters awarded President Trump with the presidency because he reassured them that America can again be the "envy" of others if we are willing to change course. President Trump knows that most of us do not envy the rich — we admire them. We may even want to emulate them. President Trump understands that for most of us, our dreams are not to hurt those who have more than we do. We just want to have good jobs that pay us enough to support our families and make us feel secure.

This is not to say that President Trump does not acknowledge that we often want to blame others when we experience hardship. And, although his message in the 2016 election was subtle, there were undercurrents of an appeal to envy in Trump's promises of "greatness" for Americans. Conservatives can, of course, be envious. As Helmut Schoeck writes, "Envy is politically neutral. It can be equally mobilized against a socialist government that has been in power since living memory, as against a conservative or liberal one."[194] The decisive difference is that the nonsocialist politician will always direct the voter's envy or indignation and resentment against certain excesses, the extravagant spending, the way of life, the nepotism of individual politicians. The conservative candidate will not pretend — as the socialist-leaning candidates do — that once he is in power, his aim will be a society in which everyone is equal and that there will be nothing to envy. Trump never promised

[194] Schoeck, *Envy*, 241.

an egalitarian society. Rather, he promised greatness—a society that others would envy—and this is what helped him win the presidency.

The demagoguery from both sides reemerged during the 2020 presidential election season, as progressive politicians in the Democratic primary rediscovered that envy can be a path to power. Attempting to outdo each other in their promises to punish those they have defined as "rich," they promoted free college tuition, a forgiveness of student loan debt, open borders, and universal health care. They castigated "greedy drug companies" and Wall Street "fat cats." And, although President Trump acknowledged the global forces that have operated to take jobs from Americans, he continued his appeal to our desire to have others envy us if we simply reelect him. This was a continuation of the political rhetoric that worked well for the president in 2016 when he told those gathered at a Michigan rally that when he wins the election, he will "end the theft of American prosperity" by bringing jobs back to the country and creating an economy that will be "the envy of the world." In a statement designed to acknowledge the resentment some feel about their jobs being shipped to Mexico or to China, Trump rallied the crowd by telling them:

> We will make Michigan the economic envy of the world once again.... The political class in Washington has betrayed you. They've uprooted your jobs, and your communities, and shipped your wealth all over the world. They put new skyscrapers in Beijing while your factories in Michigan crumbled.

Likewise, at a rally in western Pennsylvania, Trump appealed to envy by suggesting that in their pursuit of power and wealth, "our politicians have aggressively pursued a policy of globalization, moving our jobs, our wealth, and our factories to Mexico and overseas." Critical of lobbyists for international companies, President Trump encouraged voters to direct their rage against what he maintains is the "real cause" for job loss and wage stagnation: those he calls the swamp dwellers in Washington, DC—the politicians, the political action groups, the lobbyists and their enablers in the media who are promoting policies of globalization that are destroying American jobs. Rather than speaking of income inequality, Trump talked about national pride and recovering the wealth that has been "stolen" from the United States by global forces. And though he focused on the resentment that working people have toward those he called the "swamp dwellers," Trump has never pretended that as soon as he is in power, his aim will be an egalitarian society. He knows that anyone who is seriously concerned about the plight of the poor needs to be more concerned about expanding the nation's wealth rather than confiscating wealth from those who are economically successful.

In contrast, most of the 2020 Democratic Party progressive candidates for president promised a utopian world in which there is nothing left to envy. Yet the rhetoric did not always work out for them. In his failed bid to be the Democratic Party nominee for the presidency, New York City's mayor, Bill de Blasio, was unable to garner more than 0 percent of the Democratic primary voters as he promised the envious that he would actually take money out of the hands of the rich. Casting himself as an avenger sent to free the country from the rich, de Blasio warned in his State of the City speech in 2019: "Here's the truth, brothers and sisters, there's plenty of money in the world. Plenty of money in this city.... It's just in the wrong hands."[195] In that same speech, de Blasio promised

---

[195] David Goodman and Daniel Neuman, "Mayor de Blasio Says Wealth Is 'in the Wrong Hands,' Promises to Redistribute it," *New York Times*, January 10, 2019, https://www.nytimes.com/2019/01/10/ nyregion/bill-de-blasio-state-of-city.html.

The Politics of Envy

to "seize the buildings of scofflaw landlords" and pointedly framed the argument over income inequality. De Blasio thought that the demagoguery that helped him get elected mayor of New York City and has been a constant theme of his rhetoric, would get him elected on a national scale. But, when it failed, he became an early casualty of the presidential primaries.

Undeterred by the failure of de Blasio's socialist promises, the remaining progressive presidential hopefuls took up the mantle of the protectors of the poor—and the enemies of the rich. Describing the rich as "freeloaders" who are living off the capital contributions of undercompensated and exploited workers, presidential candidate Senator Elizabeth Warren proposed what she called a "wealth tax" because she claims that the rich are not paying their "fair share."[196] Warning that there would be no "loopholes" or other escapes from her proposed tax, Warren promised to penalize those who try to leave the country by levying a tax penalty of $50 million on those who try to renounce their citizenship, and she pledged dramatic increases in funding for the IRS to conduct annual audits on the "super-rich."[197] The problem with this emotional appeal to the envious to help the poor is that Warren's envy-inspired "wealth tax" guarantees that there will be less wealth to trickle down to the poor as people will find ways to avoid paying that tax.

Winston Churchill warned against this in a speech to the House of Commons on October 22, 1945, when he declared that "the

[196] Lizzie Gurdus, "Elizabeth Warren Says She Wants Billionaires to Stop Being Freeloaders," CNBC, January 31, 2019, https://www.cnbc.com/2019/01/31/sen-elizabeth-warren-i-want-billionaires-to-stop-being-freeloaders.html.

[197] Kevin Breuninger, "Elizabeth Warren Proposes 'Wealth Tax' on Americans with More Than $50 Million in Assets," CNBC, updated January 25, 2019, https://www.cnbc.com/2019/01/24/elizabeth-warren-to-propose-new-wealth-tax-economic-advisor.html.

inherent vice of capitalism is the unequal sharing of blessings. The inherent virtue of Socialism is the equal sharing of miseries." For Churchill, "socialism is a philosophy of failure, a creed of ignorance, a gospel of envy."[198] But, for the truly envious, the equal sharing of miseries is a small price to pay for the satisfaction of bringing down the rich. Demagogues know that envy is likely the most powerful political motivator. While greed is sometimes thought to be the sin of capitalism, and envy the motivation for socialism, envy can provide the inspiration for both capitalist and socialist societies. Under capitalism, when all are "free" to compete to be bigger, better, and richer than others, envy can emerge for those who are unsuccessful in that competition. Under socialism, when the goal of equality can be met only through the pursuit of the envious to take from the rich in order to provide an equal distribution of all goods, a redistribution and economic reorganization is the ultimate act of envious revenge — to destroy the rich in order to elevate those who believe they have been exploited by the rich. Calls for fairness and equitable distribution often hide the real envy that undergirds the belief that wealth is a zero-sum game: when one person gains something, the other person must lose something. Under socialism, wealth is viewed as a finite commodity, so the only way one can enjoy greater wealth is by depriving someone else of his.

The Power of Resentment

Socialism creates tremendous resentment toward those with "more." A cover story on socialism by Simon van Zuylen-Wood published recently in *New York* magazine described the annual "Red Party"

---

[198] The Churchill Project, "Socialism Is the Philosophy of Failure," July 30, 2015, https://winstonchurchill.hillsdale.edu/socialism-is-the-philosophy-of-failure-winston-churchill/.

The Politics of Envy

he had recently attended in Brooklyn. What he called the "anti-romance-themed" Valentine's Day party took place in the book-lined Jay Street Dumbo Loft that houses the radical publisher Verso Books, where "the view of the East River is splendid, the DJ is good, and the beers cost three bucks." It was a party where (without irony) attendees called each other "comrade." The author noted that those gathered were celebrating the socialist success of banishing the Amazon headquarters from the city and talked about building something great, instead of Amazon, in Queens. When asked what they might build, one of those gathered cynically quipped, "a guillotine."[199]

The guillotine has a special significance for socialists because it brings to mind the ultimate envious revenge that was exacted by the poor against the rich in the bloody Reign of Terror in France in 1793, when the Jacobins executed nobles, priests, and wealthy landowners because they were viewed as "enemies of the Revolution." Today's socialists look upon the French Revolution with a kind of yearning that they, too, might experience such startling success in destroying those with "more." During the 2020 primary, Martin Weissgerber, a well-paid senior field organizer for Democratic Party presidential primary candidate and self-described "democratic socialist" Bernie Sanders, claimed (on video) that it was time to "guillotine the rich." Weissgerber was videotaped saying that he was a communist and was in contact with groups that planned to hold mass "yellow-vest" protests in the streets of the United States, as they did in France: "I'm ready to start tearing bricks up and start fighting,... I'll straight up get armed, I'm ready for the revolution."[200]

[199] Simon van Zuylen-Wood, "Pinkos Have More Fun," *New York Magazine*, March 3, 2019, http://nymag.com/intelligencer/2019/03/socialism-and-young-socialists.html.
[200] Valerie Richardson, "Guillotine the Rich: Sanders Staffer Says He's Ready for Armed Revolution," *Washington Times*, January

Envy as the Path to Political Power

In Maine, Bre Kidman, a Democratic Party candidate for the United States Senate, has chosen the guillotine as a logo for her campaign merchandise—claiming that "it's aimed at being a sign of revolution by lower and middle classes." Adorning T-shirts and campaign buttons, the guillotine symbol is playing an increasingly prominent role in progressive politics.[201] Kidman, who decided to run for office after receiving training from the Victory Institute, which runs programs for potential LGBTQ candidates, describes herself as a "queer, feminist mermaid" and hopes to be "the first gender nonbinary queer" elected to the United States Senate, displacing Maine's long-serving Republican Senator Susan Collins.[202]

A now-popular socialist magazine, *Jacobin*, replicates the revolutionary fervor with recent cover stories on Bernie Sanders such as "I, President: How I Ended Poverty."[203] In addition to the print version, there is an online *Jacobin* blog with an article on "The Lives the Free Market Took" and another on "The Paranoid, Reactionary Dreams of Ronald Reagan," which claims that President Reagan's "hyper-nationalist worldview grew out of the paranoid jingoism of postwar America."[204] The late President Reagan has

---

21, 2020, https://www.washingtontimes.com/news/2020/jan/21/guillotine-rich-project-veritas-exposes-another-ra/.

[201] Associated Press, "Maine Candidate Picks Guillotine as Logo for Campaign Shirts," February 16, 2020, https://www.usnews.com/news/best-states/maine/articles/2020-02-16/maine-candidate-picks-guillotine-as-logo-for-campaign-shirts.

[202] Bret Scher, "'Queer, Feminist Mermaid' Surfaces to Challenge Susan Collins," *Washington Free Beacon*, April 29, 2019, https://freebeacon.com/politics/queer-feminist-mermaid-steps-up-to-challenge-susan-collins/.

[203] "Bernie Sanders: How I Ended Poverty," *Jacobin* (Winter 2019), https://jacobinmag.com/issue/a-true-story-of-the-future.

[204] Lyle Jeremy Rubin, "The Paranoid Reactionary Dreams of Ronald Reagan," *Jacobin*, March 16, 2019, https://jacobinmag.com/2019/03/reagan-american-journey-review-spitz-biography.

become yet again a target of hateful envy for the current crop of democratic socialists.

One who has capitalized on symbolic Reagan envy is democratic socialist and congresswoman Alexandria Ocasio-Cortez (D-NY), who appeared to have tapped into the envious resentment of her constituents in the fourteenth district of Queens and the Bronx in November 2018 when she ran on a socialist platform and defeated ten-term representative Joseph Crowley.[205] Now that she has a national audience, Ocasio-Cortez has escalated her attempts to use envy to divide the country, suggesting that President Reagan was a racist who "pitted white working-class Americans against brown and black working-class Americans to screw over all working-class Americans." Promising a federal job to every resident who wants to work, and government salaries even for those who do not want to work, adequate housing, free college tuition, as well as "healthy food and access to nature," Ocasio-Cortez has perfected the appeal to envy that promises to punish the rich and empower the poor.[206] At an event in January 2019 with writer Ta-Nehisi Coates, Ocasio-Cortez remarked, "I think a system that allows billionaires to exist when there are parts of Alabama where people are still getting ringworm because they don't have access to public health is wrong."[207]

[205] Jonathan Wolfe, "Who Won the Primaries," *New York Times*, June 27, 2018, https://www.nytimes.com/2018/06/27/nyregion/new-york-today-who-won-the-primaries.html.

[206] Jeffrey Cimmino, "Ocasio-Cortez Suggests America Is 'Garbage,' Claims Reagan Stirred Conflict between White Americans and Minorities," *Washington Free Beacon*, March 10, 2019, https://freebeacon.com/politics/ocasio-cortez-suggests-america-is-garbage-claims-reagan-stirred-conflict-between-white-americans-and-minorities/.

[207] Dylan Matthews, "AOC's Policy Adviser Makes the Case for Abolishing Billionaires," *Vox*, July 9, 2019, https://www.vox.com/

Ocasio-Cortez has surrounded herself with similar-minded aides, such as senior counsel and policy adviser Dan Riffle, who goes by the Twitter handle "Every Billionaire is a Policy Failure." In a profile piece in the *Washington Post*, Riffle was described as having been "raised by a single mother in trailer parks and public housing in eastern Tennessee becoming an avowed foe of the ultrawealthy."[208] Resentful about his co-workers on Capitol Hill who appeared to him to have enjoyed easier lives than his own hardscrabble childhood, Riffle told reporters that when he first started working on Capitol Hill, he thought Democratic aides would be activists and idealists. He found, however, that they were people who grew up on the Upper West Side and went to Ivy League schools: "These are people who don't think big and aren't here to change the world.... They only conceive of the world as it is, and work within that frame. They don't think, 'Here's the system; it sucks and we should burn it down.'"[209] Riffle recently retweeted a tweet from Anand Giridharadas that read: "The people up above are up above because they are stepping on people down below. And the people down below are down below because they are being stepped on." The tweet seems to encapsulate Riffle's thinking. In a wide-ranging interview with *Vox* contributor Dylan Matthews, Riffle made it

future-perfect/2019/7/9/20681088/alexandria-ocasio-cortez-dan-riffle-billionaire-policy-failure.

[208] Jeff Stein, "'Here's the System; It Sucks': Meet the Hill Staffers Hired by Ocasio-Cortez to Upend Washington," *Washington Post*, February 14, 2019, https://www.washingtonpost.com/us-policy/2019/02/14/heres-system-it-sucks-meet-hill-staffers-ocasio-cortez-has-tapped-upend-washington/?utm_term=.14f69f207686.

[209] Ibid.; see also Cameron Cawthorne, "AOC Aide Complains That Democratic Staffers Don't Want to Burn Down the Political System," *Washington Free Beacon*, February 14, 2019, https://freebeacon.com/politics/aoc-aide-complains-dem-staffers-dont-want-to-burn-down-political-system/.

clear that he wants to "eliminate" billionaires, claiming that he is not exactly sure where to draw the line on "how much" is "too much" for wealthy people to have, and he suggests that we may be allowed to vote on it: "We can have all 300 and some-odd million Americans vote on it and come up with an average that everybody thinks is a reasonable amount of money. But at some point there has to be an upper bound, right? There's nothing in this world that anybody wants or needs to do that you can't do with let's say, $10-15 million. And so at some point there has to be a line. To me, $1 billion is way, way, way, way past the line."[210] One of the ways Riffle proposes to "remove" the wealth from those he considers to have "too much money" is through the stock market:

> One of the things that I am intrigued by is what we can do about stock ownership and shareholders. Most of the galactic billionaires that we're talking about there — it's not like they have a checking account or a savings account with $100 billion in it. It's valuation of stock that they have. For Jeff Bezos, it's ownership of Amazon. For Bill Gates, it's ownership of Microsoft. So, employee-owned companies are something that we're talking about.... There's other ways that you can force the divestiture of an owner of a company once we hit a certain threshold. If you want to start a company, if you want to be an entrepreneur and start a business and that business succeeds, then you should be successful and you should be wealthy and you should be able to travel the globe and retire in your 30s and live in a big house with a big yard. But the idea that you still need

[210] Dylan Matthews, "AOC's Policy Adviser Makes the Case for Abolishing Billionaires," *Vox*, July 9, 2019, https://www.vox.com/future-perfect/2019/7/9/20681088/alexandria-ocasio-cortez-dan-riffle-billionaire-policy-failure.

to hold onto all that stock when it hits $10 million or $50 million or $100 million or $500 million or $1 billion, just isn't the case. Having more democratic control over society's resources would be helpful and having more democratic control over a company's resources would be beneficial for that company as well.[211]

The *New York* magazine article points out that today's new socialists are not just incremental welfare statists. Like the bitterly resentful Dan Riffle, they, too, are working in government to do as he suggests: "burn it down." Envy is driving this movement — just as it has always driven the envious move to socialism. While most colleges and universities had resisted much of this, the revolution is again making progress on many college campuses. Students have always been an easy target for the cult of socialism. This is even more true today as student debt has risen, and the current cohort of university professors has perfected the art of creating a resentful and envious youth culture. This is especially true on some of the most prestigious campuses. Simon van Zuylen-Wood's *New York* cover story notes that he recognized many of his Brown University classmates at the New York City gathering he attended.

Brown University seems to have made a commitment to creating a socialist culture for its students — even before they arrive on campus. In a precollege summer course called "The Idea of Socialism: Radical Political Theory from Paine to Marx," precollege students are promised to gain an understanding of "the range of views socialists hold and some of the complexities involved in socialist thought." It is a laudable goal if students were really introduced to a critical examination of the political theories surrounding socialism, but it is clear that there is another agenda — an activist agenda.

[211] Ibid.

The Politics of Envy

The instructor, an elected member of the democratic socialists of America's National Political Committee and a contributor to *Jacobin*, Sean Monahan, formerly a Brown University political science student and currently an activist for socialist causes, suggests that although the course in socialism is "historical in its organization, the class has a contemporary purpose."[212] Monahan lists the central themes for the course, which include the relationship between freedom, equality, and fraternity; the socialist conception of politics; work and leisure in socialist society; collective ownership and control of property; socialism as a religious or secular project; revolution and evolution. One of the questions Monahan lists for discussion for his students is "Does socialism have its own conception of justice or does it move beyond justice?"[213]

Of course, Brown University is not alone in its course offerings on practical applications of socialism—and moving "beyond justice." The renewed movement toward socialism is just a continuation of decades of university-based social justice, and progressive politicians' pandering in a long resentful march against those who are viewed as having more than their "fair share." Former president Barack Obama promised in 2008 that if we voted for him, he would "spread the wealth around." He tried to appeal to the resentful and the envious by taking a moment at a presidential campaign rally to reassure the very real "Joe the Plumber" that the rich would pay because some of them have "too much." President Obama simply assumed that a blue-collar worker like "Joe" would agree that the rich

---

[212] Sean Monahan, National Political Committee of the Democratic Socialists of America, Medium, https://medium.com/@seanfmonahan/sean-monahan-national-political-committee-of-the-democratic-socialists-of-america-33d6cc20c04c.

[213] The Idea of Socialism: Radical Political Theory from Paine to Marx course description, Brown University, https://precollege.brown.edu/catalog/course.php?course_code=CEPS0977.

get rich at the expense of those with less. But Joe did not conform to President Obama's biases and stereotypes about the hopes and dreams of a blue-collar worker. In fact, as it turned out, President Obama did not conform to his own stereotypes about the rich once he was wealthy enough himself to pay more than $15 million for a vacation home for his family on Martha's Vineyard in 2019.[214]

It seems that President Obama was wrong—just as the media was wrong about the broad support from the working class in 2016 for Donald Trump. While Trump won college-educated white voters by a four-point margin over Hillary Clinton, exit polls revealed that his real victory was among members of the white working class: "Twice as many of these voters cast their ballots for the president as for Clinton."[215] These working-class voters do not envy Donald Trump because he is a billionaire; they admire his courage and his willingness to take on the special interests that they believe have threatened their place in the world. Although financially troubled voters in the white working class were still more likely to prefer Clinton over Trump, few in the media, and almost no one in academia, understood Trump's broad appeal and his promise to "Make America Great Again." It was not economic anxiety or status envy that helped to elect Donald Trump; rather, postelection survey data conducted by the Public Religion Research Institute and the *Atlantic* revealed that it was "cultural anxiety"—feeling like a

---

[214] Kathleen Howley, "Barack and Michele Obama Are Buying Martha's Vineyard Estate from Boston Celtics Owner," *Forbes*, September 1, 2019, https://www.forbes.com/sites/kathleenhowley/2019/09/01/obamas-buying-marthas-vineyard-estate-from-boston-celtics-owner/#785f7adc5300.

[215] Emma Green, "It Was Cultural Anxiety That Drove White Working Class Voters to Trump," *Atlantic*, May 9, 2017, https://www.theatlantic.com/politics/archive/2017/05/white-working-class-trump-cultural-anxiety/525771/.

The Politics of Envy

stranger in America—that helped bring Donald Trump into the White House. Concerns about threats to religious freedom, family autonomy, continued access to good medical care, and anxiety about border security is what drove support for Trump—not envy of the rich.

Political Theory and Envy

The earliest philosophers warned of the evil of envy and resentment. In *On Rhetoric*, Aristotle described envy as "the pain caused by the good fortune of others." Stressing the importance of propinquity and the threat of competition, Aristotle adds that "we envy those who are near us in time, place, age or reputation," and he adds that those who envy do not necessarily want to emulate the object of the envy. In fact, in the *Nicomachean Ethics*, Aristotle suggests that emulation is felt most of all by those who believe themselves to deserve certain good things that they do not yet have. It is felt most keenly by those with an honorable or aristocratic disposition. In other words, while envy is the reaction of those with low self-esteem and a resentful outlook, emulation is the reaction of those with high self-esteem and an optimistic outlook on the future.

Philosopher Immanuel Kant (1724–1804) observed that rather than seeking their own happiness, the envious devote their energy to "destroying the happiness" of others. In *The Metaphysics of Morals*, Kant described envy as "the vice of human hate," a moral incongruity that delights in misfortune. In describing Kant's views on envy, psychotherapist Joseph H. Berke writes in *Why I Hate You and You Hate Me: The Interplay of Envy, Greed, Jealousy and Narcissism in Everyday Life* that envy is a "hate that is the complete opposite of human love.... The impulse for envy is thus inherent in the nature of man, and only its manifestation makes of it an abominable vice, a passion not only distressing and tormenting to the subject but intent on the destruction of the happiness of others, and one that is opposed to man's duty towards himself as toward other people."[216]

In her book *Envy In Politics*, New York University professor Gwyneth McClendon points out that in *Leviathan*, Thomas Hobbes (1588–1679) suggests that it is envy itself that differentiates humans and animals because "animals have no other direction than their particular judgments and appetites." While animals are driven by the need for survival, human politics emerge from a desire to be distinguished, even if that means conflict and hostility. For Hobbes, envy is grief at the prosperity of another—especially one who is close in status to the one who is envied—and is related to the drive for power. Because of this, a successful political order needs to take into account man's selfish and envious nature. John Rawls uses the term "envy" to help explain the propensity to view with hostility the greater good of others—and a willingness to deprive them of their greater benefits even if it is necessary to give up something ourselves. Likewise, Alexis de Tocqueville (1805–1859) pointed out that sometimes people can be so concerned about status that they will pursue status at the expense of their own interests.[217]

Both John Stuart Mill (1806–1873) and Adam Smith (1723–1790) viewed envy as a powerful motivating force. Mill placed envy as an antisocial vice that needed to be regulated because it involved a "breach of duty to others." While Mill calls envy "that most anti-social and odious of all passions"—placing it among the moral vices that must be regulated because the sin "involves a breach of duty to others," Adam Smith acknowledged the danger

---

[216] Joseph H. Berke, *Why I Hate You and You Hate Me: The Interplay of Envy, Greed, Jealousy, and Narcissism in Everyday Life* (London: Karnac Books, 2012), 151.

[217] Gwyneth H. McClendon, *Envy in Politics* (Princeton: Princeton University Press, 2018), 17–20.

of envy in *Wealth of Nations* but believed that the emotion is over-ridden in most people by more "prudential considerations." Smith minimized the danger posed by envy, preferring to highlight human beings' desire for admiration and distinction in the eyes of others. Claiming that such a desire for status can help one to live up to that distinction, Smith sees some value in status striving—even when driven by envy.[218]

Envy Drove the Creation of the Progressive Income Tax

Even though Adam Smith did not see envy as an evil in the way Mill and Hobbes did, Smith acknowledged the irrationality of status motivations when he suggested that we all have a basic desire to achieve distinction in the eyes of others—even when it does not bring other benefits. In this, Smith reflected the spirit of America's Founders, who rejected the envious motivation behind the current progressive income tax—that the more you earn, the larger the percentage of tax you must pay. In *Federalist No. 10*, James Madison dismissed the idea of taxing what he called the "various descriptions of property" because he knew it would begin to destroy the rules of justice. The Fourteenth Amendment promised equal protection of the law to all citizens, and early attempts to "tax the rich" met with legislative failure. In 1894, when Congress passed an income tax that was levied on only the top 2 percent of wealth holders, the Supreme Court ruled it unconstitutional because it targeted only one group. Writing for the majority, Supreme Court Justice Stephen Field repudiated the congressional action and predicted that if such a tax were al-lowed, it would be the "stepping stone to others, larger and more

---

[218] Ibid., 20–23.

sweeping, until our political contests become a war of the poor against the rich."[219]

Justice Field was prescient. Less than two decades later, campaigning on a platform of "soaking the rich," legislators promoted a constitutional amendment in 1913 permitting a progressive income tax. In these early days, the top rate was kept at a low 7 percent. But, just as Justice Field feared, only a generation later, in the midst of the Depression, Herbert Hoover and Franklin D. Roosevelt claimed that the economy demanded extreme measures. Under Hoover, the top rate was hiked to 64 percent, and once the Democrats took control of the White House, Roosevelt raised the rate to 90 percent. By 1941, Roosevelt proposed a 99.5 percent marginal rate on all incomes over $100,000. Although his proposal was not successful, Roosevelt issued an executive order to tax all income over $25,000 at the rate of 100 percent. Congress repealed the presidential order but retained the marginal tax rate of 90 percent on top incomes.[220] Today, the progressive income tax is so taken for granted that few even recall that there was ever a debate over the constitutionality of such a tax.

Psychologists have long known that achieving status within our own reference group brings pleasure and a sense of personal power and is more closely linked to self-reports of well- being than many measures of absolute welfare. When we think we are falling behind those in our reference group, we begin to feel a sense of status anxiety. And from the earliest days of the fledgling discipline of sociology in the nineteenth century, sociologists have been concerned with status issues — including status envy. Emerging in

[219] Burton W. Folsom, "The Progressive Income Tax in U. S. History," Foundation for Economic Education, May 1, 2003, https://fee.org/articles/the-progressive-income-tax-in-us-history/.
[220] Ibid.

the midst of the chaos that had accompanied urbanization and the industrialization of the economy, sociology was created to try to understand what holds social groups together during times of rapid social change and to explore possible solutions to the breakdown of social solidarity. While early sociologists such as Émile Durkheim stressed the "ties that bind us together," Karl Marx teamed with wealthy industrialist Friedrich Engels to address the growing inequality that they believed was tearing society apart. Writing at the height of the Industrial Revolution, when factory owners were accumulating wealth and factory workers remained mired in poverty, Marx and Engels attacked the growing income gap, claiming that it was capitalism that perpetuated these inequalities. Marx believed that the accumulation of capital or property was an obstacle to progress because any inequality in wealth meant that someone was exploited. For Marx, capitalism required the exploitation of the workers in order to provide profits to the owners. And although Marx viewed capitalism as an inevitable stage in the history of the world leading to "the millennium of socialism," he drew upon themes of envy toward the rich to gain support from the masses in order to destroy the capitalist system. This is still true today as the Marxist promise of "fairness" to the proletariat was a promise of a utopian world in which all conditions that produce envy will disappear.

The Myth of Social Justice

Today's Marxists argue that the egalitarian world that socialism can create removes all targets of envy so that the envious have nothing to envy. Yet envy creates its own targets, regardless of how equal people may appear to be. The fact that there has never been a socialist society that brought about such utopian classless conditions is dismissed by the Marxists, who believe that such examples of socialism have not gone far enough in redistributing the wealth equally. A recurring theme throughout much political thought has been that envy supplies the psychological and sociological foundations of the concern for egalitarian conceptions of justice. True egalitarians want to do away with the advantages of the better off. They wish to do this because they are unhappy that some have "more" than they do. According to economist Friedrich Hayek (1899–1992), "social justice rests on the hate towards those that enjoy a comfortable position, namely, upon envy." In *The Mirage of Social Justice*, Hayek suggests that social justice is a notion that lacks a rigorous meaning since no one has been able to determine, except in the marketplace, what would be the absolutely just distribution of the patrimony and income in a mass society. Suggesting that the phrase social justice had become a source of "sloppy thinking and intellectual dishonesty," Hayek believed that using the phrase was "the mark of demagogy and cheap journalism which responsible thinkers ought to be ashamed to use because, once its vacuity is recognized, its use is dishonest."[221] Describing social justice as "that incubus which today makes fine sentiments the instruments for the destruction of all values of a free civilization," Hayek warned that the continued unexamined pursuit of "social justice" will contribute to the erosion of personal liberties and encourage the advent of totalitarianism.[222]

Drawing from Hayek, Gonzalo Fernández de la Mora (1924–2002) suggests in *Egalitarian Envy*, his own treatise on the danger of envy, that "egalitarianism is the opiate of the envious and demagogues are the self-interested distributors of its massive consumption." Echoing Hayek, de la Mora writes that "the realization

---

[221] Friederich Hayek, *Law, Legislation and Liberty*, vol. 2, *The Mirage of Social Justice* (Chicago: University of Chicago Press, 1978), 97.
[222] Ibid., xii.

of what is called social justice requires economic planning and delegation to the public powers of the authority to assign work, rewards, and salaries to every citizen. Within a totalitarian system, this monopoly is equivalent to the tyranny of only one party; and within a democracy, it implies the tyranny of the majority, for in order to please its electoral clientele, it must expropriate the minorities. This is how theoretical social justice may turn out as effective inequity."[223] For de la Mora,

> what the Marxists usually call social justice is the policy of inspiring the less productive to demand that the state carry out transfers of goods by expropriating those who produce more, humbling the superior to satisfy the inferior.... This maneuver is no doubt a political use of envy. The generalization of such a practice very often makes it possible for the topic of social justice to become the pharisaic institutionalization of collective envy or a tacit concession to placate it.... Interventionism leads to increasing controls and therefore to the progressive elimination of private initiative, and actual liberties end up being destroyed by totalitarian models.... Egalitarian distribution without regard for individual merits and demerits is inequality rather than justice.[224]

In an attempt to "rescue it from its ideological captors," Michael Novak and Paul Adams provided an alternative Catholic definition of social justice in their 2015 book, *Social Justice Isn't What You Think It Is*. Challenging both progressive and conservative approaches to social justice, Novak and Adams suggest that

---

[223] Gonzalo Fernández de la Mora, *Egalitarian Envy: The Political Foundations of Social Justice* (New York: Paragon House, 1987), 94–95.

[224] Ibid., 95.

defined properly, social justice represents an "immensely powerful virtue for nurturing personal responsibility and building the human communities that can counter the widespread surrender to an ever-growing state." In the introduction, Adams dismisses the ideological version of social justice that "provides a justification for any progressive-sounding government program or newly discovered or invented right." He also criticizes the ways in which some have branded opponents as "supporters of social injustice, and so as enemies of humankind, without the trouble of making an argument or considering their views."[225] Novak and Adams emphasize social justice as a virtue and aim to recover it as a useful and necessary concept in understanding how people ought to live and order their lives together. They attempt to clarify the term's definition and proper use in the context of Catholic social teaching — applying it in the context of democratic capitalism, in which, they argue, "social justice takes on a new importance as a distinctively modern virtue required for and developed by participation with others in civil society."[226] The Catholic definition of "social justice" has the potential to counter the threat of secular, atheistic, and collectivist social movements — like the current movement toward "democratic socialism" — because it involves a readiness to "make some sacrifices" to maintain the health and strength of society. Recall that the basic idea behind true social justice has its roots in Aristotle and in medieval thought — then called "general justice." It pointed to a form of justice whose object was not just other individuals, but the community.[227] Unfortunately, as Hayek pointed out, most of those who use the term today do not talk about what individuals

---

[225] Michael Novak and Paul Adams, *Social Justice Isn't What You Think It Is* (New York: Encounter Books, 2015), 1.

[226] Ibid., 2–3.

[227] Ibid., 19.

can do. They talk about what government can do. They talk about social justice as "a characteristic of political states ... remedied by state-enforced redistribution."[228] Once social justice is redefined as a state intervention involving confiscation, it loses its status as an individual virtue, and as Hayek claims, "if social justice is not a virtue, its claim to moral standing falls flat."[229]

Contemporary political theory helps to explain the status motivations that shape voting behaviors and other political decisions. In the 1950s, research by Richard Hofstadter found that shifts in prestige across entire communities prompted individuals who had lost relative status to become progressives, so that they could push for reforms to gain higher incomes and levels of education.[230] Status inconsistencies—when individuals have high status in one dimension, such as education, and low status in another dimension, such as income—will be more likely to support progressive political parties that favor social change. This helps to explain why the majority of Ph.D.-level professors on college campuses throughout the country describe themselves as progressives and are the strongest supporters of social justice and coercive egalitarianism.

In an attempt to understand how envy operates in political behavior, Gwyneth McClendon analyzed what she sees as "puzzling" political behavior or voting behavior that is chosen even though it is contrary to one's own interests. In her book *Envy in Politics*, McClendon suggests that when looking at the policies we support and the politicians we vote for, we should pay attention to envy, spite, and the pursuit of admiration—all manifestations of our desire to maintain or enhance our status within groups. Drawing

[228] Ibid., 22.
[229] Ibid., 21.
[230] Richard Hofstadter, *The Age of Reform: From Bryan to FDR* (New York: Vintage, 1955).

from Hobbes, McClendon points out that we often pursue a higher relative position for its own sake, even when doing so incurs no material benefits, except a possible improvement in one's social status. Analyzing empirical political behavior data, McClendon began her study with these questions: "Why do citizens sometimes support redistribution and taxation policies that go against their material self-interests? Why do politicians sometimes fail to implement funded policies? Why do citizens sometimes participate in political events even though it is personally costly to do so?"[231] Her answers often focus on status motivations.

To understand status motivations, McClendon conducted an experiment in which members of an organization's LISTSERV received one of three e-mails encouraging them to attend a protest. Some were simply asked to attend; others were told that their participation was "admirable" and because of that their names would be listed in a public newsletter; and the third group was told that participation in the protest was admirable and invited the participants to post on Facebook photos of their participation. The results revealed that those offered the chance to have their names posted in the newsletter showed up at levels 76 percent higher than those who were simply invited. The desire to be admired was the major motivation for those who attended the protest.

McClendon found that "within-group status" helps us understand why people vote the way they do. She points out that people may be "willing to support costly policies and undertake costly actions when doing so wins them this other valued good.... Status motivations help explain political behavior that is materially costly to the individual but that has within-group distributive implications of income or esteem."[232] Although she expected that the widespread

[231] McClendon, *Envy in Politics*, 174.
[232] Ibid., 174.

beliefs in social mobility, individualism, and the American Dream in the United States might have muted desires to punish others for their success, she found that status concerns—including envy and spite—continue to motivate political voting behavior that hurts others' upward mobility while doing nothing to improve one's own position. The central insight from McClendon's study is that to understand more fully the political implications of inequality in any era, we need to focus on patterns of local, within-group inequality; we need to consider not only that people are self-interested, within-group biased, and concerned about fairness but also that under some conditions, they are willing to pay costs (and even see others harmed) for the sake of achieving higher status within their own groups.

The "Never Trump" movement that emerged within the Republican Party during the 2016 presidential primaries and continued through the early years of the Trump presidency relied on these concerns about within-group status among those who oppose Trump. Even though President Trump may have significantly improved the economic position of most Americans, some within the Never Trump crowd have continued to deny that he deserved any respect and certainly not their vote in 2020. To support the president openly would bring an unwelcome decline in within-group status for high-profile Never Trumpers such as Bill Kristol, the founder and editor of the now-defunct *Weekly Standard*, who has enjoyed high status because of his frequent media appearances on progressive cable television news sites where he continues his attacks on President Trump.

Still, there are many more former foes of the president who came to realize how much their opposition was mistaken. Such a course correction would effectively preserve their within-group status. The *New York Times* chronicled the journey from "Never Trumpism" to Trump support by media stars such as Glenn Beck, the radio host who once called Trump "an immoral man who is absent decency or dignity" but who now says that Trump's defeat in 2020 "would mark the end of the country as we know it."[233] Similarly, Erick Erickson, a conservative radio personality and prominent Never Trumper who said in 2016 that he would never vote for Trump, published a blog in 2019 titled "I Support the President" in a complete turnaround from his earlier stance. *The Times* pointed out that back in 2016 Erickson wrote that it was "no wonder that so many people with swastikas in their Twitter profile pics supported him.... I will not vote for Donald Trump. Ever."[234] Senator Lindsey Graham and Brent Bozell, both Never Trumpers in 2016, have since openly expressed their support for the president.

The Problem of Duplicitous Envy

One of the problems that many progressive candidates for political office face is that in order to encourage voters to defame the rich, they need to hide their own wealth. This has become more difficult as the wealth of many progressive presidential candidates far surpasses that of conservatives. *Forbes* notes that failed Democratic presidential primary competitor Elizabeth Warren has a net worth of $12 million, lives in a $3 million Victorian home in Cambridge, and has an $800,000 condo in Washington, DC.[235] Bernie Sanders, the millionaire democratic socialist candidate for the presidency for

---

[233] Jeremy W. Peters. "The Never Trump Coalition That Decided 'Eh, Never Mind, He's Fine," *New York Times*, October 14, 2019, https://www.nytimes.com/2019/10/05/us/politics/never-trumper-republicans.html.

[234] Ibid.

[235] Michela Tindera, "How Elizabeth Warren Built a $12 Million Fortune," *Forbes*, August 20, 2019, https://www.forbes.com/sites/mi-

The Politics of Envy

2020 has his own embarrassment of riches. With three homes—including a $500,000 vacation home on Lake Champlain—Sanders and his wife, according to *Forbes*, have amassed a $2.5 million net worth from real estate, investments, government pensions, and earnings.[236] A large portion of that wealth derived from the $200,000 "severance" package given to Sanders's wife, Jane, when she was removed as president of Vermont's debt-burdened Burlington College.

Indeed, during her seven-year tenure as president of the college, from 2004 to 2011, Jane Sanders pledged to double the student enrollment by spending millions of dollars of borrowed money on a beautiful new campus—thirty-three acres along the bank of Lake Champlain that was purchased from the Roman Catholic Diocese of Burlington. Mrs. Sanders predicted that the new campus would surely attract more students and donations from alumni. It didn't. The next year, Sanders took her severance package and left Burlington College in such dire straits that by July 2014, the New England Association of Schools and Colleges (NEASC) put the institution on probation for not meeting its financial resources standard. The *Chronicle of Higher Education* concluded that since the Federal Department of Education allows a college only two years of probation, Burlington College would have lost its accreditation in 2017. On May 13, 2016, the Burlington College Board of Trustees voted to close the college.

President Jane Sanders promised that "other people's money" would keep her school afloat. It didn't. Now Burlington College

---

chelatindera/2019/08/20/how-elizabeth-warren-built-a-12-million-fortune/#776ab540ab57.

[236] Chase Peterson-Withorn, "How Bernie Sanders Amassed a $2.5 Million Fortune," *Forbes*, April 12, 2019, https://www.forbes.com/sites/chasewithorn/2019/04/12/how-bernie-sanders-the-socialist-senator-amassed-a-25-million-fortune/#3172e3c136bf.

is facing allegations of loan fraud during Jane Sanders's tenure as the school's president. Coralee A. Holm, the college's dean of operations and advancement, released a statement claiming that the institution had struggled under a crushing weight of the debt that Sanders had amassed during her tenure related to the $10 million purchase of property from the Catholic diocese. Though the purchase of the property is certainly not evidence of socialism, the way Sanders was able to gain approval for the loan from the Vermont Educational and Health Buildings Financing Agency raises questions that are still unanswered.

In a lawsuit on behalf of parishioners in the Burlington Diocese, the complaint claims that "the loan transaction involved the over-statement and misrepresentation" of nearly $2 million in what were purported to be confirmed contributions and grants to the college.[237] The loans were contingent on the college's providing proof of a minimum commitment of $2.27 million in grants and donations prior to the closing. Sanders never had the confirmed grants and donations she claimed she had, and instead, the complaint alleged, she "engaged in a fraudulent scheme to actively conceal and mis-represent material facts from a federal financial institution." She left the presidency later that year, and the college defaulted on its loan from the diocese. The agreement was costly for the diocese, which was forced to accept payments totaling $1,592,000 and an unsecured $1 million investment as settlement of the $3.65 mil-lion in principal it was owed. The diocese was also forced to forgo collection of up to $923,000 in interest accrued over the five-year life of the loan.

[237] Lawsuit filed against Burlington College, January 10, 2016, https://assets.documentcloud.org/documents/2680892/LTR-to-USATTY-and-FDIC-IG-Re-Apparent-Fraud-Sen.pdf.

The Politics of Envy

Questions remain about how Jane Sanders was able to convince creditors—including the Catholic diocese, the state financing agency, and a federally insured bank—that the school qualified for the $10 million loan. The complaint filed by the "aggrieved Vermont parishioners" suggests that Sanders's privileged status as the wife of a powerful United States senator "inoculated her from the robust underwriting that would have uncovered the fraudulent donation claims she made." The public harm in this case is substantial and should be viewed as an example of crony capitalism, but it is unlikely that will be the case. Regardless, it is instructive to look at this scandal as yet another example of the fraud of socialism itself. The insolvency of Burlington College brings to mind the famous quotation from Britain's legendary Conservative prime minister, Margaret Thatcher, that the real problem with socialists is that "they always run out of other people's money."[238] A key theme of the presidential campaign of Vermont socialist Bernie Sanders was his pledge to make tuition at public colleges "free," but he promised to tax Wall Street investors to pay for his $75 billion–a-year program.

Societies flourish when people find ways to control envy, this most destructive emotion. Because envy is ever present—and powerful when aroused—a society's ability to achieve greatness depends on its ability to control this highly destructive emotion. But, as wealth grows, inequality grows with it, and there is always the seductive appeal of revengeful revolution. Dan Riffle, whose confiscatory policy suggestions reveal more about his envious resentment than any rational attempt to construct an egalitarian society,

---

[238] Margaret Thatcher, TV interview for Thames TV *This Week*, February 5, 1976, Margaret Thatcher Foundation, https://www.oxfordreference.com/view/10.1093/acref/9780191826719.001.0001/q-oro-ed4-00010826.

speaks for a new generation of envy-driven socialists. The envious are now making their way through the institutions—through politics and into the Catholic Church, where they are capitalizing on the current divisions to sow the seeds of envious discord.

7

Unholy Envy and the Religion of Humanity

The Old Testament is filled with warnings about the sin of envy. From the cautionary tale in Genesis of the deadly envy that destroyed the perfect happiness of Adam and Eve and the murderous envy that emerges between the sons of Adam, envy appears as the snake in the garden throughout the Old Testament. We see it in the rivalry of Joseph's brothers over the favored status their brother received from their father and again in Saul's animosity toward David for his beauty, his goodness, and his faithfulness to God. In Proverbs, we are told that the way of true wisdom is to avoid the company of envious people: "Let not your heart envy sinners, but continue in the fear of the LORD all the day" (23:17). The New Testament carries similar warnings. In Corinthians, we are advised that "love is to have majesty over envy" (see 1 Cor. 13:4). And in Galatians, we are warned that because of their sinfulness and depravity, those who envy others are barred from the Kingdom of Heaven (5:19–26). Matthew reminds us that it was the envy of the chief priests and the elders that led to the rejection and betrayal of Jesus into the hands of Pilate for crucifixion (Matt. 27:18). Timothy cautions that false teachings lead to envy among the people of God (1 Tim. 6:4). And, in Philippians, Paul points out that the gospel is sometimes preached out of envy and strife (1:15).

The Politics of Envy

Catholic teachings make it clear that envy is a serious sin. But as Helmut Schoeck points out, although the ethic taught by the New Testament accepted that envy was likely to emerge in a fallen world where there is bound to be inequality of outcome among people in the world, some have succeeded in adapting the anti-envy message to their own ends. Calling it a "kill-joy, ascetic morality that whispers persuasively to the joyful, lucky or successful person," Schoeck points out that the New Testament is often falsely interpreted as scolding successful people to "feel guilty, feel ashamed, for you are envied by those beneath you. Their envy is your fault. Your very existence causes them to sin. What we need is a society of equals so that no one will be envious."[239] From Schoeck's perspective, in the revisionist accounts of the New Testament, "it is no longer the envious who must discipline and control themselves and practice love of their neighbor, it is their victim who must change — and change for the worse, in conformity with envy's own yardstick." It is likely that such a distortion of the New Testament emerges from God's promise of a Heaven where "all will be equal ... whether kings or beggars when in this world; indeed, the poor have an even better chance of going to heaven."[240]

Such promises of perfect equality are promises of eternal happiness in Heaven. For Schoeck, "the doctrine [of the New Testament], progressively secularized, came to mean a mission to establish an egalitarian society, to achieve a leveling-out, a state of uniformity here and now in this world. The egalitarian utopia is respectably cloaked in the admonitions of the New Testament." The belief emerged that since all will be equal before God, all must be as equal as possible in society here on earth. Schoeck warns that "this

---

[239] Helmut Schoeck, *Envy: A Theory of Social Behavior* (Indianapolis: Liberty Fund, 1966), 160.
[240] Ibid., 160.

doctrine cannot be read anywhere in the New Testament" unless, of course, the New Testament itself is distorted, and he reminds us that "the realization of an egalitarian society would render the content of Christian ethics, for a greater part, superfluous."[241]

This has not stopped some progressive Catholic theologians, leaders, and writers from usurping the New Testament message of "all are equal before God," by changing the admonition into a secular message of "all must be equal" here on earth in the egalitarian utopian society they wish to build. In many ways, the Jesuits have led this redefinition, and it has had a negative impact on the Church over the past five decades. With more than 17,000 Jesuits worldwide, the Society of Jesus is the largest order of priests and brothers in the Catholic Church. And although the Jesuits have struggled to maintain their numbers, peaking in 1965 with 36,038 Jesuits throughout the world, the Jesuits have had tremendous influence on the culture of the Church through their elite Jesuit colleges and universities.[242] And now that Jesuits are favored at the Vatican, with Pope Francis himself a Jesuit, the progressive movement has gained influence. Originally founded by Ignatius of Loyola, the soldier turned mystic, the Jesuits moved from a primary focus on serving Christ and the Holy Father to a more secular commitment to social justice as articulated in 1968 by then–superior general Father Pedro Arrupe. Today, this has manifested itself most clearly in the progressive politics surrounding Liberation Theology, a Marxist-inspired, envy-driven ideology disguised as concern for the poor that emerged in Latin America in the 1960s and is now being restored under Pope Francis.

[241] Ibid., 161.
[242] Center for Applied Research on the Apostolate "Changing Jesuit Geography," *Nineteen Sixty-Four*, February 1, 2011, http://nineteensixty-four.blogspot.com/2011/02/changing-jesuit-geography.html.

The Politics of Envy

Though Pope Francis never claims to be a socialist or a communist, it is clear that his sympathies lie with the left. He fondly recalls learning about communism through readings provided to him by his mentor, Esther Ballestrino de Careaga, a woman he has described as "a fervent communist ... a courageous person." This commitment to educating himself about communism continued throughout Pope Francis's years as a priest in the Society of Jesus, a religious order that has been committed to redefining the very purpose of the Catholic Church—from one of spiritual otherworldliness with a concern for eternal salvation to a church of humanity involved in the here and now in the struggle to create a new sociopolitical system by helping to redistribute the earth's resources and goods. During a visit to Bolivia in 2015, Pope Francis graciously accepted from the country's Marxist president, Evo Morales, a gift of a large crucifix in the shape of the hammer and sickle—the notorious symbol of communism. Ignoring the murderous history symbolized by the hammer and sickle, Pope Francis told those on the plane ride back to Rome that "I understand this work.... For me it wasn't an offense."[243]

Continuing their commitment to the ideals of communism, the Jesuit flagship publication, *America* magazine, published a lengthy essay in July 2019 with the incendiary title "The Catholic Case for Communism." Authored by Dean Dettloff, a doctoral candidate at the Institute for Christian Studies who describes himself in his bio as "researching the intersection of media, religion, and politics," the article draws on essays, published by the Communist Party USA, "affirming the connections between Christianity and

---

[243] Associated Press, "Pope Francis Says He Wasn't Offended by Communist Crucifix Gift," *Guardian* (Manchester), July 13, 2015, https://www.theguardian.com/world/2015/jul/13/pope-francis-communist-crucifix-gift-bolivia.

communism and encouraging Marxists not to write off Christians as hopelessly lost to the right."[244] Claiming that he has "talked more about Karl Rahner, S.J., St. Oscar Romero, and Liberation Theology at May Day celebrations and communist meetings than at my own Catholic parish," Dettloff argues that "communism has provided one of the few sustainable alternatives to capitalism, a global political order responsible for the ongoing suffering of millions." Asserting that many who committed their lives to the Church worked closely with communists as part of their "Christian calling," Dettloff points out that a number of progressive priests—including Fathers Ernesto and Fernando Cardenal, S.J., the notorious priests who were suspended in 1983 by Pope Saint John Paul II for their participation in the Sandinista revolution that led to the communist takeover of Nicaragua—"have been inspired by communists and in many places, contributed to communist and communist-influenced movement as members." And although Dettloff acknowledges that "some communists would undoubtedly prefer a world without Christianity," he denies that the goal of communism is to destroy the Church. For Dettloff, "the history of communism, whatever else it might be, will always contain a history of Christianity."[245]

It is not surprising that Dettloff would cite support from the Jesuits in Nicaragua in the 1970s for his contention that there is a Catholic case to be made for communism. The 1970s was a time of great unrest in Central and South America, and communism promised to offer a solution to the tremendous inequality and social tension. Dettloff must know that it was indeed a pivotal

---

[244] Dean Dettloff, "The Catholic Case for Communism," *America*, July 23, 2019, https://www.americamagazine.org/faith/2019/07/23/catholic-case-communism.

[245] Ibid.

moment for the Jesuits because of their contribution to the revolution in Latin America. During that time, the Jesuit commitment to missionary work in Nicaragua changed from one of saving souls to a mission defined in more worldly terms. And, in important ways, some of these Jesuits drew upon the New Testament for support for their revolutionary activity in overthrowing capitalism. As Michael Novak recalls in his 1986 book, *Will It Liberate?*, Father Ernesto Cardenal, the Nicaraguan priest and leader of the Sandinista rebellion, told a reporter for a 1984 article in *National Catholic Reporter*, "Christ led me to Marx.... For me, the four Gospels are all equally communist.... I am a Marxist who believes in God, follows Christ and is a revolutionary for the sake of his kingdom."[246]

Helping to topple the corrupt and autocratic Somoza regime in Nicaragua and replace it with the Sandinista dictatorship became part of the priestly ministry of the Jesuits who were assisted by the Maryknoll Fathers in Latin America. Toward that goal, the Catholic prelates allied with Daniel Ortega and his Marxist Sandinistas conducted a guerrilla war on the Somoza regime. The priestly alliance was important to the Sandinista leadership because more than 90 percent of the Nicaraguan population were Catholic. To gain the support of the people, the Sandinistas knew they needed to enlist the Catholic Church to lend legitimacy to the communist revolution. When the Sandinistas succeeded in removing the Somoza family from power, five priests—including Fathers Ernesto and Fernando Cardenal—were given cabinet positions in the fledgling communist government in Nicaragua.

[246] Chris Hedges, "Strife within the Church Really a War of Socialist Mores," *National Catholic Reporter*, September 7, 1984, cited in Michael Novak, *Will It Liberate? Questions about Liberation Theology* (New Jersey: Paulist Press, 1986), 13.

Unholy Envy and the Religion of Humanity

Envy and Liberation Theology

The move to socialism and communism emerged in Latin America as a way for Latino Catholics to differentiate or "liberate" themselves from the ways in which Catholicism was practiced in Spain. Liberation Theology was originally a symbol of freedom — a rejection of the colonial dominance of the Roman Catholic Church. It is often claimed that the Liberation Theology movement was born in the Soviet Union's KGB, and some, such as Ion Mihai Pacepa, who served in Romania's secret police in the 1950s and '60s, claim the movement was used as a way to convert Liberation Theology into a South American revolutionary tool. The truth is that Liberation Theology was founded and given its name by Gustavo Gutiérrez, a Peruvian professor whose book *A Theology of Liberation* gave birth to the movement. In recalling these early days, Michael Novak's book *Will It Liberate?* identifies those he called the "intellectual vanguard" of the movement as including Leonardo Boff, a Brazilian Franciscan; the Uruguayan Juan Luis Segundo, S.J. (*A Theology for Artisans of a New Humanity*); the Argentinian José Míguez Bonino (*Christians and Marxists: The Mutual Challenge to Revolution*); the Brazilian Hugo Assmann (*Theology for a Nomad Church*); the Spanish Alfredo Fierro (*The Militant Gospel*); and the Mexican Jose Miranda (*Communism in the Bible* and *Marx and the Bible*).[247] In the United States in the early years of Liberation Theology, Father Arthur McGovern, S.J., of the University of Detroit suggested in his book *Marxism: An American Christian Perspective* that most liberation theologians do not "ground their theology in Marxism.... Rather, they are generally careful to modify concepts of class hatred, violence and class struggle."[248]

---

[247] Michael Novak, *Will It Liberate? Questions about Liberation Theology* (New Jersey: Paulist Press, 1986), 16.
[248] Ibid., 17.

The Politics of Envy

In his book, in a chapter titled "Look North in Anger," which might have been more aptly titled "Look North in Envy," Novak points to the resentful, envy-driven early days of Liberation Theology. He notes that although the intellectual-vanguard theorists and intellectuals were important, the more important contributors to the growth of the movement were the "hundreds of activist priests and sisters who, as teachers and intellectual guides, form the teaching body of the new theology—and of course, the hundreds of thousands who, in one way or another, have been inspired by it." According to Novak, many critics claim that Liberation Theology affected only a minority of the clergy, even among theologians, and the strength of the movement is exaggerated internationally, given the fact that books and articles by liberation theologians are far more often translated into languages not spoken by the authors. Many of those books were published in the United States by Orbis Books—a publishing house that Novak identified in 1986 as the "headquarters" of Liberation Theology in Maryknoll, New York, the international center of the missionary order of the Maryknoll Fathers and Sisters. Maryknoll Father Miguel d'Escoto Brockmann, who later became the foreign minister of Nicaragua under the Sandinistas, was the director of communications at Maryknoll. He wrote: "As Latin Americans, we knew capitalism in a way young people here don't know it. We had no New Deal, no Roosevelt to come along and soften it up. Capitalism is intrinsically wrong at its base. The basic concept of capitalism is that man is selfish, and being realistic, we should accept this and cater to it rather than change it."[249]

Novak points out that many Catholic bishops of the 1960s, '70s, and '80s were "unambiguous in their preference for Marxism."[250]

[249] Ibid., 17.
[250] Ibid., 18.

And, most of them were quite public about their Marxist lean-ings. When Dom Hélder Câmara, the archbishop of Recife, Brazil, addressed the University of Chicago's celebration of the seventh centenary of Saint Thomas Aquinas, he advised those gathered that "the best way to honor the centenary should be for the University of Chicago to try today, to do with Karl Marx what St. Thomas in his day did with Aristotle." In 1968, at a bishops' conference in Medellín, Colombia, Latin America's bishops endorsed Liberation Theology as a way to help eliminate poverty in Latin America. Driven by resentment over past injustices, social justice became defined as the uprooting of capitalist gains, which would be re-turned to the "rightful" owners, the poor people of the continent. Liberation Theology was always intended to incite Latin America's poor to rebel against what they viewed as the "institutionalized violence of poverty generated by the United States."[251] Enlisting the Jesuits in the war, the Sandinistas successfully redefined the armed violence of a Marxist-style revolution into a religious ac-tion sanctioned by legitimate Church spokesmen. Quite simply, the new goal of the Jesuits was to use the Church to help usher in a new socialist society—a Marxist Heaven on Earth.

Novak understood that while envy-driven revolutionaries in places such as Nicaragua and Cuba seem mostly to create huge armies, economic activists create jobs. He suggested that libera-tion theologians would need to learn how to create new wealth in a sustained and systematic way and proposed that they begin to "look north" to the United States "for a different kind of Liberation Theology—liberal, pluralistic, communitarian, public-spirited, dy-namic, inventive." Obviously, that suggestion was roundly rejected. In those early days of Liberation Theology, Latin America looked

---

[251] George Neumayr, *The Political Pope* (New York: Center Street, 2018), 3.

north only in envy-driven anger and resentment. The results were catastrophic for the people.

By 1982, Pope Saint John Paul II, a staunch anti-communist because of his years living under communist rule in Poland, was so concerned about the sociopolitical role that priests were playing in Nicaragua and Latin America that he rebuked them, saying, "The ways of the religious minded do not follow the calculations of men. They do not use as parameters the cult of power, riches or politics.... Your proper activity is not in the temporal realm, nor in that one which is the field of laymen and which must be left to them." On December 11, 1984, after nearly two years of conflict between the Vatican and the priests who served in the communist government in Nicaragua, the Jesuit order announced that it had dismissed Nicaragua's education minister, the Reverend Fernando Cardenal, from the order for his refusal to leave the Sandinista government.[252]

In 1983, Pope Saint John Paul II gave a stern rebuke to leading liberation theologians, publishing a letter to the Nicaraguan bishops, denouncing the movement in especially harsh terms. In a speech that was reported on in the *New York Times* on March 5, 1983, the pontiff predicted that "the Church born of the people is a new invention that is both absurd and of perilous character.... Only with difficulty could it avoid being infiltrated by strangely ideological connotations.[253] In 1984, then-Cardinal Joseph

---

[252] E. J. Dionne, "Jesuit Order Dismisses Priest in Nicaraguan Cabinet," *New York Times*, December 11, 1984, https://www.nytimes.com/1984/12/11/world/jesuit-order-dismisses-priest-in-nicaraguan-cabinet.html.

[253] Alan Riding, "Pope Says Taking Sides in Nicaragua is Peril to the Church," *New York Times*, March 5, 1983, https://www.nytimes.com/1983/03/05/world/pope-says-taking-sides-in-nicaragua-is-peril-to-church.html.

Ratzinger offered *An Instruction on Certain Aspects of the Theology of Liberation*, in which he warned about the dangers of the "diverse theological positions," and "badly defined doctrinal frontiers" of this movement. So concerned about Liberation Theology's effects on the faithful, Ratzinger called Father Leonardo Boff to Rome for dialogue in 1984. Novak recalls:

> Father Leonardo Boff left his "dialogue" with Cardinal Ratzinger in Rome smiling, confident, and cocky enough to continue upbraiding the Vatican for its alleged naiveté. Two Brazilian cardinals flanked him in Rome as cardinal protectors. Liberation theologians busily began to show how the Ratzinger declaration did not apply to them.[254]

As Pope Benedict XVI, he called Liberation Theology a "singular heresy" that "deceives the faithful by concealing Marxist dialectics within seemingly harmless advocacy for the lower classes." Drawing attention to Marxism's philosophical incompatibility with Christianity, he disputed the claim of many churchmen that Christianity could purify the Marxist elements of socialist thought.

There has been even more arrogance on most Catholic college campuses as Liberation Theology has been ascendant there for decades—with no pushback from the bishops. As Pope Saint John Paul II predicted, the movement has been infiltrated by strangely ideological connotations. Not only have many of the most prestigious Catholic colleges and universities embraced Liberation Theology, but some even rehabilitated the violent leaders of the Sandinista movement from the 1970s. In 2005, faculty at the Universities of San Diego and Notre Dame protested the decision by the U.S. State Department to deny a visa to Dora María Téllez, a Nicaraguan academic who had planned to study English at the

---

[254] Novak, *Will It Liberate?*, 31.

The Politics of Envy

University of San Diego and teach at Harvard. More than a hundred faculty members denounced the actions of the Bush administration and demanded that the State Department clear the name of Téllez by "restoring her human rights." In denying the visa, the United States general counsel in Nicaragua, Luis Espada-Platet, indicated that the Immigration and Nationality Act prevents persons who allegedly endorse or espouse terrorist activity from entering the country. After the terrorist attacks on the United States on September 11, the Patriot Act requires the federal government to exclude foreigners who, in the government's view, have used positions of prominence to endorse or espouse terrorist activity.

Although Téllez states that she is "a scholar and not a terrorist" and claims in interviews to have "no idea why I have been labeled," the reality is that in 1978, she described herself as a "combatant and guerrilla leader" when she was one of twenty-five revolutionaries who dressed as waiters and violently took over Nicaragua's National Assembly—kidnapping and holding hostage government officials. During those heady days, Téllez called herself "Commander 2" and served as the revolutionary leader in the takeover of the national palace. In an impressive show of force, she held two thousand government officials hostage at gunpoint in a two-day standoff. She later led guerrillas to rise up in the city of Leon. After the revolution, Téllez served as minister for health in the Sandinista government. During the time she was invited to be a guest at the University of San Diego, she was serving as an advocate for gay and lesbian rights in the Catholic country.

Faculty members from Notre Dame joined their San Diego colleagues in the denunciation of the Téllez denial. Most likely the Notre Dame involvement is related to the fact that in 2004, Tariq Ramadan was denied a visa to teach there. Though the faculty claimed that Ramadan was unfairly linked to terrorist groups simply because his grandfather, Hassan al-Banna, founded the Muslim Brotherhood, the most powerful Islamist institution of the twentieth century, the truth is that Ramadan has developed his own links. Islamic scholar Daniel Pipes pointed out that Mr. Ramadan was banned from entering France in 1996 on suspicion of having links with an Algerian Islamist who had initiated a terrorist campaign in Paris. The terrorist links are clear in both cases, yet none of this information is included in the faculty response to neither the Ramadan nor the Téllez protests. And not a single bishop expressed concern about any of this. In fact, in the San Diego Téllez case, faculty were reminded by those who invited her that Dora María Téllez could not be a terrorist because she had been allowed to visit the San Diego campus in 2001 to receive a prestigious honor from the university. Besides, in its continuing commitment to social justice, the university has honored other members of terrorist organizations. Luz Mendez, a Guatemalan National Revolutionary Unity Party member, received the university's 2004 PeaceMaker Award, despite the fact that the State Department has listed the Revolutionary Unity Party as a left-wing terrorist organization.

Today, after decades in the shadows, Liberation Theology is once again ascendant, as the current Jesuit pope has used every opportunity to promote what he appears to view as the Liberating Theology of his Latin American home. In one of his first interviews after his election as pope, Francis said that liberation theologians have a "higher concept of humanity." On March 13, 2013, a few months after he became pope, Francis welcomed the founding father of Liberation Theology, the Peruvian priest Gustavo Gutiérrez, to the Vatican as an honored guest. Gutiérrez had been absent from ecclesiastical circles under Pope John Paul II and Pope Benedict XVI after making a Marxist appeal for "effective participation in the struggle which the exploited classes have undertaken against their oppressors."[255] In 2015, Pope Francis elevated Leonardo Boff, the liberation theologian from Brazil, who had been disciplined in 1984 by Cardinal Ratzinger's Congregation for the Doctrine of the Faith, by inviting Boff to serve as an adviser for *Laudato Si'*, his 2015 papal encyclical on climate change. Pope Francis also reinstated the priestly faculties of Miguel d'Escoto Brockmann, who had been suspended because of his participation in Nicaragua's Marxist revolutionary government. D'Escoto now lobbies for the Libyans, remains a member of the Sandinista National Liberation Front, and continues to serve as an adviser to Daniel Ortega, the left-wing Nicaraguan guerrilla leader, member of the Sandinista junta that took power in 1979, and the current three-term president of Nicaragua.

Liberation Theology has been strengthened by the movement to Popular Catholicism in Latin America — and beyond. The descriptor "Popular" does not refer to prevalence; rather, it refers to the religious practices and beliefs that emerge from the people — that is, laypeople, as opposed to priests. Emphasizing the contextual nature of theological reflection, Popular Catholicism maintains that theology must always be cultural and historical. From this perspective, any attempt to deculturate the theological and religious expressions of a community is dehumanizing because it rejects the authentic experience of the people. Many of today's most radical proponents of Popular Catholicism draw from the same ideology, and implement the same language and radical methods, of the liberation theologians of the past. In some ways, they are even more ambitious in their agenda than those of the past because they are now provided with the envious motivating rhetoric and theological cover from Pope Francis. Pope Francis recently affirmed the importance of what he called a "free and

---

[255] Neumayr, *The Political Pope*, 4.

responsible" form of Catholic theology—what he called a "creative fidelity"—in the life of the Church, and he privileges a form of Popular Catholicism.[256]

The influence of Popular Catholicism—or theology emerging from the people—was especially evident with the 2016 release of *Amoris Laetitia*, the pope's document on the family. Latin for "the joy of love," *Amoris Laetitia* was described in a guide that the Vatican sent to Catholic bishops before its release as "reflecting the pope's concern to re-contextualize doctrine at the service of the pastoral mission of the Church.... The Gospel must not be merely theoretical, not detached from people's real lives. To talk about the family and to families, the challenge is not to change doctrine but to inculturate the general principles in ways that they can be understood and practiced."[257] Fallout from *Amoris Laetitia* and its suggestions—emerging from the people—for a consideration of the right of divorced-and-"remarried" Catholics to receive the Holy Eucharist caused great consternation for faithful Catholics. Similar kinds of demands emerging from the people have focused on the goodness of same-sex relationships and civil unions, the removal of the celibacy requirement, and women's ordination.

Proclaiming the Gospel in a "new way" to a rapidly changing world, this embrace by Pope Francis of Popular Catholicism, which includes many elements of Liberation Theology, is in contrast to

---

[256] Devin Watkins, "Pope to Italian Theologians: Creative Fidelity Needed to Confront Modern Challenges," Vatican News, December 29, 2017, https://www.vaticannews.va/en/pope/news/2017-12/pope-to-italian-theologians--creative-fidelity-needed-to-confron.html.

[257] Joshua McElwee, "Vatican Guide Says Francis' Family Document Puts Doctrine at Service of Pastoral Mission," *National Catholic Reporter*, April 6, 2016, https://www.ncronline.org/news/vatican/vatican-guide-says-francis-family-document-puts-doctrine-service-pastoral-mission.

his papal predecessors. Both Pope Saint John Paul II and Pope Benedict spoke harshly about the dangers of a Church that was "born of the people." The Synod of Bishops for the Pan-Amazon Region (commonly referred to as the "Amazon synod"), held in Rome in October 2019, provides a very public window into the problems that a "people's church" poses. Indeed, the Amazon synod, as announced by Pope Francis in 2017, promised to work to "identify new paths for the evangelization of God's people in that region." Pope Francis specifically addressed the problems of the indigenous peoples of the area who he believes "are often forgotten, and without the prospect of a serene future." The synod included representatives from Bolivia, Brazil, Colombia, Ecuador, French Guiana, Guyana, Peru, Venezuela, and Suriname, most of which are countries in which Roman Catholicism is the dominant religion. They are also countries in which Liberation Theology—and the "people's church" movement—have made inroads. Critics of the synod claim that the participants are attempting to undermine the Church's consistent teaching on moral and sacramental absolutes, especially with regard to the indissolubility of marriage, homosexuality, contraception, and abortion.

Father Luke Hansen, S.J., reported from the synod for *America* magazine and described the opening speeches at the official synod as focusing on the need to be "open to change." Cláudio Cardinal Hummes emphasized several themes of Liberation Theology—and Pope Francis's pontificate: the church must "throw open her doors.... God always brings newness ... one must not fear what is new." According to Father Hansen, Cardinal Hummes concluded that the Church needed to go out and create "new pathways, embracing the Amazonian face of the church, inculturation, and interculturality; the role played by women; integral ecology and listening to the earth and the poor; the church in urban reality; and issues concerning water." There was the usual

Liberation Theology denigration of capitalism as discussion turned to climate change, with one suggestion being "an end to the use of fossil fuels, especially in industrialized nations which produce the most pollutants."[258] According to Father Hansen, participants discussed the need for inculturated celebrations of the sacraments, and "a proposal was put forward to establish—*ad experimentum*—an Amazonian Catholic rite to live and celebrate faith in Christ."[259] This "Amazonian" approach to Catholic doctrine and practice is exactly what Pope Saint John Paul II was concerned about when he warned of the dangers of the "people's church." The "people's church" in the Amazon has proposed that women's ordination, a married priesthood, and changing Church doctrine on the indissolubility of marriage are all up for discussion. Father Thomas Weinandy described the synod as "teeming with participants sympathetic to and supportive of all of the above."[260]

Although progressives continue to applaud the many ways in which Pope Francis has embraced change and inculturation and denigrated capitalism—excoriating what he claims are the profit motives of those he views as the "greedy" business owners—many faithful Catholics have experienced a growing unease about the Holy Father's public pronouncements on the evils of capitalism. These concerns emerged in the earliest days of his papacy and grew

[258] Carol Glatz, "First Synod Talks Look at Climate Change, Priests, Inculturation," *National Catholic Reporter*, October 8, 2019, https://www.ncronline.org/news/earthbeat/first-synod-talks-look-climate-priests-inculturation-vatican-says.

[259] Luke Hansen, S.J., "Here's What Happened on the First Day at the Synod," *America*, October 8, 2019, https://www.americamagazine.org/faith/2019/10/08/heres-what-happened-first-day-amazon-synod.

[260] Thomas G. Weinandy, OFM Cap., "Pope Francis and Schism," *The Catholic Thing*, October 8, 2019, https://www.thecatholicthing.org/2019/10/08/pope-francis-and-schism/.

with the release of his 2013 papal document *Evangelii Gaudium*, in which Pope Francis denounced capitalism as a "new tyranny" and decried the "idolatry of money." Conservative radio host Rush Limbaugh called the pontiff's economic principles and denouncement of capitalism "pure Marxism."[261] Michael Savage, the radio host of *Savage Nation*, took to Twitter to call Pope Francis "Lenin's Pope."[262] And, in the summer of 2015, the *Economist* published an essay describing the pontiff as "The Peronist Pope."[263]

The Peronist Pope?

It has been alleged by many that the young Jorge Bergoglio, raised in Argentina, was captivated by the anti-clericalist, envy-driven Peronist political movement based on the political ideology and legacy of former President Juan Domingo Perón and his wife, Eva. The Peronist ideal rejects both capitalism and communism but views the state as the savior in negotiating conflicts between managers and workers. The negotiations under Peronism favored the workers because the Peronist movement emerged from the working class and sympathetic unions. Rather than looking to social, spiritual, or political measures to help the poor, Pope Francis, like the Peronists, looks to the state to redistribute existing wealth.[264]

[261] Cheryl K. Chumley, "Rush Limbaugh Decries Pope Francis' 'Pure Marxism' Teachings," *Washington Times*, December 3, 2013, https://www.washingtontimes.com/news/2013/dec/3/rush-limbaugh-decries-pope-francis-pure-marxism/.

[262] Michael Savage (@ASavageNation), "LENIN'S POPE SAYS THERE IS NO HELL!," Facebook, March 29, 2018.

[263] Bello, "The Peronist Pope," *Economist*, July 9, 2015, https://www.economist.com/the-americas/2015/07/09/the-peronist-pope.

[264] Daniel J. Mahoney, *The Idol of Our Age: How the Religion of Humanity Subverts Christianity* (New York: Encounter Books, 2019), 99.

Pope Francis has called for such redistribution several times. For example, in an address to the United Nations Secretary General Ban Ki-moon and other United Nations leaders gathered in Rome for an audience with the pope in 2014, *Time* magazine reported that Pope Francis "railed against an economy of exclusion," and "called for a state-led global initiative to close the widening gap between rich and poor through redistribution."[265]

Proletarian in nature, the Peronist movement was driven by the rhetoric of envy and resentment to inspire its devoted followers. Resentful supporters describe the Peronist doctrine as a way to "take back" what has always rightfully belonged to the workers. The redistributionist policies of the Peróns confiscated wealth and property and disbursed some of it to the people—and much to themselves. Progressives often laud its populist roots, citing President Perón's universal social security, free health care, and free higher education. Soviet-style low-income housing projects were created for "workers," and employers were forced to provide paid vacations for all employees. According to Fordham Professor Paul McNelis, S.J., followers of Peron split into two groups: the traditional Catholics who saw Peronism as the embodiment of Catholic social teaching, and those who saw Peronism as a path to Argentine-style Marxism.[266]

By 1954, Peronism attempted to extend state control over the churches as the country saw denunciations of clergy and confiscation of Catholic schools and Church property. Many Catholic

[265] Dan Kedmey, "Pope Francis to World: Redistribute the Wealth," *Time*, May 9, 2014, https://time.com/94264/pope-francis-redistribute-wealth/.

[266] Paul McNelis, S.J., "Argentine Capitalism and the Economic Memories of Pope Francis," Papal Visit 2015, September 21, 2015, http://papalvisit.americamedia.org/2015/09/21/argentine-capitalism-and-the-economic-memories-of-pope-francis/.

churches throughout Argentina were destroyed, and priests were persecuted. Despite all of this, Pope Francis appears to have found much that was good in the Peronist ideology of protecting the poor at the expense of the rich. But is it fair to call Pope Francis a "Peronist Pope"? Samuel Gregg, research director at the Acton Institute, cautions against reading too much into the fact that some of the pontiff's rhetoric mirrors that of Peron and his followers. In an article published in *Catholic World Report*, Gregg writes that although it is no secret that Francis is, like Perón, skeptical about free markets, it doesn't automatically make the pope a Peronist.[267] Still, Gregg acknowledges that "it was impossible for an Argentine of Jorge Bergoglio's generation *not* to have a position vis-à-vis Peron.... It would also be unsurprising for an Argentine Catholic like Bergoglio to have Peronist sympathies." Gregg points out that Perón wanted the support from Catholics and occasionally referenced Pius XI's 1931 encyclical *Quadragesimo Anno* as one of his inspirations. At one point, a Jesuit priest, Father Hernán Benitez, functioned as a Perón adviser. Gregg points out that, according to Armando Rubén Puente's book on Bergoglio, *La Vida Oculta de Bergoglio*, the pontiff grew close to one particular Peronist movement in the early 1970s: the Guardia de Hierro (Iron Guard).[268]

Though Gregg concludes that "while it is possible to describe Francis as a Peronist, one should hesitate before drawing too close a link between the pope and Peron himself." The fact remains that in the model of the Peronists, Pope Francis claims that he

---

[267] Samuel Gregg, "The Pope and Peron," *Catholic World Report*, August 3, 2016, https://www.catholicworldreport.com/2016/08/03/the-pope-and-peron/.

[268] Armando Ruben Puente, *La Vida Oculta de Bergoglio* (Spain: Libros Libres, 2014).

identifies with the poor and has said on more than one occasion: "My people are poor and I am one of them."[269] His refusal to wear the traditional gold papal cross and his rejection of the papal residence in favor of the humble papal guesthouse were intended to send the message that he was a man of the people. Posting on his public Twitter account in 2014 that "Inequality is the root of all evil," Pope Francis showed clearly his distrust of those with "more." Dismissing traditional Catholic teaching that Satan's envy of God's superiority is the root of all evil, Pope Francis has often lauded communist friends of his and denigrated capitalism. In Paraguay, he created a kind of caricature of capitalism by telling a large gathering "not to yield to an economic model which is idolatrous, which needs to sacrifice human lives on the altar of money and profit."[270] And, during the welcoming ceremony at Jose Marti International Airport in Havana on September 19, 2015, when Pope Francis visited the communist island, he spoke of his "sentiments of particular respect" for Fidel Castro,[271] a totalitarian tyrant who subjugated the people of Cuba for more than fifty years and viciously persecuted the Catholic Church.

Echoing these concerns about the inability of the current pontiff to criticize dictators such as Castro and Peron, Assumption College

[269] See, e.g., "Biography of the Holy Father Francis," Vatican, http://www.vatican.va/content/francesco/en/biography/documents/papa-francesco-biografia-bergoglio.html.

[270] Philip Pullella and Daniela Desantis, "Pope Rails against Unbridled Capitalism, 'Idolatry of Money,'" Reuters, July 11, 2015, https://www.reuters.com/article/us-pope-latam-paraguay/pope-rails-against-unbridled-capitalism-idolatry-of-money-idUSKC-N0PL0Q420150712.

[271] Inés San Martín, "Fidel Castro, the Communist Leader Who Received Three Popes," *Crux*, November 26, 2016, https://cruxnow.com/global-church/2016/11/fidel-castro-communist-leader-received-three-popes/.

politics professor Daniel Mahoney suggests in his book *The Idol of our Age* that "Pope Francis seems to be rather indulgent towards despotic regimes that speak in the name of the poor." Critical of the fact that, during his visit to Cuba, Pope Francis stayed silent about the persecution of mainly Catholic dissidents in Havana, Mahoney suggests that "all of this is disappointing to say the least. The poor need political liberty too, and the opportunities that come with private property and lawfully regulated markets." It is all the more striking that Pope Francis never reiterates the Church's defense of private property, a central concern of Catholic social teaching going back to the first social encyclical, issued by Pope Leo XIII: *Rerum Novarum*. In his 2013 papal encyclical, *The Joy of the Gospel*, Francis refuses to defend private property as necessary for personal dignity and ignores the benefits of the market economy rooted in the rule of law and sound mores. Mahoney writes: "Gone are the Church's warnings against ideological utopianism," as Pope Francis completely ignores the socialist confiscation of human freedom. Elsewhere in his book, Mahoney writes that Pope Francis "almost always identifies markets with greed, inequality, economic imperialism and environmental degradation. Moreover, he is silent about the horrendous environmental devastation that accompanied and characterized totalitarian socialist systems in the twentieth century."[272]

Referring to the secularization we are witnessing now, Mahoney concludes, if secular modernity has a religion, it is undoubtedly "the religion of humanity." The idea of a secularized Christianity — a Christianity without Christ or transcendence — was first promoted in the nineteenth century by early sociologist August Comte. A proponent of the "science of society," Comte's *System of Positive Polity* was anti-theological and anti-metaphysical — viewing the

[272] Mahoney, *The Idol of Our Age*, 98.

morality of "positive science" as superior to the morality of revealed religion because it has substituted "the love of Humanity for the love of God." An atheist, Comte regarded questions about "meaning in life" as pointless, preferring to remove the focus from metaphysical questions to "the true science" of a positivist spirit of society.[273] Under the "religion of humanity" the concepts of truth and meaning are excluded, and envy flourishes as the humanist morality puts feelings ahead of what is morally "right." Although Comte recognized that people should defer to what is best or most admirable in people, true nobility involves subordinating what is human to what is "above man." When there is nothing above man, nothing humane or truly spiritual can arise from what Eric Voegelin's *Science, Politics, and Gnosticism* has called "an apocalypse of man" that has been built on the death of God. As a result, man risks becoming a monster to himself, "enslaved by his own self-deification."[274] For those who continue to search for meaning in Christianity, the humanitarian impulse to regard man "as the measure of all things" has corrupted the value of much of organized religion, reducing it to an inordinate concern for social justice, radical politics, and an increasingly fanatical egalitarianism.

No Mercy for the Faithful Catholics in China

Mahoney concludes that humanitarians have confused equitable social arrangements with socialism, and moral judgment with utopianism and sentimentality. Pope Francis lauded the "positive" relationships he has with the leaders of Communist China. In an interview with a journalist in May 2019, Pope Francis said, "My

[273] Ibid., 9.
[274] Ibid.

dream is China … Relations with China are good, very good."[275] Dismissing concerns about the marginalized and imprisoned Catholics — including priests and bishops — in the underground Church in China, Pope Francis claimed that the Sino-Vatican agreement "united" Catholics in the communist country. In September 2018, representatives of the Vatican and the communist government in China signed what they described as a "provisional agreement" on the appointment of bishops. Pope Francis lifted the excommunications or regularized the status of seven of China's bishops who had been ordained by the communist government without the Vatican's consent, marking the first time since the 1950s that all the Catholic bishops in China were in "full communion" with the pope. But this agreement has not meant the end of the arrest and imprisonment of priests and bishops or the end of the persecution of Catholics.

Yet Pope Francis continues to dismiss these concerns — claiming that China is united now: "The other day two Chinese bishops came to me, one who came from the underground church and the other from the patriotic church, already recognized as brothers…. They know that they must be good patriots and that they must take care of the Catholic flock."[276] Pope Francis appears to be unaware that during the previous month, April 2019, Chinese government officials detained Father Peter Zhang Guangjun, an underground priest of the Diocese of Xuanhua, after Palm Sunday Mass. Father Guangjun was the third priest to be held in detention by the communist government during that single month of April 2019. On

---

[275] Courtney Mares, "Pope Francis Responds to Heresy Accusation, China Concerns," Catholic News Agency, May 29, 2019, https://www.catholicnewsagency.com/news/pope-francis-responds-to-heresy-accusation-china-concerns-16641.

[276] Ibid.

June 8, 2019, Monsignor Stefano Li Side, the underground bishop of Tianjin, died in captivity. The bishop had refused to be a part of the Communist-sanctioned church and had been exiled to a mountain village under house arrest since 1992.

According to *Catholic News World*, Bishop Li suffered years of imprisonment and seventeen years in forced labor camps for refusing to belong to the Patriotic Association, the communist government–approved church in China. The Patriotic Association forbade a Catholic funeral in the Cathedral of St. Joseph in Tianjin and refused the burial of Bishop Li in a Catholic cemetery. A few underground priests courageously defied the government and entered the funeral parlor to hold a funeral prayer service for ten minutes. However, they were not allowed to participate in a funeral Mass for their bishop.

Pope Francis has had nothing to say about the persecution of priests and bishops in China and the brutal history of the formation of the government-created Patriotic Association to control the Catholic Church under communist dictator Mao Zedong. Following the formation of the Patriotic Association church, Bishop Li was arrested in 1958 and sentenced to forced labor camps. Although he was released in 1962, he was again arrested and imprisoned in 1963 until 1980 — again assigned to forced labor camps. Today, the Diocese of Tianjin has forty "official" communist-appointed priests and twenty underground priests. Tianjin also has a coadjutor underground bishop, Monsignor Melchiorre Shi Hongzhen, ninety-two, who remains under house arrest by the communist government in the region's mountains.[277]

[277] Wang Zhicheng, "Catholic Underground Bishop Dies under House Arrest by Government in China," *Catholic News World*, June 12, 2019, http://www.catholicnewsworld.com/2019/06/breakingnews-catholic-underground.html.

The Politics of Envy

Today, there is no religious freedom in China. The release of four hundred pages of internal Chinese government documents obtained by the *New York Times* revealing the mass detention, torture, and re-education of as many as one million predominantly Muslim minorities in the Xinjiang region should give pause to Pope Francis and some of his top Vatican officials who have spent the past few years praising the communist state. When Pope Francis says that his "dream" is China, he seems to ignore the nightmare experienced by those incarcerated in the detention camps. Yet Bishop Marcelo Sánchez Sorondo, the chancellor of the Pontifical Academy of Social Sciences, told an interviewer last year that "right now, those who are best implementing the social doctrine of the Church are the Chinese." Citing China's "concern for the environment and human dignity," Sorondo claimed that when he visited the country earlier in the year, "What I found was an extraordinary China.... What people do not realize is that the central value in China is work, work, work.... There is no other way fundamentally, it is like St. Paul said: he who doesn't work, doesn't eat.... You do not have shantytowns, you do not have drugs, young people do not take drugs. Instead there is a positive national conscience." Suggesting that the communist country is "developing well," Sorondo dismissed any concerns about China by pronouncing that "you cannot think that the China of today is the China of the time of John Paul II, or Cold War Russia." Sorondo concluded that China now has "many points of agreement" with the Vatican.[278]

---

[278] Staff Reporter, "'China Is the Best Implementer of Catholic Social Doctrine,' Says Vatican Bishop," *Catholic Herald* (London), February 6, 2018, https://catholicherald.co.uk/china-is-the-best-implementer-of-catholic-social-doctrine-says-vatican-bishop/.

Maybe not. At least one Vatican official, concerned about what he called "Sorondo's adulation" of Chinese culture, published an editorial with the headline "Sanchez Sorondo in Wonderland," claiming that Sorondo's praise of the totalitarian dictatorship in China "makes a laughingstock of the Church."[279] But Sorondo is not alone in his naïveté. Pope Francis has gone out of his way to accommodate China's demands to regularize the state-sponsored Catholic Church, which is beholden to the Communist Party and not to Rome.[280]

These are perilous times for the Catholic Church as the "people's church" continues to gain ascendancy under the current pontiff. It is difficult to predict where the envy-driven ideology will take the Church. In his book *The Power of Silence*, Cardinal Robert Sarah, the prefect of the Congregation for Divine Worship and the Discipline of the Sacraments, suggests that the Church is in danger of sliding into the same kinds of envy-driven worldly preoccupations that the Church in Latin America concerned itself with in the 1970s and '80s. Moving away from Christianity's focus on the salvific mission of the Church toward a renewed commitment to addressing the needs of the here and now, there is growing concern that Pope Francis is steering the Church toward a new socialist society. While Pope Francis elevates the liberation theologians and the social-justice-warrior priests and bishops, many orthodox theologians in the Vatican have been publicly humiliated and removed from their positions. In 2017, Pope Francis publicly rebuked Cardinal Sarah for endorsing traditional liturgical practices. The pope promotes

---

[279] Philip Pulella, "Unholy War of Words Breaks Out over Vatican Rapprochement with China," Reuters, February 8, 2018, https://www.reuters.com/article/us-pope-china/unholy-war-of-words-breaks-out-over-vatican-rapprochement-with-china-idUSK-BN1FS2F4.

[280] Mares, "Pope Francis Responds."

instead a doctrinal vision that is "born of the poor" in prioritizing the lived experiences of ordinary Catholics over the authoritative teachings of the Church.[281] Such policies have only compounded a long-term negative trend in Catholic church attendance.

A 2015 Pew Foundation poll found that within Christianity, the greatest net losses, by far, have been experienced by the Catholic Church. Nearly one-third of American adults say that they were raised Catholic. Among that group, fully 41 percent no longer identify with Catholicism. This means that almost 13 percent of American adults are former Catholics, while just 2 percent of U.S. adults have converted to Catholicism from another religious tradition. No other religious group has experienced such a lopsided ratio of losses to gains.[282] While the downward trend began before Bergoglio became pope, his papacy has only made matters worse. But, in the envy-driven culture that remains, there seems to be little that can be done at an institutional level while he leads the Catholic Church. This is not to say that the faithful will continue to stay silent in the face of what they see as a Church adrift. In 2019, theologian Father Thomas Weinandy published an article on what he sees as an "internal papal schism" in which the pope himself is the de facto leader, for all practical purposes, of a schismatic church. "Because he is the head of both, the appearance of one church remains, while in fact there are two."[283]

[281] Marco Tosatti, "The War against Cardinal Sarah," *First Things*, October 23, 2019, https://www.firstthings.com/web-exclusives/2017/10/the-war-against-cardinal-sarah.

[282] "America's Changing Religious Landscape," Pew Foundation, May 12, 2015, https://www.pewforum.org/2015/05/12/americas-changing-religious-landscape/.

[283] Thomas Weinandy, OFM Cap., "Pope Francis and Schism," *The Catholic Thing*, October 8, 2019, https://www.thecatholicthing.org/2019/10/08/pope-francis-and-schism/.

The real concern in this growing age of envy is that as individuals move away from organized religion, they begin to search elsewhere for meaning in life. Some turn to relationships, or to work, or to politics. In some important ways, this has contributed to the current culture of envy because once the realm of the metaphysical is rejected, individuals become creatures not of God but of society and politics. This is why everything is now political. It is also why people become anxious and consumed with political campaigns and the outcomes of elections. Those who continue to try to depend on their traditional religious institutions have found that, in many cases, religion itself has become corrupted by politics—losing its transcendental reference points while it undermines balanced political judgment.

Still, the Church is filled with faithful Catholics who are beginning to recognize the danger posed by the current ideologically driven regime in Rome. It is clear that many of the cardinals and bishops are aware that the Francis pontificate has been a threat to the unity of the Catholic Church. In June 2019, Cardinal Raymond Burke, Bishop Athanasius Schneider, and three other high-ranking prelates signed a declaration designed to address the "current widespread confusion concerning Catholic Church teaching" under the Francis pontificate. Titled "The Declaration of Truths Related to Some of the Most Common Errors in the Life of the Church in our Time," the document affirms the unchanging teachings on forty Catholic truths and dismisses any idea of a theology based on the "lived experiences" of the people. It opens with the statement that the "right meaning" of the expressions "living tradition" and "development of doctrine" must include the truth that any "new insights" that may emerge can never be "contrary to what the Church has always proposed in the same dogma, in the same sense, and in the same meaning."[284] Whether Catholics will begin to rally around their faithful leaders, such as Cardinal Sarah and Cardinal Burke — rejecting the envy-driven ideological turn to the left in Rome — remains to be seen.

[284] Cardinal Raymond Burke and others, "The Church of the Living God: The Pillar and the Bulwark of the Truth: Declaration of the Truths Relating to Some of the Most Common Errors in the Life of the Church in Our Time" (June 10, 2019), http://www.ncregister.com/images/uploads/Declaration_Truths_Errors_final_version_clean.pdf.

8

Envy of Excellence in Academe

Several years ago, American writer Gore Vidal, a public intellectual known for his piercing prose and clever witticisms, famously said: "Whenever a friend succeeds, a little something in me dies."[285] While Vidal may have made the remark in jest, the truth is that there are many people who feel a sense of envious resentment whenever a close acquaintance or a competitor accomplishes something extraordinary—something that they wished they had been able to accomplish themselves. And, although Vidal, who died in 2012, had won many literary awards throughout his richly rewarding writing life—including the National Book Award for nonfiction and the Medal for Distinguished Contributions to American Letters from the National Book Foundation—he was long haunted by an envious resentment over what he viewed as the "advantages" of his peers. His resentment resulted in vicious public feuds with other famous writers, including Truman Capote, William F. Buckley Jr., and Norman Mailer. Most of these battles were provoked by

<hr/>

[285] Wilfrid Sheed, "Writer as Wretch and Rat," book review section, New York Times, February 4, 1973, https://www.nytimes.com/1973/02/04/archives/writer-as-wretch-and-rat-the-good-word.html.

The Politics of Envy

Vidal's caustic wit. The clashes were entertaining for onlookers, but they were never in jest, as grudges were held for decades. In fact, when his nemesis, William F. Buckley Jr., died in 2008, the then eighty-two-year-old Vidal suggested in an interview with a *New York Times* reporter that "hell is bound to be a livelier place as he joins those whom he served in life, applauding their prejudices and fanning their hatred."[286]

It is possible that Vidal's resentment emerged back in 1948, following the furor that accompanied the publication of his third novel, *The City and the Pillar*. It was a compelling story about a young man coming to terms with his homosexuality—and the love of his life. It was also purported to be semiautobiographical, about the struggles and lost loves of Vidal himself. Published two or three decades before the country was ready for a novel about a loving same-sex relationship, it caused a scandal in the publishing world—and beyond. Vidal claimed that the *New York Times* book-review editor, Orville Prescott, refused to review the book and blocked other critics from reviewing any book by Vidal. According to an obituary published in the *Free Thinker*, Vidal claimed that an editor at Dutton told him, "You will never be forgiven for this book."[287] It was true, as the scandalous novel ended his ability to find publishers for his writing for decades. To pay his bills, Vidal published detective stories under a pseudonym. And, although his career recovered in the 1970s, and he achieved greatness during

---

[286] Deborah Solomon, "Literary Lion: Questions for Gore Vidal," *New York Times*, June 15, 2008, https://www.nytimes.com/2008/06/15/magazine/15wwln-Q4-t.html.

[287] Barry Duke, "Farewell Gore Vidal, Gay Atheist Extraordinary," *Free Thinker*, August 1, 2012, https://web.archive.org/web/20180108041016/http://freethinker.co.uk/2012/08/01/farewell-gore-vidal-gay-atheist-extraordinary/.

his lifetime of publishing award-winning books and screenplays, his bitter resentment continued throughout his life.

Joseph Epstein, the author of the brief treatise *Envy*, would be unsurprised by Vidal's openly expressed resentment. Epstein suggests that writers and American academics, especially those in the humanities, are the "most likely candidates" for a large group existing in a state of resentment:

> They feel themselves, simultaneously, greatly superior and vastly undervalued, above their countrymen, yet isolated from them and insufficiently rewarded and revered by them. They have about them a perpetually disappointed air; one senses they feel that the world has, somehow, let them down. Sometimes this will reveal itself in a general sourness; sometimes it takes the form of hopelessly radical political views. These political views, it does not take long to recognize, usually feature a complex shifting and reorientation of society so that people like themselves will be allowed a justly deserved role of power.[288]

When the resentment becomes strong enough, and other faculty members with similar resentments are enlisted, there is danger of an organized "mobbing" action to be taken against an individual on campus—usually a high-status and highly productive individual—in order to destroy the perceived threat to the faculty.

Faculty mobbings are most often preceded by resentment—a complex, multilayered emotion that frequently accompanies feelings of envy and a sense of having one's abilities and goodness "unrecognized." It is most often characterized by bitterness. When we feel resentful, we may feel a sense of injustice that someone else got something that we believe should have been given to us. A few

[288] Epstein, *Envy*, 80.

The Politics of Envy

years ago, a colleague told me that every time he gets his copy of the prestigious quarterly *American Sociological Review* in the mail, he gets angry that so many "inferior" sociologists are published on its pages, while he—with his Princeton Ph.D.—has never had an article accepted for publication. He is resentful and has often denigrated the journal, claiming that the publication has devolved into an economics journal, neglecting theory and dependent on too many statistical tables.

To understand how resentment emerges, it is helpful to read the work of the early twentieth-century German continental philosopher Max Scheler, author of the seminal study *Ressentiment*. Scheler followed Friedrich Nietzsche, who used the Kierkegaardian term *ressentiment* to describe the existential distinction between the two basic character options available to the individual: the strong master and the weak slave. The master type understands his burden of goodness and freedom and chooses his destiny, while the resentful slave type chooses to blame his submissiveness on the dominant master man and his entire class. Scheler draws from Nietzsche's phenomenology to create his own observations on the relationship between envy and *ressentiment*, offering insights on what he calls "a special form of human hate." Scheler uses *ressentiment* throughout his book in order to retain the meaning of the original French word, which helps to express the repeated experiencing and reliving of a particular emotional reaction against someone else. The continual reliving of the emotion "sinks it more deeply into the center of the personality.... It is not a mere intellectual recollection of the emotion and of the events to which it responded—it is a re-experiencing of the emotion itself. A renewal of the original feeling." Secondly, for Scheler, as for Nietzsche, the word "*ressentiment* implies that the quality of this emotion is negative—it contains a movement of hostility." For Scheler, the word *ressentiment* is closest to the German word *Groll* (rancor). Both words express the ways in which "a suppressed wrath, independent of the ego's activity,... moves obscurely through the mind" — taking shape through the repeated reliving of the intentionalities of hatred or other hostile emotions.[289]

In Scheler's view, *ressentiment* begins in a feeling of powerlessness that emerges when we recognize that we cannot change the circumstances we find ourselves in, but we refuse to resign ourselves to them. When we are resentful, we denigrate the thing we cannot do or have. Like the resentful fox and his just-out-of-reach grapes, we become bitter — and sometimes revengeful toward those who may have figured out a way to get to those grapes when we were unable to do so. Scheler calls this a "poisoning of the mind. It is a lasting mental attitude caused by the systematic regression of certain emotions and affects which, as such, are normal components of human nature. Their repression leads to the constant tendency to indulge in certain kinds of value delusions and corresponding value judgments." For Scheler, "a thirst for revenge is the most important source of *ressentiment*."[290] In fact, envy, hatred, revenge, and spite are often the interactive emotional effects of resentment, and Scheler suggests that *ressentiment* frequently ends in "embittering and poisoning" the personality. There is a progression of feeling that starts with revenge and runs via rancor, envy, and the impulse to detract all the way to spite, coming close to *ressentiment*. Usually revenge and envy have specific objects, and they arise against definite objects. But Scheler points out that those who suffer from *ressentiment* "seek those objects out, those aspects of men and things, from which it can draw gratification. It likes to disparage and to smash pedestals, to dwell on the negative aspects

[289] Max Scheler, *Ressentiment* (Milwaukee: Marquette University Press, 2007), 20.
[290] Ibid., 25.

of excellent men and things, exulting in the fact that such faults are more perceptible through their contrast with the strongly positive qualities.... In spite, this impulse has become even more profound and deep seated—it is, as it were, always ready to burst forth and to betray itself in an unbridled gesture, a way of smiling, etc. An analogous road leads from simple Schadenfreude to malice."[291]

If the desire for revenge remains permanently unsatisfied, and if the feeling of "being right" is intensified, Scheler suggests that the resentful individual "may actually wither away and die." The truly vindictive person is instinctively and without a conscious act of volition drawn toward events that may give rise to vengefulness. He or she tends to see injurious intentions in all kinds of perfectly innocent actions and remarks of others. Truly resentful people are often described as "easily offended" or "touchy," as they are always in search of people and things to be resentful about. As an atheist, Gore Vidal was famously touchy about moralism and appeared to despise those he judged as excessively religious. Feeling hurt by views against homosexuality held by those such as the very public Catholic William F. Buckley, Vidal fought back against Buckley as a proxy for religion itself.

Current research on academic mobbing indicates that the successful career of a person can inspire envy, resentment, and fear in others, and they try to eliminate that person by organizing and attacking or making that professor's life "a burden." In his book *Workplace Mobbing in Academe: Reports from Twenty Universities*, Kenneth Westhues suggests that it is the high status and the professional expertise of targeted professors that tends to "invite" the envy of others and opens the door to mobbing actions against them. While mobbing actions can occur in all workplace settings, Westhues has found that the worker most vulnerable to being mobbed

[291] Ibid., 26.

is a high-achieving professor whose productivity or prior success may embarrass or shame his or her colleagues. It is more common in the professional service sector—especially in the university setting—where "work is complex, goals ambiguous, best practices debatable, and market discipline far away." Westhues suggests that "the impulse to gang up, to join with others against what is perceived to be a common threat, lies deep in human nature. It is not easily outlawed."[292]

A frequent lecturer on mobbing and what he calls the "social elimination" of high-performing professors and administrators, Westhues often tells audiences that "in every human being are three appetites: for food, for sex, and for humiliating somebody else."[293] Westhues writes that his method in his books on mobbing are "similar to that of René Girard" in that the method in his studies of scapegoating was to make a critical, structural analysis of documents (what Girard called "persecution texts"), looking for common themes (what Girard called "stereotypes"), and carefully sifting out the empirical facts of the matter from the meaning or interpretation given by those in charge.[294] People caught up in the scapegoating movement, Girard believed, are "too naïve to cover the traces of their crimes."[295] Scapegoaters are "imprisoned in the illusion of persecution."[296] Girard believes that the social eliminative impulse, or what Westhues calls "the lust to wipe another person out," is categorically similar to the impulse

[292] Kenneth Westhues, *Workplace Mobbing in Academe: Reports from Twenty Universities* (Lewiston, NY: Mellon Press, 2004), 8.

[293] Kenneth Westhues, *Envy of Excellence* (Lewiston, NY: Mellon Press, 2005), 27.

[294] Ibid., 13.

[295] René Girard, *The Scapegoat* (Baltimore: Johns Hopkins University, 1986), 8.

[296] Ibid., 40.

for food and sex because it can consume a person to the point of obsession, spreading like a virus through a group, becoming the driving force behind collective energy. Much of that impulse emerges from envy. In his book *Envy of Excellence: Administrative Mobbing of High-Achieving Professors*, Westhues writes that the most basic clue that a mobbing action is occurring is that the eliminators' focus is on the targeted person, rather than on the allegedly offensive act: "The guilty person is so much a part of his offense that one is indistinguishable from the other. His offense seems to be a fantastic essence or ontological attribute."[297] When an individual is being mobbed, there is an attempt to break that individual's bond with everyone else by humiliating him or her. Social eliminations are carried out by people who have fallen into what social psychologists call "fundamental attribution error," identifying some alleged offense so closely with the offender's identity that they cannot see the latter as a human being like themselves. They have lost sight of the truth and the dignity of the human being they have targeted.

A Faculty Mobbing at Mount St. Mary's University

One of the most bitter academic mobbings began in 2015 at Mount St. Mary's, a small Catholic university in Emmitsburg, Maryland, after the school's board of trustees hired as its new president Simon Newman, a successful Los Angeles private equity and strategic-planning professional. The board of the financially struggling school hoped Newman would turn things around. Newman had a long and successful business career helping companies regain profitability. Though Mount St. Mary's was ranked highly in terms of academics among regional colleges by *U.S. News and*

[297] Westhues, *Envy of Excellence*, 28.

World Report, *Forbes* ranked it one of the "least financially fit schools in America" in 2013, assigning it a grade of D in "financial fitness." Mount St. Mary's was one of 107 schools to receive the low grade — ranking 888th out of 927 in terms of balance sheets and operational strength. In 2015 — before Newman was hired — Fox Business News listed Mount St. Mary's as one of the next 18 universities most likely to go out of business. Shortly before Newman arrived on campus, the university unexpectedly ran out of cash and required an emergency loan from its endowment to meet payroll. The university had been losing money for more than a decade but had survived by amassing a high level of junk-rated debt that was three times the level considered prudent for a college with a small endowment. According to a strategy review conducted by external consultants in June 2015, Mount St. Mary's labored under a convoluted governance structure that was heavily criticized in the accreditation reports; this indicated that the school did not adequately or appropriately define, exercise, or implement the roles, responsibilities, and structures of authority and governance. The school had a declining retention rate; the lowest return on a degree compared with its peers; a tuition discount rate above 60 percent; and a declining matriculation rate that had dropped to below 12 percent. None of this was sustainable.[298]

Newman was chosen because the school needed a new strategy for solvency and sustainability. A number of colleges and universities — including Catholic colleges — had been turning to business leaders to run their institutions. But it is still a very low number, and it appears to bring with it some serious threats to faculty morale. According to a 2017 study by the American Council on Education, 15 percent of U.S. college presidents came from fields

---

[298] *Mount St. Mary's University Strategy Review*, June 2015. Confidential.

outside academia—down from 20 percent in 2012.[299] As the *Atlantic* pointed out, while "proponents of the non-academic candidates say that leaders from the world of business or government or law are needed to innovate, control costs and manage a complex organization," faculty resistance is strong.[300]

This was evident in the Newman case. Despite opposition from some faculty members from the moment he stepped on campus, Newman was making progress based on years of experience of turning around major corporations. He implemented the best business practices he had gleaned from his experiences in the corporate consulting world and applied them on the Catholic university campus. He also relied on the expertise of outside consultants to provide strategic advice. That may have been his first mistake. Most academics, especially in the humanities, are hostile to those who work in the corporate world. Some of that hostility emerges from envy and resentment over the large salaries business leaders receive—in comparison with their own. Epstein notes this envious resentment when he writes that most college professors, because of their superior performance in school, have been told over and over again how bright and extraordinary they are, and some of them are angry that they are not well compensated in comparison with their corporate peers. According to Epstein, resentful and envious faculty members

> remain in the environment, that of the classroom, that has long been the scene of all their rewards, by becoming teachers.

---

[299] American Council on Education, "Path to the Presidency," 2017 Overview, American Council on Education, https://www.aceacps.org/summary-profile/#path-to-the-presidency.

[300] Laura McKenna, "Why Are Fewer College Presidents Academics?" *Atlantic*, December 3, 2015, https://www.theatlantic.com/education/archive/2015/12/college-president-mizzou-tim-wolfe/418599/.

It all seems like a good life, but soon it is spoiled by the realization that people who did less well than they in school seem to be faring rather better in the world. Not quite first-class lawyers are making hundreds of thousands of dollars a year; dullish boys and girls, now practicing medicine, have large summer homes near gentle lakes. Coarse creeps are scoring heavily in the stock and commodities markets. While they, once the darlings of their teachers—who bestowed all those lovely A's upon them—are struggling along, not only financially but spiritually. No, it's not working out at all, and it's damn unfair.[301]

Simon Newman was everything that resentful faculty members despise. He was a cheerful, financially successful, handsome young business leader of a private equity firm who had made enough money to leave the corporate world and devote his efforts to helping turn around the struggling school. Rather than being grateful that he was willing to offer his business expertise to the university, some on the faculty were resentful that he had been chosen. Some of those willing to speak on condition of anonymity for this book, complained that the new president was "arrogant" and "wore expensive suits." On private (and sometimes public) Facebook pages, others pointed to his wearing cuff links, his painting the walls in his office, his wife's hair, his car, his accent, and his refusal to have his family move into the presidential home—which Newman says was structurally unsafe. Newman had tremendous confidence—the kind of confidence that was interpreted by his faculty detractors as arrogance. To others, Newman seemed happy and genuinely committed to turning the school around so it could once again succeed.

[301] Epstein, *Envy*, 81.

The Politics of Envy

Realizing that he had to act quickly to save the struggling school, Newman was able to reduce costs by $3 million during the first year, reducing debt and long-term obligations by $12 million. But, in the process, he made some very unpopular decisions: he reduced administrative bloat by removing six administrators, and he ended a costly health insurance plan that provided retiree health benefits, as well as up to $100,000 in fertility treatments for employees. These decisions created tremendous resentment. On November 18, 2015, three retirees published a letter to the editor in the student newspaper, decrying Newman's decision to end the health benefits to retired employees and setting the stage for later battles with the faculty. Blaming Newman personally for the decision and claiming to be angry that the new president failed to meet with them "in person" to discuss the decision on ending health benefits for retirees, the retirees accused the president of failing to handle the retiree health-benefit issue "as graciously" as previous administrators had done—concluding that "this is not the Mount we knew for decades."[302]

Beyond cost cutting, in an attempt to recruit students to the struggling school, Newman upgraded university common areas, built new classrooms, upgraded campus technology, and instituted a partnership with Cambridge University to send top Mount St. Mary's students to study in the UK during the summer. He also arranged to offer Cambridge programs at the Mount St. Mary's campus, including an International Security program to be headed by the former head of MI6. The Cambridge in America program was to later include Creative Writing and Philosophy. In addition, the faculty developed five new degree programs in high-demand areas,

---

[302] "Letter to the Editor from Retired Mount Professors," *Mount Echo*, November 18, 2015, http://msmecho.com/2015/11/18/letter-to-the-editor-retired-mount-professors/.

including forensic accounting, philosophy-politics and economics, entrepreneurship, data sciences, and cyber-security. Under Newman's guidance, and with faculty leadership, the faculty reduced the unpopular and bloated core curriculum from 68 credits to below 49. Although there was no reduction in the number of required English, philosophy, or theology courses, it is no coincidence that most of the resistance to Newman emerged from faculty in the liberal arts. Whatever the motivation, it was clear that from the moment of the announcement of Newman's hiring, a small group of faculty members and a few mid-level administrators appeared to be determined to oppose his presidency. Two of the most hostile members of the faculty protest had applied for the presidency, but neither were considered for the position.

One of the early concerns focused on what some faculty members called a "frivolous lawsuit" filed by Newman in the summer of 2015 against a Catholic college in Los Angeles with the same name. The previous president of the Mount St. Mary's Maryland campus had approved of the name change in a letter to the California institution dated the previous year. But, Newman believed it was a trademark infringement and the wrong decision to allow another university to have the same name. The faculty sided with the previous well-liked president, and some suggested that this was indicative of the ways in which Newman's governing style differed from his predecessor.

The rumors about Newman proliferated. The first rumor was that Newman was hostile to the school's Catholic identity because he wanted to broaden the appeal of Mount St. Mary's to non-Catholic students. Using data from consultant's reports, Newman concluded that the strong Catholic identity was no longer as great a draw for students as in the past and it seemed to faculty that he de-emphasized the Catholic character of the university in marketing materials. Some on the faculty have stated that Newman was especially critical of homeschooled students—claiming that they were excessively religious and judgmental of other students. A rumor circulated that Newman had objected to those he allegedly called "Catholic Jihadists" among the student body, and that he had complained about "all the bloody crucifixes" around the campus.[303]

According to a *Washington Post* column titled "Why So Many Are Alarmed by the Ongoing Controversy at Mount St. Mary's," Michael Bayer suggested that Newman did not embrace the liberal arts and instead pursued policies that appealed to career-minded students.[304] In his view, the controversy is a reflection of the national debate over the relevance of the liberal arts at a time when parents and students alike increasingly believe job training is the purpose of higher education. Critics claimed that Newman "disliked" and sought to remove students who struggled due to depression and learning disabilities. Some faculty said his retention plan was intended to target these struggling students. By October 2015, at a meeting of the advisory board of the College of Liberal Arts, when the conversation turned to the need for additional academic support for struggling students, an academic-affairs administrator who was present contradicted President Newman in front of the visiting advisory-board members about the president's opinions of some homeschooled students on campus. According to some of those who had attended, Newman also suggested that some of

---

[303] Adelaide Mena and Matt Hadro, "More Allegations Emerge as Mount St. Mary's Controversy Boils" Catholic News Agency, February 11, 2016, https://www.catholicnewsagency.com/news/more-allegations-emerge-as-mount-st-marys-controversy-boils-48348.

[304] Michael Bayer, "Why So Many Are Alarmed by the Ongoing Controversy at Mount St. Mary's," *Washington Post*, February 17, 2016, https://www.washingtonpost.com/news/acts-of-faith/wp/2016/02/17/why-so-many-are-alarmed-by-the-ongoing-controversy-at-mount-st-marys/.

the "at-risk" first-year students did not appear to want to be on the campus. At the advisory-board meeting, the administrator disagreed with Newman and accused him of "casting aspersions on the Mount's students."[305] Although others at that meeting had a different interpretation of Newman's description of struggling students, the unflattering version of events carried the day—adding to the campus gossip about a president who was hostile to the Catholic identity and the students. Within two weeks of the Advisory Board meeting, on November 3, 2015, President Newman demoted the administrator and returned him to his tenured faculty position. That was likely a mistake because it caused the former administrator to be viewed as a martyr of an autocratic president—garnering more hostility toward Newman.

In the corporate world, employees serve at the pleasure of the CEO, and when an employee does not agree with the direction that the organization is going, the unhappy individual is asked to leave. Newman had the right to fire members of his senior leadership team—including one at the dean's level—but in this case, the demotion of an administrator who criticized Newman only contributed to the public perception that Newman was a despot. Beyond the dean's level, on university campuses, all hirings and firings are done by committees and departments. It can take years to replace a department chairman. On some dysfunctional college campuses, department chairs can "serve for life" because no one wants to confront the now-powerful chair of the department. In some ways, this all helped to ready the battlefield for the final confrontation between the president and the faculty that emerged

[305] Susan Svrluga, "The Controversy at Mount St. Mary's Goes National after Professors Are Fired," *Washington Post*, February 9, 2016, https://www.washingtonpost.com/news/grade-point/wp/2016/02/09/the-controversy-at-mount-st-marys-goes-national-after-professors-are-fired/.

the following month when Newman found himself at the center of a firestorm over some remarks he made in a private conversation with a faculty member about his alleged retention plan that would "remove" at-risk first-year students from campus.

Retention had long been a problem at Mount St. Mary's. Prior to Newman's arrival, the school had a retention plan that Newman said was unjust for students. It was a strategy in which every year, in late December, up to thirty first-year students left the school with no transferable credits and a bill for the full semester's tuition and board of about $15,000. The transfer-out rate was more than 31 percent. Newman said this was unfair to students and set out to remedy this by enlisting faculty members to help him identify struggling students early and step in with an intervention and an invitation for those students to be allowed to withdraw without incurring tuition costs. But this retention plan—which involved using a survey to help identify struggling students—was interpreted by faculty critics as a plan that would remove students without giving them a chance to succeed because the high-risk freshman students needed to be identified by September 25 when enrollment numbers must be reported to the Department of Education. The survey (a nationally normed survey used by many colleges and universities) that was used to identify students with depression or mental-health issues was widely opposed, and those objections were amplified by critics involved in the campaign to oust President Newman.[306]

---

[306] John Schwenkler, February 11, 2016, comment on Magicalersatz, "Mount St. Mary's Student Survey Tried to Find Out Which Students Were Depressed," *Feminist Philosophers* (blog), February 11, 2016, https://feministphilosophers.wordpress.com/2016/02/11/mount-st-marys-student-survey-tried-to-find-out-which-students-were-depressed/.

Newman denies claims that he ever wanted to "remove" struggling students without first offering to help them stay. In fact, he has said many times in media interviews and in private conversations with faculty that he was trying to remedy the past retention programs in place at Mount St. Mary's that would financially penalize the failing students by keeping their tuition money even though most of them had never even attended classes during the semester of their enrollment. But the truth is, there was already a retention plan that allowed students to be removed if they did not attend class during the early weeks of the semester. Unfortunately, Newman began to be defined as someone who was "hostile" to students, and so the plan to "eliminate" at-risk students was easy for others to believe. At one point, the rumors had gotten so far out of control that an e-mail was circulated around the large faculty and homeschool community at Mount St. Mary's, claiming that an undergraduate student on campus was pregnant and terrified that she would become one of those students who would be removed from campus. It is uncertain whether the story of the pregnancy was even true, but the report of the young woman's crisis pregnancy was circulated to thousands through private Facebook accounts and homeschooling networks associated with the school. The rumors were always accompanied by a call for the resignation of the president—and a demand that the recipients contact the board to demand Newman's removal.

To help facilitate the mobbing action, several of the most resentful faculty members recruited their wives to help lead a social media campaign against Newman. Many of these faculty members were part of an extensive homeschooling network in the area, and faculty used that network to recruit others in the surrounding town and in the greater Washington, DC, area. Angry about the rumors that Newman did not appreciate homeschooled children, some of the wives in that network helped to recruit a few alums and at least one former faculty member and his wife living out of state. The wife of this former faculty member was especially adept in her organizing ability and vicious in her online postings on Facebook—posting on her own Facebook page that she was "happy to organize [the protest] from here." One of this woman's more incendiary posts about President Newman produced more than 2,200 comments—all piling on the beleaguered president. According to insiders, this woman attempted to enlist seminarians and former seminarians who were enrolled in Mount St. Mary's Seminary to protest Newman's presidency. In Facebook postings, she promoted an inflammatory YouTube documentary that portrayed President Newman as a mentally unstable individual who goes on profanity-filled rants throughout the campus—promising to kill students. This woman's Facebook posts claimed that the documentary was created by one of her most talented former students at Mount St. Mary's (during the time she had served as an adjunct faculty member).[307] The Mount St. Mary's graduate who allegedly created the satirical documentary had been a top student at the university—enjoying four tuition-free years at the school. He is currently a Ph.D. candidate, teaching as an adjunct professor at Mount St. Mary's University. The video is still posted today with more than 10,400 views on YouTube. Attempts to interview the filmmaker to try to understand his motivation for creating the documentary were unsuccessful.

The campus chaos reached a peak when faculty members allegedly forwarded a confidential e-mail to the *Mountain Echo*, the student newspaper, which claimed to "expose" what they said was President Newman's plan to remove "at-risk" students in order to "boost the retention rate 4-5%." Worse, a Mount St. Mary's faculty "whistleblower" disclosed what the faculty member called "offensive" verbal remarks that Newman made to him when he was speaking privately and informally with him about retention strategies for students. According to the published accounts in the school newspaper, the faculty member claimed that Newman told him that the faculty and administration were too protective of failing students: "This is hard for you because you think of the students as cuddly bunnies, but you can't; sometimes you just have to drown the bunnies ... put a Glock to their heads." In interviews, Newman stated that the context and the sentiment was false. He said that his comment was meant to be a lighthearted remark about helping failing students leave the school without incurring costs. He believed that the professor he was speaking to also knew it was certainly not a serious remark.

Unfortunately, the faculty member used the bunny-drowning remark as "proof" that Newman disliked students.[308] According to insiders, the remark was fed to student editors at the school newspaper, the *Mountain Echo*, and the *Washington Post* published its own reporters' accounts of the story. It quickly became national news as more than three hundred major newspapers published articles about the now-sensationalized bunny-drowning aspect of the story. Newman made headlines in more than thirty countries, and he became known as the "bunny-drowning-president." At the height of the controversy, Newman's office received more than three thousand e-mails each day — most of them hate-filled.

[308] Rebecca Schisler and Ryan Golding, "Mount President's Attempt to Improve Retention Rate Included Seeking Dismissal of 20–25 First Year Students," *Mountain Echo*, January 19, 2016, http:// msmecho.com/2016/01/19/mount-presidents-attempt-to-improve-retention-rate-included-seeking-dismissal-of-20-25-first-year-students/.

The Politics of Envy

The two faculty members who were thought to have been complicit in organizing the mobbing were promptly fired and removed from campus. One of them — a tenured faculty member — had allegedly used social media to organize what the faculty called "BlackOut Friday" in an attempt to end donations to the school. The other faculty member had served as the faculty adviser to the *Mountain Echo*.[309] Newman and the board obviously believed that the firings were justified. But the termination process was fatally flawed, denying due process for either of the faculty members and with no attempt to implement shared governance procedures, which are highly valued on all college campuses.

And although confidential e-mails among the faculty demonstrate that the attempt to oust Newman began several months before the faculty firings, it was the violation of shared governance in faculty firing that sealed the fate of his presidency. The two fired faculty members immediately became defined in the media and on campus as victims of an autocratic president. The faculty mobilized at once — using social media and their wives' homeschooling network to enlist national support for their action.[310] One of the faculty wives posted on her Facebook page that Newman and the board at Mount St. Mary's were "evil." John E. Coyne III, then chairman of the board of trustees at Mount St. Mary's, was also deluged with phone calls after he was doxed on Facebook posts that revealed his home address and phone number. When he was asked to comment on the story prior to publication in the student

---

[309] Susan Svrluga, "Mount St. Mary's President Resigns," *Washington Post*, February 29, 2016, https://www.washingtonpost.com/news/grade-point/wp/2016/02/29/mount-st-marys-future-direction-on-the-table-as-leaders-meet-today/.

[310] "Academics' Statement of Protest Regarding Faculty Firings at Mount St. Mary's, https://docs.google.com/spreadsheets/d/1ewOmme-BiUmGlDw12gi9Xi5cSkcDQ5av12jRmIIZtc0/edit#gid=0.

newspaper, he responded by calling the story "the product of a disgruntled employee and the creative and destructive imagination of a student [editor] being spoon fed his information."[311] Coyne believed that the small group of angry faculty members had encouraged the student to publish the damaging information. And one of the student editors of the newspaper allegedly admitted this to a senior administrator at the school, but since the senior administrator was hostile to Newman, this news was not revealed until much later—after Newman had left the university.

In published interviews with the media, Coyne identified "incontrovertible evidence of the existence of an organized, small group of faculty and recent alums working to undermine and ultimately cause the exit of President Newman."[312] Coyne concluded that the disgruntled faculty group's issues were "born out of a real resistance to positive change at Mount St. Mary's." Writing on behalf of the university's board of trustees, Coyne sent a formal letter to the student newspaper describing its article as a "grossly inaccurate impression on the subject of the Mount's effort to improve student retention and to intervene early on to assure that incoming students have every opportunity to succeed at our university." Coyne concluded that the ultimate goal of the group was "to undermine the president by circulating mischaracterized accounts and flat out falsehoods."[313]

---

[311] John E. Coyne III, "Letter to the Editor: A Message from John Coyne, Chair, on Behalf of the Board of Trustees of Mount St. Mary's University," *Mountain Echo*, January 1, 2016, http://msmecho.com/2016/01/19/letter-to-the-editor-a-message-from-john-coyne-chair-on-behalf-of-the-board-of-trustees-of-mount-st-marys-university/.

[312] Ibid.

[313] See the longer version of the letter, posted on Fire, February 9, 2016, https://www.thefire.org/letter-to-the-editor-a-message-from-john-coyne-chair-on-behalf-of-the-board-of-trustees-of

The Politics of Envy

Newman had some supporters on the faculty and the board, but they, too, were demeaned and denigrated by those intent on ousting the president. Faculty members who supported Newman became fearful for their families in light of the warnings from the much larger mob. Some wrote heartfelt letters to Newman apologizing for their inaction—claiming that they could not speak out publicly for fear of reprisals from angry faculty members. Three members of the Mount St. Mary's alumni who attended the Liberal Arts advisory-board meeting where Newman was challenged by an administrator contradicted the version that the faculty presented and claimed that President Newman had "praised the strong Catholic identity." In published interviews, these advisory-board members also added that they understood that Newman had to make unpopular decisions to help make the school sustainable. The three advisory-board members tried to point out that Newman's statements were being mischaracterized; they told reporters that the increased competition for students demanded that the university no longer rely only on its strong Catholic identity to recruit high-achieving students. They added: "We did not view President Newman's comments as showing either disdain for or hostility to our beloved Mount, only a realistic determination to identify, confront and resolve the issues that it must grapple with at this time in its history."[314] Because many faculty and alumni had already concluded that Newman was hostile to Catholic identity and to at-risk students, observers on

-mount-st-marys-university/; Anne Hendershott, "A Violation of Trust at Mount St. Mary's," *Chronicle of Higher Education*, February 12, 2016, https://www.chronicle.com/article/a-violation -of-trust-at-mount-st-marys/.

[314] "Faculty Asked the Mount St. Mary's President to Resign. He Didn't," *Washington Post*, February 3, 2015, http://www.washingtonpost.com/news/grade-point/wp/2016/02/15/faculty-asked-the -mount-st-marys-president-to-resign-he-didn't/.

campus and off paid little attention to the members of the advisory board who were supportive of Newman.

Besides, Newman's supporters on the advisory board were overshadowed by a more vocal and pro-active contingent on that same board who published an open letter to the students and faculty to demand Newman's resignation. They wrote, "After reading the accounts of President Newman's bizarre behavior and heavy-handed methods in the *Mountain Echo*, *Washington Post*, and other news media, we have decided to come forward." These three advisory-board members—all alumni of Mount St. Mary's—wrote that Newman had shown "contempt for the Mount's Catholic identity and tradition." Claiming that Newman "had called for a radical de-emphasis of the liberal arts education for which the university has been justly noted," the three board members concluded their open letter with this statement: "Whether it be the administration of questionable surveys to profile students, the manipulation of faculty to advance dubious purposes, or the vulgar and defamatory language directed at the Mount and her students, Simon Newman and his collaborators have brought shame on this university and therefore relinquished the authority to lead it."[315]

To bring attention to what they viewed as the "dangerous" president of their school, faculty protestors revealed in confidential e-mails and on social media that they were willing to destroy their own school by organizing several initiatives, including holding a "Blackout Friday" to depress fundraising and contacting the attorney general of the state of Maryland to complain about the university's ethics violations related to the retention survey that had been sent to students. The faculty protestors claimed that the survey did not have the approval of the institutional research board

[315] Open Letter from John Singleton, Joseph Baldacchino, and David McGinley, in Svrluga, "Controversy at Mount St. Mary's."

of the school. This was false: the survey was a national survey that had gained approval by the institutional research board at Mount St. Mary's. The disgruntled faculty at Mount St. Mary's also made formal complaints about their president to the Cardinal Newman Society, a Catholic watchdog organization, and to the Middle States Accreditation Board. E-mails circulated by the same small group of disgruntled Mount St. Mary's professors and their alumni enablers revealed that, to garner support for their cause of eliminating the president, the group had enlisted organizations such as the American Association of University Professors and the American Philosophical Association as well as the Foundation for Individual Rights in Education (FIRE). The *Daily Nous*, a blog that describes itself as "providing news for and about the philosophy profession," was integral to organizing opposition to Newman. In the end, more than six thousand professors throughout the country—mostly in the humanities—joined in the mobbing action by signing the petition, which denounced the faculty firings and lamented the loss of shared governance at Mount St. Mary's.

The attacks on Newman and long-time board members such as board chairman John E. Coyne took a great toll. Under the intense pressure from accreditors concerned about the firings and the very real lack of shared governance, Newman began to lose the support of the board—the same board that had hired him just a year before. Newman was asked to resign. So he resigned. Coyne also resigned. In response, the faculty organizers of the campaign to oust Newman—both on campus and off—celebrated. Some of the leaders of the mobbing action promised additional campaigns to oust unpopular administrators on other campuses. The former Mount St. Mary's professor who protested Newman's presidency from his perch at an out-of-state university by organizing the national petition celebrated publicly his success in forcing the president out—telling a *Chronicle of Higher Education* reporter that the statement of protest he had organized "helped to make a national story out of what otherwise could have been just another incident of administrative overreach at a small college. . . . I hope this is a clear signal to other academics—and administrators at other institutions—to what can happen when scholars join together in solidarity for justice."[316] As part of his victory lap, the professor took to the comments section of an article posted on the *Daily Nous* to celebrate and warn of additional faculty actions: "Seriously philosophers, you should all feel pretty great right now. The momentum behind that statement was awesome to witness and played a huge part in making this a national story. This incident should be a message to administrators everywhere about the power of the academic community to unite. Now let's do it more."[317]

Open Season on College Presidents and Productive Faculty Members

Newman was not the only college president from the business world who was under attack by his faculty during the fall semester of 2015. During the same months that battles were waged on the Mount St. Mary's campus in Maryland, Timothy M. Wolfe, the former president of the University of Missouri, also paid a high price for poor relations with faculty when he was forced to resign for failing to consult with faculty and students about several major decisions. Some charged that Wolfe's nonacademic roots meant

[316] Katherine Mangan and Nick DeSantis, "Simon Newman Resigns as President of Mount St. Mary's," *Chronicle of Higher Education*, March 2016, https://www.chronicle.com/article/Simon-Newman -Resigns-as/235541.

[317] Justin Weinberg, "Bunny Drowning University President Resigns," *Daily Nous*, February 29, 2016, http://dailynous.com/2016/02/29/ bunny-drowning-university-president-resigns/.

that he was not interested in fostering dialogue with students. Still, it is more likely that envy and resentment over Wolfe's business success played a more important role. Wolfe was a successful business leader like Newman, and it is likely that the cost-cutting strategies that Wolfe had implemented led — in part — to the poor relations he developed on campus. The *Chronicle of Higher Education* pointed out that Wolfe had allowed the graduate-student health-insurance subsidy to expire. Similarly, Mount St. Mary's president announced major changes to the retiree health-insurance plan a few months before the retention scandal and eventual elimination. The decision engendered tremendous hostility toward the new president.[318]

It is difficult to predict what kind of professor or administrator is most likely to be mobbed. On dysfunctional campuses, one can be mobbed just because he or she is "next in line." René Girard's work on scapegoating helps us understand the role that the scapegoat plays in the workplace — and in the world. Girard suggests that campuses in chaos — like the culture at Mount St. Mary's even before Newman arrived — are vulnerable to such episodes of scapegoating. But sometimes a professor or an administrator is mobbed simply for making colleagues look bad or threatening their status on campus. Proposing a new major that may skim students away from a rival discipline has incited mobbing behavior. Making curricular changes — as Newman proposed — poses an existential threat to program viability and can incite mobbing behavior. Westhues points out that there really is no checklist but "to calculate the odds of your being mobbed, count the ways you show your workmates up: fame, publications, teaching scores, connections,

---

[318] Professor Emeriti, "Letter to the Editor: Retired Mount Professors," *Mountain Echo*, November 18, 2015, http://msmecho. com/2015/11/18/letter-to-the-editor-retired-mount-professors/.

eloquence, wit, writing skills, athletic ability, computer skills, salary, family money, age, class, pedigree, looks, house, clothes, spouse, children, sex appeal. Any one of these will do.... And don't forget, refusing to run with the herd, any herd, is reason enough for the herd to turn on you."[319]

Sometimes these kinds of faculty-led mobbings can have deadly consequences. In his research on mobbing behaviors, Heinz Leymann, a scholar who pioneered research on mobbing behaviors in Sweden in the 1980s, has noted that the "mental effects [of being mobbed] were fully comparable with PTSD from war or prison camp experiences." Some victims develop alcoholism or substance-abuse disorders. Family relationships suffer. Workplace targets and witnesses may even develop brief psychotic episodes. In his research, Leymann estimated that 12 percent of suicides in Sweden could be directly attributed to workplace mobbing. He estimated this by surveying Lutheran pastors in the Diocese of Stockholm who interview bereaved families about the circumstances leading up to deaths.[320]

There are many examples of the negative effects of mobbing on those targeted. In 2006, University of California at Santa Cruz chancellor Denice Denton leapt to her death from a forty-two-story San Francisco high-rise building in the wake of a well-orchestrated faculty-led attack that included death threats, harassment, vandalism of her home, and a hostile media campaign waged against her. It was driven entirely by envy over Denton's "compensation package" and spousal hiring. According to the *San Francisco Chronicle*, the UC faculty unions protested the "spousal hiring" of Denton's longtime partner, Gretchen Kalonji, as part of her

[319] Westhues, *Envy of Excellence*, 163.
[320] John Gravois, "Mob Rule," *Chronicle of Higher Education*, April 14, 2006, https://www.chronicle.com/article/Mob-Rule/36004.

recruiting package. A distinguished scholar herself, Kalonji was given a well-paid and well-publicized administrative position in the UC system. But a brutal media campaign followed that focused on Denton's alleged demands for costly improvements to her university-provided house on campus—including fencing for her dogs and a new sound system. In some ways, it was the dog enclosure that focused the attention on the envy-driven mobbing action, as it became like the "bunny-drowning" statement from President Newman. At the height of the mobbing, someone threw a large metal pole through a window in Denton's home, scattering shattered glass throughout her living room. The *San Francisco Chronicle* reported that Denton, who had received a doctorate in electrical engineering from the Massachusetts Institute of Technology and won a prestigious national award for encouraging women and girls in science, had "very high standards.... She expected people to perform and she also worked like crazy.... She really set an example."[321] In an article entitled "Too Much, Too Fast," in the *Chronicle of Higher Education*, Paul Fain suggested that Denton never understood the University of California culture, and her expectations were too high.[322]

Westhues provides several case studies of similar tragedies. For example, following a faculty mobbing at McGill, Justine Sergent, a professor in the Montreal Neurological Institute at McGill University who was accused of failing to get ethics-committee approval for her research on the brain function of pianists, was found dead

[321] Cecilia Vega and Jackson VanDerbeken, "Santa Cruz Chancellor Jumps to Her Death in San Francisco," *San Francisco Chronicle*, June 24, 2006, https://www.sfgate.com/news/article/UC-Santa-Cruz-chancellor-jumps-to-her-death-in-2517073.php.

[322] Paul Fain, "Too Much, Too Fast," *Chronicle of Higher Education*, January 19, 2007, https://www.chronicle.com/article/Too-Much-Too-Fast/14537.

in her car—with her husband—in the garage of their home on April 12, 1994. The double suicide occurred three days after the Montreal *Gazette* published on April 9, 1994, an "anonymous letter" it had received. Headlined "Researcher Disciplined by McGill for Breaking Rules," the letter suggested that Sergent's entire career was built on fraud. In a suicide letter found at the scene, Sergent described the "nightmare" and "harassment" of the previous two years. She said that

> there was no end in sight now that it was exposed in a newspaper and blown out of proportion, and it allows a discredit on myself, my work and my career, which I cannot tolerate.... I love research too much to even consider tampering with data or making false claims, and anyone working in my research field or participating in my experiments could testify that I have always paid much attention to the quality and rigor of my studies and to the welfare of the subjects or patients participating in them.[323]

On news of the suicides, McGill administrators announced that the investigation into "scientific fraud" in Sergent's work would continue. But on March 20, 1997, McGill shut the investigation down, without a resolution and without findings of guilt, but with a continued refusal to exonerate Sergent.[324]

In July 2020, University of North Carolina at Wilmington (UNCW) criminology professor Mike S. Adams took his life after enduring nearly a decade of mobbing by leftist faculty. The mobbing peaked after Adams angered the faculty over a satirical tweet he posted in the early days of the coronavirus lockdown, in March 2020. The tweet read: "Don't Shut Down the Universities. Shut

[323] Westhues, *Workplace Mobbing in Academe*, 25.
[324] Ibid., 25.

Down the Non-Essential Majors like Women's Studies."[325] The
mobbing escalated and drew national attention to Adams when
he posted a tweet on May 28, 2020, mocking North Carolina's
governor for expecting the population to obey what Adams saw as
the state's draconian rules surrounding the coronavirus pandemic:
"This evening I ate pizza and drank beer with six guys at a six-seat
table-top. I almost felt like a free man who was not living in the
slave state of North Carolina. Massa Cooper, let my people go!"
Defining the Tweet by Adams as "racist," UNCW faculty demanded
his removal from campus—and the academic administration com-
plied. Adams was due to retire on the first of August—a week after
he took his life, on July 23.

In recalling the bullying that Adams had endured for nearly a
decade on the UNCW campus, Houston Baptist Professor Robert
A. J. Gagnon posted on Facebook on July 26 that "Mike was a good
and decent man of God, a courageous man of God, who stood up
to the bullies and haters on the Left for years, often using satirical
humor. He started out as an unbelieving leftist, became a Christian, and defended the pro-life cause and free speech on college
campuses. I weep at our loss and for the pain he must have felt in
the last two or three weeks of his life."[326]

Beyond the role that the scapegoat plays in all academic mobbings, the previous productivity and success of Newman, Sergent,
Wolfe, Denton, and dozens more that Westhues has documented is
key to understanding academic mobbing by envious and resentful

[325] Mark Tapson, "Confessions of a Conservative College Professor,"
    FrontPage Magazine, July 14, 2020, https://www.frontpagemag.com/
    fpm/2020/07/confessions-conservative-college-professor-mark-ta
    pson/?fbclid=IwAR3NS6waSHBhdTN6xrfwWYnPIfIR5RghHH
    cODkxeCnHPYvL0sWIk_TOx1fA.
[326] Robert A. J. Gagnon, Facebook, July 26, 2020, 6:36 p.m., https://
    www.facebook.com/robert.a.gagnon.56.

faculty. Westhues's *The Envy of Excellence* reveals that mobbing victims in the faculty and administrative ranks is almost always highly successful in their professional lives. In her essay "The Anatomy of an Academic Mobbing," Florida Atlantic University professor Joan Friedenberg suggests that "productive, inner-directed individuals who also often act on their principles" are the most likely to be targeted.[327] For example, Saint Louis University's longtime president, Father Lawrence Biondi, devoted twenty-six years to leading the Jesuit university to prominence—increasing both the number and the quality of its faculty and its students, doubling the acreage of the school, and stabilizing a huge swath of the city, making the Grand Center Arts District and extending SLU's influence throughout the city and the world. In an article for *St. Louis Magazine*, the mayor of the city, Francis Slay, told a reporter that "those who remember SLU when he arrived and examine the one from which he will retire know the truth: Larry Biondi is one of America's great college presidents."[328] But that did not stop a faculty-led mobbing action against him over a tenure dispute and an unpopular academic vice president.

As Girard would predict, current research on academic mobbing reveals that it is the successful career of another person that inspires envy and fear, and the mob tries to eliminate that person from their campus. Newman's bunny-drowning statement, the favored status given to Denton's partner, and the personnel decisions by Wolfe and Father Biondi were all used by faculty members to justify an extreme reaction. These incidents provide a "moral" reason for

---

[327] Joan Friedenberg, "Anatomy of an Academic Mobbing" (paper presented at the University of Waterloo, Canada, April 11, 2008), The Mobbing Portal, http://www.mobbingportal.com/friedej.html.

[328] Jeannette Cooperman, "The Complex Legacy of Father Lawrence Biondi," *St. Louis Magazine*, September 20, 2013, https://www.stlmag.com/The-Complex-Legacy-of-Father-Lawrence-Biondi/.

the overt mobbing behavior to begin. For researchers of mobbing behavior, these kinds of incidents are just the "struck match.... The kindling's been stacking up for years, dry and brittle and some of it drenched in gasoline."[329] This is what *ressentiment* looks like.

Jeanine Stewart, professor of psychology at Washington and Lee University, has proposed that the design of the academic workplace itself fosters these kinds of counterproductive behaviors. In a paper titled "Dysfunctional by Design: Mobbing and Harassment in the Academic Workplace," published in *Women in Higher Education*, Stewart suggests that in a campus community in which large numbers of faculty members might report to a single dean or provost, informal pecking orders can emerge. She calls these virtual power structures "soft hierarchies," in contrast to the hard hierarchies one sees on an organizational chart. It is within the highest tiers of the soft hierarchies—the rank and file workers—that power is concentrated.[330]

On most campuses, tenured faculty—especially tenured faculty in the humanities—hold most of the soft-hierarchical power because the curricula on liberal-arts campuses such as Mount St. Mary's require students to enroll in large numbers of core courses in the liberal arts. This mandate results in full employment for faculty who do not have to recruit students to enroll in their courses. Any change in the core requirements in these areas becomes an "existential threat" to the status of humanities faculty because it endangers their power and status. In a threat to the power of the

---

[329] Ibid.

[330] Jeanine Stewart, "Hierarchical Dysfunction and Mobbing in the Academy," *Women in Higher Education*; Katherine Hermes et al., "Workplace Bullying and Sexual Harassment," Central Connecticut State University Committee on the Concerns of Women, December 11, 2008, https://www.ccsu.edu/ccw/files/archive/ReportWBandSH.pdf.

philosophy and history professors on the Mount St. Mary's campus, President Newman questioned the comparatively high number of core courses that students were required to take. Potential and incoming students were unhappy about what many of them saw as the bloated sixty-five-unit core. To attract career-minded students, Newman enlisted the assistance of a committee consisting of some of the strongest students on campus and a number of faculty members to consider reducing the number of required core liberal-arts courses and giving students more freedom to choose the courses they would like to take. This change, of course, would dramatically alter the pecking order—the balance of power at the university—creating tremendous resentment within the humanities faculty on that campus.

Beyond threats to power, Kenneth Westhues's research on mobbing behavior within faculties reveals that the faculty member or administrator who is most vulnerable to being mobbed is a high achiever who is perceived to "threaten or put to shame co-workers." In some ways, the eliminative impulse is driven by fear. Westhues believes that the need to "gang up" or to join with others against what is perceived to be a common threat lies deep in human nature—as in original sin. Westhues has found that what he calls "the lust to wipe another person out" is categorically similar to a biological need since "it can consume a person to the point of obsession, spread like a virus through a group, and become the driving force behind collective energy. Yet, unlike the appetites for food and sex, this one has come to be proscribed in the process of civilization. It is supposed to be held in check by universal compassion, common allegiance to the brotherhood of man."[331] But, as we have seen at a growing list of colleges and universities, these checks appear to be absent.

[331] Westhues, *Workplace Mobbing in Academe*, 11.

The Politics of Envy

A Faculty Mobbing at Providence College

Westhues's "common allegiance to the brotherhood of man" was certainly absent at Providence College in 2016 when an especially vindictive faculty mobbing occurred. World-class scholar Anthony Esolen, author of sixteen books and more than five hundred published articles and the most outstanding faculty member in the history of the midsize Catholic college in Providence, Rhode Island, was the target of a protracted mobbing by faculty and at least one administrator. The mobbing culminated in a loud protest outside his campus office, with about sixty students brandishing bullhorns and demanding that he be removed from campus. Accompanied by a female senior level administrator who claims she was there just to "keep order," there was plenty of faculty assistance in the student action. Indeed, faculty members contributed to the mobbing by circulating their own campus petition, which originated with the school's Black Studies Program faculty. It stated that Esolen had "openly, publicly, and unabashedly articulated a disdain for racial, ethnic, gender, sexual and religious inclusion." At the same time, there was what the participants in the mobbing defined as a triggering incident: the publication of two online articles by Dr. Esolen in *Crisis Magazine*, a journal of orthodox Catholic thought. The articles were critical of the recent "diversity" movement on the Providence campus and the establishment of a "Bias Response Protocol." Dr. Esolen had the temerity to describe the diversity movement as misguided and destructive—and the students, and presumably the administrator who participated in the protest, were outraged by his criticisms.

As Westhues suggests, the critical incident over the two offending articles that had been published in the weeks before the student protest was just the most recent, and most overt, attack on Esolen. Esolen became a target on campus long before the appearance of the two offending articles because he had been "openly critical" of the school's new "Bias Response Protocol." In an interview about the mobbing published by Rod Dreher on the *American Conservative* website, Esolen recalls: "It's a long story.... It involves five Catholic colleagues who had been treated disgracefully by their secular colleagues or have suffered under the inquest of the 'Bias Response Protocol.'"

Esolen correctly understood that the emergence of a Bias Response Team was a red flag on the Catholic campus; he was aware that this new bias reporting mechanism was proliferating on many campuses—and was ensnaring Catholic faculty who may not have been on board with the prevailing zeitgeist of the secularizing faculty. The Foundation for Individual Rights in Education (FIRE), a national organization whose mission is to defend and sustain the individual rights of students and faculty members at America's colleges and universities, has viewed as alarming the creation of more than 230 Bias Response Teams throughout the country. On its website, FIRE has warned that over the past several years, it "has received an increasing number of reports that colleges and universities are inviting students to anonymously report offensive, yet constitutionally protected speech to administrators and law enforcement through 'Bias Response Teams.' These teams monitor and investigate student and faculty speech; offensive statements are reported to law enforcement and student conduct administrators."[332] Esolen was appalled at the campus threats to the freedom of speech, freedom of association, due process, legal equality, religious liberty, and sanctity of conscience that such "bias response" teams posed. He had already witnessed several colleagues becoming ensnared in

---

[332] "2017 Report on Bias Reporting Systems," Foundation for Individual Rights in Education, https://www.thefire.org/research/publications/bias-response-team-report-2017/report-on-bias-reporting-systems-2017/.

the bias reporting. One of his friends on the faculty was reported to the Bias Response Team because he had the temerity to send e-mails to former students to offer to send them pamphlets on the Rosary, Confession, and Theology of the Body at his own expense—and only if the students requested it. Another professor was so upset by her ordeal with the Bias Response Team that she had to take a medical leave of absence and considered early retirement.[333]

Esolen's *Crisis Magazine* article titled "My College Succumbed to the Totalitarian Diversity Cult" reflected his concern about the bias reporting mechanism on campus—referring to it as the "Star Chamber" whose constitution and laws and executive power no one will know. Esolen warned readers that "the quest for diversity has made life hell for more than one of my friends. All, now, in the name of an undefined and perhaps undefinable diversity, to which you had damned well better give honor and glory. If you don't—and you may not even be aware of the *lèse-majesté* as you commit it—you'd better have eyes in the back of your head."[334] According to Esolen:

> Someone at school then got hold of them [the articles] and before I knew it, I was in the middle of an outrage, coming mainly from a group of students who I believe have been misled by radical professors who have adopted politics as their god, whether these professors are aware of it or not. The students accused me of racism, despite my explicit

[333] Michael J. Rubin, "Providence College and Dr. Anthony Esolen: An Alumnus Speaks Out," *Catholic World Report*, November 29, 2016, https://www.catholicworldreport.com/2016/11/29/providence-college-and-dr-anthony-esolen-an-alumnus-speaks-out/.

[334] Anthony Esolen, "My College Succumbed to the Totalitarian Diversity Cult," *Crisis Magazine*, September 26, 2016, https://www.crisismagazine.com/2016/college-succumbed-totalitarian-diversity-cult.

statements in the articles that I welcome people of all ethnic and racial backgrounds, and despite my appeal at the end of one of the articles, that they and their secular professors should join us in that communion where there is neither Greek nor Jew, etc. They were angered by my suggestion in one article that there was something narcissistic in the common insistence that people should study themselves rather than people who lived long ago and in cultures far removed from ours by any ordinary criterion, and that there was something totalitarian in the impulse of the secular left, to attempt to subject our curriculum to the demands of a current political aim.[335]

As Westhues would predict, the foundation for the mobbing had begun years before Esolen ever published the two articles that the faculty, members of the administration, and students claim to have been offended by. Envious of his scholarly productivity and the thousands of dedicated students who continue to support him today, several members of the faculty were determined to eliminate him from campus. According to an article authored by one of his many devoted former students and published in *Crisis Magazine*, Esolen had been nominated several times for Providence College's Accinno Teaching Award. But, as the former student pointed out, "despite more than a dozen nominations by students like myself, he never won it, and never will.... A friend and colleague of Esolen's informed him years ago that he should never even bother applying for it, such was the disdain that members of the selection committee had for him."[336] In an interview published in the *Na-*

[335] Rod Dreher, "Tony Esolen Contra Mundum," *American Conservative*, November 1, 2016, https://www.theamericanconservative.com/dreher/anthony-esolen-contra-mundum-catholic/.
[336] Rubin, "Providence College and Dr. Anthony Esolen."

tional Catholic Register, Esolen said that the "turning point" for him came when Reverend Brian Shanley, the president of Providence College, refused to meet with him and a small group of Catholic professors concerned about the attacks on faithful Catholic faculty members.[337] Worse, rather than meeting with Esolen, Father Shanley sided with the mob and sent a campus-wide e-mail stating that Professor Esolen "speaks only for himself.... He certainly does not speak for me, my administration, and for many others at Providence College who understand and value diversity in a very different sense from him."[338]

Esolen responded on the pages of the *National Catholic Register*:

And what can you do against slander and detraction? Stand on a stump and shout your innocence to all passersby?... I could live with a somewhat Catholic school that was really committed to the humanities, such as we were for many years. I could live with an unreservedly Catholic school where the humanities needed shoring up. But to live at a used-to-be-Catholic school no longer committed to the humanities, where all the big decisions are basically secular in their inspiration and their aim, on a campus that is highly politicized and therefore treacherous ... no, that's not for someone of my years. I wrote, 10 years ago, that we had never really lost our identity, and what we lost we were well on

---

[337] Peter Jesserer Smith, "Anthony Esolen in His Own Words," *National Catholic Register*, May 4, 2017, http://www.ncregister.com/blog/pjsmith/anthony-esolen-in-his-own-words-why-i-left-providence-college-for-thomas-mo.

[338] Fr. Brian Shanley's letter to the faculty, in Rod Dreher, "Tony Esolen *Contra Mundum*," *American Conservative*, November 1, 2016, https://www.theamericanconservative.com/dreher/anthony-esolen-contra-mundum-catholic/.

the way to recover. I could not write those words now.... Saving the school is no longer my battle.[339]

As the college term drew to a close in the spring of 2016, Esolen, prolific author and translator of a highly regarded edition of Dante's *Divine Comedy*, packed up and got ready to leave the school where he had taught since 1990. He would renounce his tenure, give up his well-earned sabbatical, and accept a teaching position at a smaller and more faithfully orthodox Catholic college. Esolen's choice to leave one Catholic school for another had nothing to do with a desire for greater status or a higher salary. He wasn't swayed by the offer of an endowed chair or a lighter teaching load. Rather, he was attracted to the curriculum at the faithful Catholic college — the commitment to a classical Catholic education "that values the theology of Thomas Aquinas more than diversity studies." Today, Esolen teaches at Magdalen College in Warner, New Hampshire — a small faithful Catholic college where his gifts are better appreciated. According to Esolen, he left Providence because "students are meant to be surrounded by beauty and sanity" and because he wanted to "be part of delivering a curriculum that was based on the Truth."[340] It appears that he has found that at Magdalen.

The Esolen mobbing best illustrates the influence of the soft hierarchies on college campuses. As mentioned earlier, in disputes like this, the real power resides within the soft hierarchies — often emerging from the envy-driven faculty and lower-level administrators. For nearly fifteen years — beginning with the faculty-fueled attack on Harvard University president Lawrence Summers in 2005 — faculty have been increasingly willing to organize mobbing

---

[339] Smith, "Anthony Esolen in His Own Words."
[340] Ibid.

The Politics of Envy

actions to bring down productive professors and senior-level administrators. Social media has facilitated these mobbing actions. Summers was targeted after he suggested at an academic conference that innate male-female differences might possibly provide a partial explanation why mathematics, engineering, and hard-science faculties remain so heavily male. And although that was the triggering incident that eventually brought Summers down, resentful female faculty members in Harvard's Caucus for Gender Equality had already been pressuring Summers to hire more women. Although there was no evidence of discrimination in hiring, the Caucus charged the president with having "reduced diversity" by failing to hire enough female professors. In response to the powerful faculty demands, Summers retracted his suggestion on innate gender differences and issued what the *Atlantic*'s Stuart Taylor Jr. called "a groveling, Soviet show-trial style apology."[341] Still, the faculty held a "no-confidence" vote and Summers resigned.[342]

Mobbings continue and, on some campuses, seem to be escalating. Yet, when a mobbing action is begun, it is always denied by those involved in the mobbing behavior—obscured by the pretense of serving some lofty goal of commitment to the core, academic excellence, or equality and diversity. Those involved in mobbing often see themselves as holding the higher moral ground, claiming that the targeted individual is not supportive of a specific diversity initiative on campus or is blocking "progress" in some new campus

---

[341] Stuart Taylor Jr., "Why Feminist Careerists Neutered Larry Summers," *Atlantic*, February 2005, https://www.theatlantic.com/magazine/archive/2005/02/why-feminist-careerists-neutered-larry-summers/303795/.

[342] Alan Finder and Kate Zernike, "Embattled President of Harvard to Step Down at End of Semester," *New York Times*, February 21, 2006, https://www.nytimes.com/2006/02/21/education/embattled-president-of-harvard-to-step-down-at-end-of-semester.html.

initiative. Westhues views this as a "persecutory unconscious" operating in those caught up in the snowballing process. The envious are likely not even aware of their own envious resentment. Westhues, who spent several years in the seminary, says these mobbing actions can be analogous to "what Jesus referred to in his prayer on the cross: Father forgive them because they do not know what they do."

Westhues may be too kind. Social elimination reflects a fundamental attribution error, the tendency in all of us to overestimate the extent to which behavior reflects underlying personal qualities (dishonesty, for instance, or untrustworthiness) and to underestimate the extent to which it reflects the particular situation or context.[343] Social eliminations are carried out by people who have fallen deeply into a fundamental attribution error, by identifying some alleged offense so closely with the offender's identity that they cannot see the person as a human being like themselves. The target becomes the "other" and needs to be eliminated.[344]

Westhues provides a checklist of identifiable symptoms and empirical indicators that an exclusionary process has "escaped the bounds of reason and civilization" and moved toward mobbing. These are "reliable signs that a mobbing is occurring and that elimination in its savage sense is underway." The first is that the person being pursued is a *popular high-achieving target*. Mediocre performers tend not to arouse the eliminative impulse in leaders or peers. They do not show others up. But, when the person targeted has a record of success, suspicion grows that something more lies behind the mobbing action. Second, there is a *lack of due process*. Standard procedures, rules of fairness and natural justice, and all that the term "due process" includes hold eliminative impulses in check and encourage mutual tolerance. Effective mobbing behavior

[343] Westhues, *Workplace Mobbing in Academe*, 11.
[344] Ibid., 12.

may look fair to outsiders, but the evidence suggests that those leading an envy-driven exclusionary effort are making up rules as they go along or have become a law unto themselves.

Unanimity is another empirical indicator that a mobbing is taking place. Westhues's research demonstrates that

> the loss of diverse opinion is a compelling indication that eliminative fury has been unleashed. When all decent people agree on the need to put somebody down, when they demand it with one voice in mass meetings, when one by one they put their names to long denunciations (or angry petitions generated by disgruntled former faculty members with scores to settle) alarm bells should go off. Decency and unanimity seldom coincide. The late French philosopher, Emmanuel Levinas, liked to quote the Talmudic principle, "If everyone is in agreement to condemn someone, release him for he must be innocent."[345]

In addition, there is often evidence of *prior marginalization* of the target. In this, the punishment precedes the "crime" that the individual is being eliminated for. The University of California, Santa Cruz's chancellor Denice Denton created tremendous resentment among the faculty because of her demands for faculty productivity. She worked very hard, and she expected the faculty to produce also. In nearly every case of envy-driven mobbing, there were months—or even years—of subtle hints of mobbing behaviors, including rumors, gossip about her lesbian partner, innuendo, and minor ostracism, that preceded the critical incident. *Secrecy* is also an important component of a mobbing as eliminators prefer to keep their proceedings confidential and their organizing secretive. In *Things Which Are Done in Secret*, a book about faculty

[345] Ibid., 15.

eliminations at McGill University, author Marlene Dixon describes the star chamber proceedings that preceded each of the mobbings she investigated.

Envy-driven mobbing behavior is not bullying behavior, although sometimes the two look quite similar, and the effects on the victim are similar. But the motivations for bullying and mobbing are very different. With bullying, there is usually a stronger and more powerful individual who oppresses a person of lower status. With mobbing, the target is more often a high-status individual who inspires envy and fear. Insecure faculty members and mid-level administrators are more likely to initiate mobbing actions against high-status faculty members who appear to threaten them with their excellence. No one wants to be reminded of his or her own mediocrity, so when there is an especially high-achieving member in a faculty, that person needs to be eliminated. As Joseph Epstein points out in *Envy*, for some academics, "envy can mix with snobbery, with impotence added, all mounted against a background of cosmic injustice, to put a large class of persons into a permanent condition of *ressentiment*."[346] For Scheler, *ressentiment* has its genesis in negative psychic feelings such as envy and jealousy, hatred, spite, malice, and joy over another's misfortune. It always involves "mental comparisons" or value judgments with other people who allegedly have no feelings of *ressentiment* and who usually exhibit positive values. The truly resentful faculty member ends up coveting the personal qualities and goods of another, such as the person's talent, writing ability, education, persuasive speaking, publications, or rapport with students. In the early stages of *ressentiment*, there are feelings of inferiority. But, as time goes on and the resentful individual realizes that he or she can never acquire the talents or the abilities of the envied colleague, he or she begins to seek out

[346] Epstein, *Envy*, 82.

colleagues of lower value as a source of solace. Scheler calls this "Man's Inherent Fundamental Moral Weakness" because this tendency to seek surrogates to compensate for frustration with higher-value attainment inserts itself into the scenario.[347] It is a moral weakness because it is a sense of hopelessness and meaninglessness that drives an individual to enlist similar aggrieved surrogates, to create a scapegoat, and to attack.

Faculty Mobbing and Original Sin

Westhues once told an interviewer that "there's only two kinds of people in the world, those who believe that there's original sin and those who don't.... Mobbing research as a whole is more on the side of the original sin folks." Westhues, who studied for the priesthood, is, of course, on the side of original sin—even though he has since left the Church. From a sociological perspective, mobbing is a direct contradiction of the work of Max Weber, one of the earliest sociologists. Weber believed that the bureaucracy and hierarchy of the university would ensure rational behavior of its members. It doesn't. And although tenure was designed to protect the academic freedom of faculty from outside interference, it does nothing to protect faculty members and administrators from the mob within their own university's walls. Westhues suggests that faculty mobbings are the collective expression of the eliminative impulse in formal organizations—the ghost in the machine.[348] Few can survive when a conspiracy of faculty members mobilizes to denigrate, humiliate, and eliminate a colleague or a feared administrator.

There is little that can be done to prevent mobbings. Mobbing is not easily outlawed. In fact, Westhues believes that a policy

[347] Scheler, *Ressentiment*, 23–25.
[348] Westhues, *Envy of Excellence*, 42.

forbidding mobbing behavior may, in practice, become a weapon for convicting some mobbing target of a punishable offense and thereby aiding in his or her humiliation. There is much evidence that policies against sexual harassment have often been used as tools for harassing innocent but disliked colleagues.[349] Esolen's criticisms of the Providence College Bias Response Teams are a case in point. Europe is much more likely to acknowledge the irrationality inherent in campus mobbings. France already has anti-mobbing legislation, and several European universities have attempted to pass anti-mobbing laws. According to Westhues, *Das mobbing* is a household term in Germany. Some schools in the United States have attempted to pass their own "anti-bullying" laws for faculty, but they have ended up ensnaring conservative faculty members—such as Esolen—who may not be supportive of the kinds of initiatives pushed by progressive faculty members. A few years ago, a Committee on the Concerns of Women at Central Connecticut State University attempted to promote the passage of a state "Act Concerning Bullying in the Workplace." In 2010, H.B. 5285, the Act Concerning State Employees and Violence and Bullying in the Workplace, was passed unanimously by the Labor and Public Employees Committee, but it did not get to the floor and was not passed by the Committee on Government Administration and Elections.[350]

Rather than legislative initiatives, Westhues suggests that we should be cultivating a campus culture that is aware of the herd instinct in all of us. Once the mob emerges, the administration can (and should) do something to stop it. Sometimes all it would take would be for one senior administrator just to tell the faculty to stop it. Mobbing actions cannot succeed without the backing

---

[349] Westhues, *Workplace Mobbing in Academe*, 8.
[350] Hermes et al., "Workplace Bullying and Sexual Harassment."

of senior administrators and members of the board of trustees. But if the targeted professor or administrator is in the minority on campus, most cowardly campus leaders' first instinct will be to side with the majority—especially if the majority contains powerful faculty members such as those in the Black Studies Program at Providence. If Providence College's Father Shanley could have found the courage to agree to meet with Esolen and his attackers, much of the mobbing could have been avoided. But it is possible that for Father Shanley, the secularization path he appears to have charted for Providence College has been made much easier with Anthony Esolen gone.

In most cases, the victim of the mobbing chooses to leave or is forcibly separated from his or her university home. Like Esolen, victims cut their losses. Some find other jobs, but most often, professors who have been mobbed leave academia entirely. For those who have been mobbed, the stress from the mobbing has led to heart disease and other stress-related illnesses. In some of the cases Westhues studied, the mobbing has been so spiteful and vengeful that victims have received large court settlements for harassment, wrongful firing, and defamation. But few targeted faculty and administrators want a protracted and expensive court case, which would require them to relive the horrors of the mobbing and threaten to bankrupt them and their families. That is unfortunate because if envious faculty members and complicit administrators are not confronted for their role in a campus mobbing, the mobbings will continue.

9

Envy in the Age of Social Media

While envy-driven workplace mobbings like those described in the previous chapter have always been possible without the use of social media, the mobbing actions at Mount St. Mary's and Providence College demonstrate what happens when a group of envious or resentful faculty members utilize social media to destroy an individual they view as a threat to their well-being. Both of these campus attacks were well organized, and both exploited social media to mobilize the masses.

In the Mount St. Mary's mobbing, a former professor there—an individual who had never had any contact with the new president—collaborated with campus faculty members to use social media to try to destroy his presidency. In this case, social media was effective in converting what should have been a local workplace dispute into a national call to action.[351] This faculty member used social media not only to help push the president out but also to congratulate the mob—sending a message to warn all administrators "about the power of the academic community to unite." Promising additional mobbing actions, the faculty member mobilized his social media followers by promising to do it again—and again—to

[351] Weinberg, "Bunny Drowning University President Resigns."

anyone else who attempts to undermine shared governance in hiring and firing or who tries to make the kind of curricular or campus cultural changes that the former Mount St. Mary's president had attempted.[352] Three years after the mobbing, this faculty member still feels justified in doing what he did. When asked (by e-mail) whether he had any "second thoughts" about his role in removing the president of Mount St. Mary's, he responded quickly: "I don't know what reason there would be to have had second thoughts about anything. The president of Mount St. Mary's attempted to fire two faculty members, and discipline several more, due to their role in reporting on his administration and raising perfectly legitimate criticisms of his behavior. And I think the willingness of philosophers and other academics to unite behind their colleagues on this massive scale should send a warning to administrators about the consequences of ignoring faculty rights, especially for such self-serving ends."[353]

In the Esolen mobbing, social media was used to organize a kind of a campus flash mob, replete with faculty and student leaders carrying bullhorns to shout angry denunciations outside the besieged professor's office windows. At least one senior administrator was present at the mobbing that took place outside Esolen's office window. In a scene reminiscent of Henrik Ibsen's *Enemy of the People*, Esolen was denigrated through chants and taunts by the angry students and faculty enablers. And although he had many student and faculty supporters on campus, most were too afraid of the angry mob to offer public support to their colleague — telling him privately that they were "with him" but

[352] Ibid.
[353] Personal e-mail from a philosophy professor following a query on whether he had any "second thoughts" about his role in the Mount St. Mary's–Simon Newman debacle, November 22, 2019.

242

could not publicly help. Some feared for their safety. Most just wanted to save their jobs and worried about the wrath of the mob being turned on them. Even though Esolen, an internationally renowned Dante scholar, has many friends and thousands of admirers of his published work, all of that was little consolation for the Esolen family when they were in the middle of a social media–driven mobbing action that persisted from November 2016 through the following spring semester, when Esolen finally was driven out of Providence.

In these two cases, and in many more examples of what are increasingly being defined as a part of "cancel culture," individuals who are envied and feared by others are increasingly being targeted and mobbed through social media in an attempt to "cancel" their very existence. Cancel culture is a form of boycott in which the targeted individual is eliminated from his or her job or social circle. These now targeted individuals are then said to be "canceled" or eliminated. This is becoming a much bigger problem than most realize. In 2019, former President Barack Obama warned about cancel culture, saying that it would "not bring about change." Obama decried the culture of eliminating people by saying that going online to destroy people "is not activism."[354]

Former First Lady Michelle Obama tried to end online bullying, and Melania Trump, the current First Lady, has made online bullying a focus of her "Be Best" campaign for children and teens. Still, bullying is very different from the kind of envy-driven cancel culture that is the topic of this book. In fact, unlike bullying, which now causes the bully to be stigmatized in today's renewed

---

[354] "President Barack Obama on Being Woke and Cancel-Culture: That's Not Activism," video, 1:00, *Politico*, October 30, 2019, https://www.politico.com/video/2019/10/30/obama-woke-cancel-culture-activism-069022.

anti-bullying culture, the very act of leading or joining a mobbing action against an envied individual can actually increase the status of the leaders of the mob. Faculty members gained national status for their savvy use of social media to promote the mobbing of the Mount St. Mary's president. Some got promoted. Others spent time online gloating about their success in removing the "bunny-drowning" president.

Social media mobbing is much like the mobbing activity among birds. Heinz Leymann, a German-born Swedish citizen, was the first to apply the zoological term "mobbing" to human behavior. Previously, the term mobbing was used almost exclusively in the animal kingdom, characterizing the behavior of small birds aggressively ganging up on a larger predator bird in order to force the predator to retreat. In some ways, these campus mobbings replicate the kind of bird mobbing behavior I often witness in my own backyard on the Long Island Sound. Having lived on the New England coastline for more than a dozen years, my husband and I have grown to appreciate the changing tides and the extraordinary behavior of the birds who make their home on the shoreline. A variety of birds are attracted by oyster beds that surround our home—a century-old Victorian home that had once been the site of a thriving oyster farm in the early 1900s. The oyster beds are still here today; and even though commercial oyster fishermen continue to fill their boats with oysters each September and October, the marshlands still attract the most fascinating birds—including the great blue heron, the hawks, as well as the grackles, sparrows, songbirds, bluebirds, and of course, the insatiable seagulls. Most of the birds on the coast are territorial and have created some serious disputes over turf and status hierarchies.

When our family first moved here in the spring of 2007—at the height of the bird mating season—we witnessed our first bird mobbing action when we were drawn outside by a noisy flock of birds aggressively zooming in and out of the trees near our dock. Clearly agitated, more than a dozen of them—all angry little songbirds—appeared to be terrorizing what seemed to be a helpless but very large hawk hiding out in the trees. Like kamikaze pilots, the fearless little birds would zoom toward the hapless hawk, almost touching him, screaming at him and sometimes even defecating on his head. Paying no attention to my presence, the attack continued for several minutes until eventually, the tiny terrorists seemed to have made their point, and the predator hawk finally escaped their wrath, covered with the stain of his shame. The attack by the mob of songbirds continues until the predator skulks away in defeat. This is mobbing behavior—its purpose is to drive the predator away. Or, in the words of the eminent Austrian ethologist, Konrad Lorenz, to "make the enemy's life a burden."[355]

It is difficult to understand why the hawks do not fight back. They are so much bigger and more lethal than the common songbirds. But, as the bird experts point out, hawks, owls, ospreys, and great blue heron have been killed or severely injured "when the mob turns ugly." It is likely that the hawks have learned that it is better to remain calm and endure the aggressive attack, doing nothing to further inflame the much smaller, but more abundant, birds. Large hawks are rarely quick enough to catch the little birds, and the birds know this. Seldom do birds mob smaller hawks, as the more agile predators can easily catch songbirds and, as one fellow birdwatcher posted online, "would love to have the little birds visit them for lunch."[356] A study published in 1978 determined that the main payoff from mobbing birds is increased knowledge of the

---

[355] Gravois, "Mob Rule."
[356] "Hawks Getting Mobbed," Bird Watcher's General Store, May 11, 2001, http://www.birdwatchersgeneralstore.com/mobbing.htm.

local predators. And that has remained the accepted explanation for years. However, a recent article reveals that birds mob to assess the quality of the neighborhood. Just like people, birds shy away from areas that seem unsafe. And, just as birds signal when they find a full bird feeder, their calls help other birds avoid risks and find food. In that sense, one writer claims, "birds mob for the same reasons people go to parties. It's a way to see and be seen—and that, in the forest, is critical. They're judging each other's performances, seeing who's well fed, who's aggressive, who would be a good mate." It turns out that many, if not most, species are able to eavesdrop on each other's communications and learn critical news about the neighborhood.[357]

Bird mobbing increases dramatically in the spring months because, in addition to defending territory and protecting nesting areas, mobbing is an important way for male birds to demonstrate their courage and their prowess to potential mates. It is an important activity that male birds use to gain higher status, attracting the most desirable young female birds for mating. Female birds are attracted to the most daring of the young mobbers—the ones who zoom in closest to taunt the predator. The aggressive behavior and the bid for higher status in the bird kingdom is very much the same as that of mobbing behavior in the workplace. Just as the birds send signals to initiate a mobbing when a predator threatens them, social media provides a similar function in disseminating a "call to action" for a mobbing. But, unlike bird mobbings, which are initiated when a smaller bird feels physically threatened by a predator, social media mobbings most often emerge when people feel envious or resentful and want to eliminate the source of their painful emotions.

[357] Emily Wurtman-Wonder, "Why Birds Love Mobs," *Nautilus*, January 18, 2017, http://nautil.us/blog/why-birds-love-mobs.

Envy in the Age of Social Media

Envy Is Woven throughout Social Media

More than fifty years before the term "social media influencer" was coined, René Girard identified the social role played by those whose attractiveness and authenticity inspired others to want to be like them. The advertising industry has always known of our mimetic desires. Marketers appeal to our envy by pointing out the ways in which their products will make us the "envy of our peers." Just as Shakespeare makes mimetic desire explicit in *The Two Gentlemen of Verona* when he chooses the name Proteus, the Greek god of transformation, for a character who personifies his envious desire to "become" his friend Valentine, so today's social media influencers create and interpret trends by inspiring desire—often envious desire.

In the case of envy, social media works in three closely related ways: by increasing social proximity, by eliminating encapsulation, and by rejecting concealment.[358] A growing body of social science research indicates that envy is so deeply woven into our use of social media that we may not even be aware that we are in the process of eliminating many of the social norms and structures that had been built to mitigate our envy. Although, in the past, we tended to envy those closest to us geographically or socially, proximity kept envy in check because we could envy only those we "knew" or were in contact with. Social media has changed all of that by reducing the barriers to *social proximity*. Prior to the expansion of social media, including Facebook and Instagram, we could not envy those we did not "see" or have exposure to. And, although we may have secretly envied celebrities or those we read about in newspapers or magazines, envy remains an issue of propinquity.

---

[358] Alexandra Samuel, "What to Do When Social Media Inspires Envy," *JSTOR Daily*, February 6, 2018, https://daily.jstor.org/what-to-do-when-social-media-inspires-envy/.

The Politics of Envy

As Aristotle's *Rhetoric* suggests, the objects of envy have always been characterized by nearness in time, place, age, and reputation:

Kin can even be jealous of their kin.... Also our fellow-competitors ... we do not compete with men who lived a hundred centuries ago, or those not yet born, or the dead, or those who dwell near the Pillars of Hercules, or those whom, in our opinion or that of others, we take to be far below us or far above us. So, too, we compete with those who follow the same ends as ourselves, we compete with our rivals in sport or in love, and generally with those who are after the same things; and it is therefore those whom we are bound to envy beyond all others. Hence the saying: "Potter against potter."[359]

Aristotle knew that we envy "those whose possession of, or success in a thing is a reproach to us." He understood that the objects of envy are most often "our neighbors and equals; for it is clear that it is our own fault we have missed the good thing in question; this annoys us and excites envy in us." We envy those who have what we ought to have or who have what we once had:

Hence old men envy younger men, and those who have spent much, tend to envy those who have spent little on the same thing. And men who have not got a thing, or not got it yet, envy those who have gotten it quickly. We can see what things and what persons give pleasure to envious people and in what states of mind they feel it; the states of mind in which they feel pain are those under which they will feel pleasure in the contrary things. If therefore, we ourselves

[359] Aristotle, *Rhetoric* (N.p.: Create Space Independent Publishing, 2013), 96–97.

with whom the decision rests are put into an envious state of mind, and those for whom our pity, or the award of something desirable is claimed are such as have been described, it is obvious that they will win no pity from us.[360]

Social media has greatly expanded the number of those we call our "friends," giving us access to every aspect of what seems to be their perfect lives. Social media has created an illusion of intimacy with those who are distant from us geographically or in terms of social class. While in the past, we might have envied classmates, or friends from work, or neighbors who seemed to enjoy advantages we may have coveted, we are now constantly bombarded with the ever-growing number of elaborate vacations, beautiful new houses, and fulfilling jobs of our Facebook "friends." Their triumphs are posted on our news feeds—taunting the envious—demanding to be "liked."

A recent study from the United Arab Emirates (UAE) reveals that "as many as 41 percent of survey takers in the UAE admitted to feeling envious when they see the seemingly happier lives of their friends on social media." While the individuals surveyed in the UAE study cannot be viewed as representative, the data suggest that envy on social media is a crosscultural phenomenon. The desire for "likes" plays a central role in this, with a majority of people feeling upset when their friends get more likes than they do. The study, which surveyed 16,750 people worldwide, found that individuals "often experience negative emotions after spending time on social media due to a variety of reasons, and these overpower the positive effects of social media." Dr. Jamilah Motala, clinical psychologist at Light House Arabia in Dubai, explained that the tendency of feeling jealous due to the number of likes is similar to

The Politics of Envy

the insecurity and lack of self-esteem in a person: "Jealousy and envy may be underpinned by core beliefs such as my value depends on what others think of me or I am not good enough."[361]

These concerns are especially true regarding Instagram, a free social networking service built around sharing photos and videos, where the posting of likes has been paramount in placement of posts. Instagram launched in October 2010 but was purchased by Facebook in April 2012. Like Facebook and Twitter, Instagram allows people to follow users and creates a feed on the homepage, allowing people to like the photos or video posts of others. The importance of likes on Instagram cannot be understated, as the more likes a post gets on social media, the faster it rises to the top of people's timelines and the longer it stays there. According to social media strategist Farrukh Naeem, "more likes indicate content that is more popular, however there is also genuine content not being noticed and mediocre content rising up because of users and accounts who have learned how to game the algorithm."[362]

From the earliest days of Instagram, celebrities and social media influencers have found ways to game their Instagram feed to indicate a greater popularity than actually exists. Some of that may end soon: in July 2019, Instagram's CEO, Adam Mosseri, announced that the platform was removing the public likes count for certain users as "a test of the feature." After testing the "hiding the like" count in Australia, Brazil, Canada, Ireland, Italy, Japan, and New Zealand, Mosseri claimed that the decision was made to make the "likes" private in order to take the pressure off users and create a positive environment on the platform where people

[361] Jumana Khamis, "Number of 'Likes' on Social Media Cause of Envy," *Gulf News*, February 10, 2017, https://gulfnews.com/going-out/society/number-of-likes-on-social-media-cause-of-envy-1.1976152.
[362] Ibid.

feel comfortable expressing themselves.[363] While it is laudable for Instagram to minimize envy through status competitions by removing the public likes count on the platform tally, it will do little to mitigate the relentless pursuit of status on social media. Even though the likes will be hidden from the envious eyes of the public, the tally of likes will still be provided to the individual who is posting the content. In some ways, it is like the current practice of not keeping score for the youngest Little League ball players. Any parent knows that the little players keep score on their own, and they know who won the game, even though no one has posted the score or spoken of the score aloud. Everyone knows the score.

Because Facebook owns Instagram, it will likely follow suit. In September 2019, Facebook experimented with removing the likes counts on posts; and Twitter CEO Jack Dorsey has hinted at wanting to remove "public likes" from tweets for over a year now. At the WIRED25 Summit in 2018, Dorsey told of his unhappiness with what he called "the big like button with a heart on it."[364] However, the blowback was immediate, and Twitter's vice president of communications, Brandon Borrman, reassured users by tweeting that they had "considered" removing the button, but "there are no plans" to do so anytime soon.[365] It seems that some

[363] Sophia Ankel and Jenni Ryall, "Earlier This Year Instagram Started Removing 'Likes' Counts from Posts, but They Also Started Removing Likes Altogether as the Result of a Global Bug," *Business Insider*, August 14, 2019, https://www.businessinsider.com/instagram-test-could-be-scrapping-likes-altogether-experiment-platform-2019-08.

[364] Paige Leskin, "Twitter CEO Hinted at Removing Like Button Next Year and Users Freaked Out about It," *Business Insider*, October 29, 2018, https://www.businessinsider.com/twitter-ceo-hinted-removing-like-button-users-freaked-out-2018-10.

[365] Brandon Borrman (@bborrman), "Short story on 'like.' We've been open that we're considering it. Jack even mentioned it in

people have become dependent on the validation that the "like" button provides for them.

A research article on "Examining the Influence of Frequency of Status Updates and Likes on Judgments of Observers," published in *Media Psychology*, explored how the number of status updates and "markers of approval" or likes affected observers' impressions of a profile owner's personality and character. The aim of the study was "to examine whether the presentation of content on profiles affects inference making of the profile owner's character." Using an experimental design within a population of college students, the findings indicate that "fewer status updates and 'likes' on a profile led to judgments of the profile owner as more depressed and socially unskilled" than those who post status updates more frequently. These impressions biased later judgments of the owner's attractiveness.[366]

A growing body of research indicates that social media may be making people unhappy. In fact, studies have suggested that many people report "being happier" after they take a break from social media. A study on the happiness of 1,095 people conducted in Denmark in 2015 by the Happiness Research Institute found that staying away from Facebook can significantly increase people's levels of contentment. Almost 95 percent of the users visited Facebook every day prior to the study, and 78 percent of them used it for more than thirty minutes a day. The study required half of the

---

front of the US Congress. There's no timeline. It's not happening 'soon.'" Twitter, October 29, 2019, 7:25 a.m., https://twitter.com/bborrman/status/1056915020422860800.

[366] Robert S. Tokunaga and Justice D. Quick, "Impressions on Social Networking Sites: Examining the Influence of Frequency of Status Updates and Likes on Judgments of Observers," *Media Psychology* 21, no.2 (2018): 157, https://www.tandfonline.com/doi/full/10.1080/15213269.2017.1282874.

participants to stay off the network altogether; the others used Facebook as usual. After a week, those who did not use Facebook reported significant jumps in happiness, while those who continued to use Facebook were 55 percent more likely to say they felt stressed, and 39 percent were more likely to feel less happy compared with those who did not use the social media site.[367]

It looks as if envy may be to blame for much of this unhappiness. A growing body of research suggests that Facebook in particular may have adverse effects on mental health. In a large number of studies, Facebook use has been associated with increases in envy, loneliness, stress, social comparison, and depression as well as decreases in life satisfaction and social capital.[368] A scholarly study that explored the relationship between envy and social media was conducted by researchers from Technische Universitat Darmstadt in Germany and the University of British Columbia. Surveying 1,193 college-age Facebook users recruited from a mailing list at a German university,

> researchers assessed how envy played out on social networks by asking participants to describe their emotions about Facebook and to describe which emotions they thought their friends experienced when looking at Facebook statuses (as a way to trick people into revealing their more guarded feelings). They found that people readily described feeling envy while reading social network statuses, especially statuses about travel and leisure.... More than 37 percent of

[367] Shaunacy Ferro, "Avoiding Facebook Might Make You Happier, Study Finds," *Mental Floss*, November 12, 2015, https://www. mentalfloss.com/article/71133/avoiding-facebook-might-make -you-happier-study-finds.

[368] H. Appel, A. L. Gerlach, and J. Crusius, "The Interplay between Facebook use, Social Comparison, Envy and Depression," *Current Opinion in Psychology* 9 (2016): 44–49.

respondents noted that they were unlikely to find out about the kind of information that caused them envy (news of an awesome party, perhaps) in an offline encounter, suggesting that services like Facebook are generating envy that we would not otherwise feel.[369]

In June 2019, the Happiness Research Institute conducted a follow-up study to their 2015 research on the relationship between social media and happiness. The 2019 study took a more nuanced approach to looking at the relationship between social media usage and unhappiness for young people by surveying 1,160 Nordic young people ages fourteen to twenty-nine and analyzing data collected from 77,600 Nordic teenagers ages fifteen or sixteen. Those surveyed were from five Nordic countries: Denmark, Finland, Iceland, Norway, and Sweden. Participants were recruited from Facebook and were asked a series of questions about their current mood—whether they felt happy, lonely, connected, interested, anxious, proud, ashamed, or bored. Respondents were also asked about what they had been doing on Facebook immediately prior to answering the survey. The goal of that part of the experiment was to uncover any significant relationships between specific digital activities on Facebook and momentary happiness. Although there were no direct questions about feelings of envy or jealousy, questions about what the researchers called "social comparison" were included and provide some helpful indicators of the kinds of feelings that suggest envy.

The Happiness Research Institute researchers acknowledge that it is impossible to judge the effects of social media without

[369] Shaunacy Ferro, "Posting a Status Update? It's Probably out of Envy, Study Says," *Mental Floss*, December 10, 2015, https://www. mentalfloss.com/article/72275/posting-status-update-its-probably -out-envy-study-says.

at the same time addressing the context in which social media is used. In addition, the researchers suggest that it is difficult to talk about the "effects of social media because causality cannot be assumed—we cannot claim that social media causes envious feelings or causes young people to be unhappy without considering that young people who are already unhappy or envious are likely to make more use of social media." Since most research in this area is based on survey data that looks at an individual's behavior at a single point in time, we cannot confidently state that social media causes changes in the individual's happiness or self-esteem without longitudinal data. Still, it is helpful to review the happiness study as it suggests areas for future research on the relationship between envy and social media.

Findings reveal that young people in the five Nordic countries are well above the European average in terms of social media use. According to Eurostat figures from 2011 to 2018, Nordic young people make up three of the top five European countries with the highest social media use among young people. In Denmark, in particular, one in four fifteen-year-old girls reports spending at least four hours a day on social networking sites and other forms of digital communication. But, surprisingly, the findings from the study indicate that there is no significant relationship between time spent on Facebook and an overall positive affect—or negative affect. Rather, the statistically significant links between the amount of time users spend on Facebook and their current mood has more to do with whether the user of Facebook is an "active" or a "passive" user. Active users engage in direct communication with others. Passive users consume content without directly communicating with others. Findings indicate that passive users are much more likely to have an increased negative affect, and active users are much more likely to have an increased positive affect. Communicating directly with others has a positive effect even

The Politics of Envy

for those with few close ties. Conversely, more time spent simply scrolling through the news feeds of friends on Facebook is related to significantly lower levels of happiness. As the authors point out, "Looking at friends' pages is the strongest predictor of changes in young people's mood. This particular activity is associated with decreased feelings of interest and pride, as well as increased feelings of loneliness and shame."[370]

The authors of the Happiness Research Institute survey concluded in 2019 that its findings seem to support what has previously been referred to as the "highlight reel effect" because people tend to share more positive experiences than negative experiences online. As a result, "the more time young people spend on Facebook passively observing the lives of others, the more likely they are to make upward negative social comparisons."[371] These negative social comparisons can result in feelings of envy. Young people without close social relationships are particularly vulnerable on Facebook. Among those respondents who reported having fewer than two close relationships, the researchers found a link between increased social media use and feelings of loneliness and anxiety. The more time these more isolated young people spent on Facebook, the more likely they were to feel lonely or anxious.

Presentation of Self in Everyday Life, written by sociologist Erving Goffman in 1959, might have predicted the anxiety that social media users seem to be experiencing. Goffman argued that our public lives represent the "front stage" where we all play a role to impress others by presenting our very best "self." The Danish researchers might have called the "front stage" the "highlight reel."

[370] Michael Birkjaer and Micah Kaats, *#SortingOutSocialMedia: Does Social Media Really Pose a Threat to Young People's Well-Being?* (Copenhagen: Happiness Research Institute, 2019), 24, http://norden.diva-portal.org/smash/get/diva2:1328300/FULLTEXT01.pdf.
[371] Ibid.

Envy in the Age of Social Media

The message is that impressions matter to those of us on the "front stage." But, in 1959, there was plenty of backstage room for us to be ourselves. For Goffman, backstage is where we do not have to "play roles." Rather, in the backstage world, we can step out of the character we have created for the front stage.[372] But, as Katherine Omerod wrote in *Why Social Media Is Ruining Your Life*:

> The all-seeing, all-knowing, 24/7 world of social media has ramped up the sheer volume of public information that we're all sharing and the culture of Periscope, Instagram, and Snapchat, which encourage a near live-streamed existence have significantly upped our "on stage" time.... Today our "front stage" idealized personas are becoming more and more how we define ourselves. As our ability to maintain this supercharged, "photo-shopped" good impression layer is fast evolving, we have less and less time with the off duty "backstage" side of ourselves.[373]

Reducing Encapsulation and Rejecting Concealment

Beyond expanding proximity to include a much broader comparison group, social media has increased envy by reducing *encapsulation* (the ability to segregate by class and status) and rejecting concealment (the ability to maintain our privacy). Social media accelerates the elimination of social class and status segregation by giving us a glimpse of what goes on inside the walls of the exclusive vacation destinations, the private clubs, the gated communities, and the elite fraternities, sororities, and eating clubs on prestigious university

---

[372] Erving Goffman, *Presentation of Self in Everyday Life* (New York: Anchor Books, 1959).

[373] Katherine Omerod, *Why Social Media Is Ruining Your Life* (London: Cossell, 2018), 38.

campuses. Instagram and Twitter take us into those venues—giving us a front-row seat on what "others" enjoy, but we do not.

Anthropologist George Foster first discussed the threats to encapsulation in 1972 in his book *The Anatomy of Envy*. Long before the advent of social media, Foster was already seeing a reduction in the separation in American society by class and status. He and his contributors provided an anthropological perspective on how the gated clubs and communities of the past functioned as a way to protect those inside who might be envied. It was always thought that envy could be minimized if no one saw the luxury and opulence within the enclosures. And, in some ways, the locked gates and impenetrable walls diminished many of the disruptive effects of envy. Foster writes that "encapsulation in America, in the form of caste, class, and family groups, has been a potent factor for generations in suppressing envy between groups, and thereby contributing to a basic social stability. It is clear that in the future this device will work much less well. How envy can be controlled, or if it can be controlled, remains to be seen."[374] Encapsulation disappeared once the first visitors behind those walls took their first selfies, posted them on Instagram, and inspired the envy of countless social media followers.

Bergün, a picturesque Swiss town in the canton of Graubünden, is so beautiful that it supposedly attempted to ban photography and social media in 2017 as a precaution against what has been called "holiday envy." Throughout its rolling hills, cobbled streets, and fairy-tale architecture, the town has posted signs that read: "Photographs of our picturesque landscape, shared on social media, can make others unhappy because they themselves cannot

---

[374] George M. Foster et al., "The Anatomy of Envy: A Study in Symbolic Behavior," *Cultural Anthropology* 13, no. 2 (April 1972): 165–202.

be here." And, although it is obviously impossible to ban anyone from posting their vacation photos, the ban is ostensibly enforced by some of those in the town who want to protect the charm of their little village. The more cynical among us would conclude that the initiative has been implemented as a "clever ploy by the Swiss tourism board, or their version of the Chamber of Commerce, to gain more interest and photographs of the town.... If it is a ploy, it has worked well because Instagram is filled with photos with the hashtag #Bergün and the mayor, Peter Nicolay, offers a 'friendly special permit' that allows you to take photos within city limits."[375]

It is most likely that Bergün is simply capitalizing on the tremendous potential of social media marketing initiatives that thrive on reducing encapsulation and inspiring holiday envy. As an image-based app, Instagram has enabled millions of users to share their photos of their spectacular adventures. According to Google trends, #travel has been used 318 million times—one of the most popular hashtags on Instagram. Even more revealing, 48 percent of Instagram users rely on Instagram photos and videos to help choose their next travel destination, and 35 percent of users look to Instagram to discover new places—and capture their own "Instagrammable" moments. According to a study conducted in the UK, 40 percent of millennials choose a travel spot based on how "Instagrammable" that location is perceived.[376]

In a scholarly attempt to explain when and why people feel envious when scrolling through Facebook or Instagram posts, researchers have found that it is "experiences" such as fabulous

[375] Rachel Macbeth, "The Town That's So Instagrammable, It Banned Social Media to Prevent Holiday Envy," *Elle*, July 6, 2017, https://www.elle.com/uk/life-and-culture/travel/news/a36245/instagrammable-town-bergun-bans-social-media/.

[376] "How Instagram Is Changing How We Travel," Mediakix, https://mediakix.com/blog/instagram-travel-location-trends/.

vacations or adventures that elicited more envy than material purchases. University-based researchers from Germany and the Netherlands collaborated on three studies, using three methods to evaluate which type of content on social media triggered the most envy. Their goal was to determine whether it was material purchases or what the researchers called "experiential purchases" that triggered the most intense envy. Experiential purchases are those purchased or arranged with the primary intention of acquiring a life experience—an event or series of events that one lives through, such as a vacation, an elaborate dinner, or an exciting adventure. Material purchases are obviously those made with the primary intention of acquiring a material good—an object that is kept in one's possession. The researchers hypothesized that experiential purchases enhance social relations more than material purchases do because they improve well-being. Experiential purchases tend to be more closely associated with one's central identity than material purchases are. Acquiring them is therefore likely to have a strong positive effect on well-being. The authors write: "When people look back on their lives, they indicate that experiences were more important parts of their life than material purchases were."[377]

To study the relative effect of material purchases or experiential purchases on the emergence of envy, the researchers used an experimental method in the first of three studies: they asked subjects to look at their own Facebook feeds and report the first instance in which a friend shared an experiential or a material purchase. They were also asked to report how frequently they see posts in

[377] Ruoyun Lin, Niels van de Ven, and Sonja Utz, "What Triggers Envy on Social Network Sites? A Comparison between Shared Experiential and Material Purchases," *Computers in Human Behavior* 85 (August 2018): 271–281, https://www.ncbi.nlm.nih.gov/pmc/articles/PMC5990704/.

each category. For each reported post, subjects were asked how important the shared topic was for their own identity, how easy it was to compare the shared purchase to other possible purchases, and how intense the envy was. The results indicated that posts about experiential purchases are much more frequent on their Facebook feeds than posts about material purchases. These posts about vacations or adventures not only elicit a higher degree of envy but also elicit envy more frequently. The authors also conclude that posts about "experiential purchases triggered more intense envy than posts about material purchases." But Facebook users also encounter posts about experiential purchases more often, and this probably gives rise to more frequent envy as well. The researchers conclude that this increased incidence of intense envy is due to the experiential purchases being seen as "more self-relevant" and important to one's identity.[378]

The two follow-up studies used different populations, including college students and American workers. In one of the studies, participants were asked to report how frequently they tend to post status updates. Then they were asked to report the extent to which they like to see status updates from other people in each post category. Envy was measured with one question: "When someone posts about experiences (or material purchases), does such a post make you feel a little envious?" The results of the studies replicated the first study in that experiential purchases elicit much more intense envy than material purchases did. Posts about appearance and "relationships and family" triggered the least envy, but experiential purchases triggered the most frequent and the most intense envy.

Part of the reason experiential purchases trigger the most envy is because, as mentioned above, people tend to post more about their experiences than their purchases. The study found that participants

[378] Ibid.

do this because they tended to like people who post about experiential purchases more than they like people who "brag" about material purchases they made. This fits with prior research that shows that sharing of experiences can improve social bonds. A second reason experiential purchases lead to more envy is simply that people do not seem to realize that experiential purchases are likely to elicit more envy in others, and so they post these experiences more than other types of posts. Experiential purchases are life enhancing and satisfying compared with material purchases, which people sometimes regret. Also, there is a "story" element to experiential-purchase posts and people are more likely to post their travel stories or their adventures.

Even though reading about another's experiential purchases led to much more envy than reading about material purchases, it is also confirmed that sharing experiential purchases is better for social bonding than is sharing material purchases. Still, envy is detrimental for social relationships and can lead to negative behavior toward the envied person. And, although the researchers claim that sharing about experiential purchases may not trigger the malicious form of envy and instead incite only the "benign form of envy," this is a difficult claim to make. As we have seen throughout this book, true envy is never benign. What may start out as admiration of another often ends up as envy. As people become more engaged with each other through the reduction in encapsulation, they have less tolerance for any given level of inequality of access to both material and experiential purchases. Envying Facebook friends and Instagram contacts can lead to a vicious envy spiral resulting in diminished general satisfaction with their lives.[379]

[379] Peter Buxmann, "Facebook Makes Users Envious and Dissatisfied," Humboldt-Universität January 21, 2013, https://www.hu-berlin. de/en/press-portal/nachrichten-en/archive/nr1301/nr_130121_00.

Katherine Omerod refers to all of this as the "self-promotion-envy spiral.... Triggered by a range of positive content uploaded by our Facebook friends or Instagram contacts, we end up using even greater self-promotion and impression management in reaction to help cope with our feelings of envy.... The rampant sharing of positive information about our own lives and identities causes our friends to up the ante with their own posts until we all feel under pressure to project a more and more impressive version of who we are."[380] *JSTOR Daily* author Alexandra Samuel suggests that the "solution" to the envy spiral is to avoid what she called "envy farmers"—those who share only their finest moments, as if the whole purpose of their social media presence is to inspire envy. Suggesting that "we should share our disappointments and our pain on Facebook to remind one another that whatever we envy is just one slice of a much larger and more complicated picture," this author claims that we need to "demand honesty and vulnerability from our online friends, and from ourselves."[381]

Although Samuel's suggestions may be well intentioned, they are naïve. People will not be willing to post their problems and their defeats on Facebook so others can feel better about themselves. In fact, those on Facebook who continually post problems and requests for help are not going to maintain their friends for long. Although there are specific Facebook support groups for sharing similar problems, it is not likely that most Facebook users will be attracted to a platform that provides a space to complain about personal problems. Facebook was not designed for this, nor was Instagram. The sites were designed for sharing our lives—our best "front stage" lives—our photoshopped lives. We are still a society

---

[380] Omerod, *Why Social Media Is Ruining Your Life*, 39.
[381] Alexandra Samuel, "What to Do When Social Media Inspires Envy."

The Politics of Envy

fueled by Darwinian competition. People who constantly demand that others feel sorry for them and respond to their constant calls for assistance may not inspire envy, but they will not inspire much of anything else either.

Still, Snapchat is one social media site that predicts more social enjoyment and positive mood than Facebook, Twitter, and Instagram. Snapchat is a mobile application known as a form of "ephemeral social media," meaning that content is displayed for only a limited time—only for seconds, as opposed to forever on Facebook and Twitter. A study done in 2015 by University of Michigan researchers revealed that Snapchat brings more happiness to the user than the other social media platforms. Of course, this could be, in part, because Snapchat is also known as the "sexting" app, as it has been most often used to communicate spontaneously with close friends in a "more enjoyable way." But, beyond "sexting," college students indicated that Snapchat was associated with much more positive emotions than Facebook and other social media. The Michigan researchers concluded that whereas "Facebook has become a space for sharing crafted big moments such as babies, graduations, and birthdays, Snapchat seems to provide users with distinct space for sharing the small moments. Participants focused more attention on Snapchat messages than archived content on platforms like Facebook.... There is less concern about self-presentational concerns ... less worrying about whether shared pictures seem ugly or conceited."[382] One of the most revealing findings that emerged in the follow-up interviews from the Michigan study was that participants viewed

---

[382] Jared Wadley, "Snap Decisions: More Happiness Gained by Using Snapchat than Facebook," *University of Michigan News*, October 20, 2015, https://news.umich.edu/snap-decisions-more-happiness-gained-by-using-snapchat-than-facebook/.

Snapchat as similar to face-to-face conversations because they were mundane, not recorded, and typically occurred in close relationships. Envy is less likely to emerge in these kinds of pseudo-face-to-face conversations. We are less likely to compare ourselves with someone we are engaging closely with in one-on-one conversations. In contrast, Instagram and Facebook make the lives of our "friends" look wonderful—and almost attainable. Social comparisons to others create what sociologists have called "relative deprivation," a term that refers to the dissatisfaction people feel when they compare their slightly smaller lives with their friends' slightly larger ones. Young mothers with their own expensive strollers for their babies speak of "stroller-envy" of their peers with the latest two-thousand-dollar European stroller. Young families with beautiful homes in enviable locations speak of the "kitchen-envy" they endure when seeing their neighbors' open-concept kitchens. The family vacation to the Grand Canyon cannot compare to their Facebook friends' extended European holiday. Relative deprivation can spark envy, even when the envier may be a target of the envy of others.

Still, at least one study of the effect of social media on relative deprivation demonstrated that communication on social media with "influential" others—especially higher-status, older individuals—helped to reduce relative deprivation. Focusing on the value of social media for enhancing personal connections and networking, the author stresses that personal connections are often a crucial condition for gaining social success in Korea's Confucian culture; he therefore designed a study that would assess whether enhancing access to social capital through building personal networks and personal trust would decrease relative deprivation. To test the hypothesis that engaging in social media to enhance social capital would reduce relative deprivation, Jaehee Cho surveyed 2,169

The Politics of Envy

citizens of South Korea—a country in which more than 82 percent of adults use the Internet, and more than three-quarters of them are highly reliant on social media. The average age of participants in the study was thirty-three, with equal gender representation. Participants were asked to rate the extent to which they communicated with "influential others," including friends, family, and colleagues, about personal concerns; social life, including school and work life; hobbies; and social and political issues. To measure relative deprivation, specific survey questions included:

It is unpleasant for me to see people who are higher social status than me?

It is unpleasant for me to see people who have better career experiences than I have?

It is unpleasant for me to see people who are richer than I am?

It is unpleasant for me to see people who have better natural abilities than I have?[383]

The results indicated that in South Korea, where there is greater access to "influential others" through social media, developing personal ties through social networking on social media decreased feelings of relative deprivation by creating social capital through interpersonal communication about important issues.

Obviously, this South Korean study cannot be viewed as generalizable to the United States because of dramatic differences in culture. But the findings suggest that there can be a role for social

---

[383] Jaehee Cho, "Will Social Media Reduce Relative Deprivation? Systematic Analysis of Social Capital's Mediating Effect of Connecting Social Media Use with Relative Deprivation," *International Journal of Communication* 8 (2014): 2811–2833.

media sites to reduce relative deprivation and envy by increasing access to social capital through interactions with influential others. LinkedIn, the American business and employment-oriented social media site that is primarily used for professional networking, could possibly play a role in helping users make personal connections. But LinkedIn, which advertises itself as a site where you can "find people who can help you," does not offer the kind of personal-story sharing that enables South Korean social media users to build trusting relationships with others. Even though family ties and personal networks can help one build a career, our culture does not embrace the South Korean Confucian culture of strong personal ties as the strongest determining factor of social success. It is unlikely that negative social comparison, relative deprivation, and envy will ever be reduced in this country through social media. Nearly every scholarly study of the effects of social media on well-being reveals that although social networking may be enhanced, envy and resentment are much more likely to emerge through extended use of social media in a more individualistic, consumer-driven, and competitive culture like ours.

The evidence strongly suggests that engaging in social media for extended periods of time can create problems of envy and social comparison for users. There is a reason Silicon Valley tech leaders routinely ban their children from using social media. In a 2018 article for UK's *Independent* titled "The Tech Moguls Who Invented Social Media Have Banned Their Children from It," we learn that Susan Hobbs, chief of staff at the security firm Cloudflare and a former venture capitalist, "completely banned" her daughter, now sixteen, from using social media. Hobbs told a reporter for the *Independent* that the banning "actually became a bit of a point of contention. I would leave town and she would download Instagram. So, I changed the restrictions on her phone so the App Store [from which she could download the app] didn't even show up."[384] Instagram founder Kevin Systrom admits that he was unable to stamp out the problems of "online harassment and bullying" and says that his then-nine-month-old daughter, Freya, had made him think harder about his own legacy. Tech leaders such as Apple's late founder, Steve Jobs, Facebook's Mark Zuckerberg, and Yahoo's Marissa Mayer have all spoken out on limiting their children's screen time. Microsoft's Bill Gates did not allow his children to have cell phones until they were thirteen years old. The Waldorf School, based near Google's Mountain View campus and a popular school choice for tech workers, bans technology for children before seventh grade because "it can hamper their ability to develop strong bodies, healthy habits of discipline and self-control, fluency with creative and artistic expression and flexible and agile minds."[385] And although Waldorf does not include "decreasing social comparisons and envy" through banning social media for children, it is implied in their rules. Children are as vulnerable to feelings of envy as adults are, and encouraging engagement on social media for young children is always a mistake.

The fact that Instagram announced the removal of the like count from its social media platform is a step in the right direction toward reducing envy on social media. Jack Dorsey, CEO of Twitter, has highlighted what he has called "conversational health" as a priority, and Mark Zuckerberg wrote an "open letter" to his infant daughter imploring her to "go outside and play," and to "stop and

[384] Olivia Rudgard, "The Tech Moguls Who Invented Social Media Have Banned Their Children from It," *Independent* (London), November 6, 2018, https://www.independent.ie/life/family/parenting/the-tech-moguls-who-invented-social-media-have-banned-their-children-from-it-37494367.html.
[385] Ibid.

smell the flowers" in their day-to-day activities.[386] As the scholarly studies reveal the effects that social media can have on our happiness and well-being, there is a new movement of tech insiders and outsiders both arguing for a more nuanced approach. As Katherine Omerod writes: "Structurally, social platforms are being altered in an attempt to lessen the worst of the media's negative effects—a development being labelled humane tech.... Compassionate design may be trending in Silicon Valley circles, but you'd be forgiven for raising a serious eyebrow in skepticism."[387] Tech leaders may be able to reduce the occasion of the sin of envy by removing the like count or redesigning the news feeds, but in a free and competitive society like ours, the potential for envy—online or offline—can never be eliminated in our social interactions.

---

[386] Marc Beaulieu, "Surprise Emoticon: Mark Zuckerberg, Father of Facebook, Says Stop and Smell the IRL Flowers," CBC.ca (August 29, 2017), https://www.cbc.ca/life/wellness/surprise-emoticon-mark-zuckerberg-father-of-facebook-says-stop-and-smell-irl-flowers-1.4267554.

[387] Omerod, *Why Social Media Is Ruining Your Life*, 237.

10

Recovering the Sacred

Those who are envious never speak of envy — denying it even to themselves. And those who are envied by others would never think of acknowledging it because it would be unseemly to pronounce oneself worthy of envy. Few in academia are willing to study the emotion of envy, and although there are a few theologians willing to explore the ways in which envy continues to seep into our day-to-day lives, most speak historically of the sin of envy, providing us with a long list of biblical references documenting the demonic source of the evil emotion. While there are political scientists who are willing to speak of the role that envy plays in voting behavior and public policy, sociologists rarely speak of it — except for Marxists, who promise us that when we move to socialism, there will be nothing left to envy. Even sociologists who do research on the social construction of emotion devote little space in their published work to understanding envious desire. Psychologists in academe — other than the rare Freudian still hanging on to discredited theories about the Oedipal complex — rarely speak of envy at all. Contemporary philosophers hardly touched the subject, except those, such as Rawls, who promise that envy can be contained in a well-ordered society that is truly committed to justice.

The Politics of Envy

This is perplexing to those of us who study envy because we know that envious desire is a universal phenomenon — a part of the human condition — and potentially, the most destructive emotion of them all. We know that envy can be controlled but never eradicated. As Friedrich A. Hayek writes in *The Constitution of Liberty*, "envy is not one of the sources of discontent that a free society can eliminate. It is probably one of the essential conditions for the preservation of such a [free] society that we do not countenance envy, nor sanction its demands by camouflaging it as social justice, but treat it in the words of John Stuart Mill, as 'that most anti-social and odious of all passions.'"[388]

While most of today's demands for social justice and egalitarianism claim to be based on a more just distribution of "the good things of the world," the truth is that these demands are usually based on envy. Hayek understood that "it is one of the great tragedies of our time that the masses have come to believe that they have reached their high standard of material welfare as a result of having pulled down the wealthy." He taught that "in a progressive society, there is little reason to believe that the wealth which the few enjoy would exist at all if they were not allowed to enjoy it. It is neither taken from the rest nor withheld from them.... To prevent some from enjoying certain advantages first may well prevent the rest of us from ever enjoying them. If through envy we make certain exceptional kinds of life impossible, we shall all in the end suffer material and spiritual impoverishment."[389] Those who study envy know that a world in which the majority could prevent a minority from attaining that which is envied by the majority would be an apocalyptic world — a world of violence, destruction, and death.

---

[388] F. A. Hayek, *The Constitution of Liberty* (Chicago: University of Chicago Press), 155–156.

[389] Ibid., 196.

Durkheim, Girard, and the Role of Religion

René Girard's groundbreaking theoretical work on mimetic desire in 1962 opened the door to helping us understand that all of our noninstinctual desires are mimetic, shaped by others' desires. Social discord originates in mimetic rivalries — competitions in which the envied object becomes secondary to the rivalry itself. For Girard, all violence in society is rooted in envy: "I want what you have and if you won't give it to me I am going to take it."[390] Despite our autonomous belief that our desires are original to us, arising from within our being, Girard draws from biblical narratives to illustrate that all of our desires — including our envious desires — are the desires of others. As contained in the Genesis narrative, Eve exhibits no spontaneous desire for the fruit of the forbidden tree. It is only when the serpent boasts about the desirability of such forbidden fruit that Eve's envy is aroused. Eve begins to question why the serpent — and not she and Adam — should have access to such wondrous fruit. The forbidden nature of the fruit and the fact that the serpent has access to it make Eve's desire for the fruit even stronger. As Girard points out in a radio interview in 2001:

> With Adam and Eve, the thing which is fascinating is that neither one really desires the apple. Eve comes first because she is approached first by the serpent, and it is the serpent who instills in her the desire for the apple. He says, you will be like God.... She then transmits that desire to Adam and gets him to do it. Then, the scene is played back in reverse, when God asks Adam what happened. Adam replies

[390] Fr. Dwight Longenecker, "Rene Girard, Sacred Violence and the Mass," Fr. Dwight Longenecker, March 13, 2018, https://dwight-longenecker.com/rene-girard-sacred-violence-and-the-mass/.

something like, "she made me eat of the forbidden fruit."
Eve then says, "the serpent made me do it."[391]

Girard points out that desire, including most significantly, envious desire, is not rooted in the object. Rather, it is rooted in the subject or the person who possesses the object. Envy emerges when we want to become the one who possesses what we think we want, yet we are blocked by that rival. To deny that fact is to defend the impossibility of spontaneous desire or what Girard calls "the illusion of autonomy to which modern man is passionately devoted."[392]

As Cynthia Haven's *Evolution of Desire: A Life of René Girard*, points out: Girard's mimetic theory "saw imitation at the heart of individual desire and motivation, accounting for the competition and violence that galvanizes cultures and societies.... Girard claimed that mimetic desire is not only the way we love, it's the reason we fight. Two hands that reach towards the same object will ultimately clench into fists."[393]

Once envious conflict over an object or an advantage begins, it tends to intensify and spread as people copy one another's violence. Violence is a contagion that spirals to ever greater dimensions, spurred on by reciprocal violent acts between groups of individuals. Unchecked, mimetic rivalry threatens the very existence of any human society.[394] To understand the current anti-Semitic violence in places such as Crown Heights, or the turf-related gang violence

---

[391] David Cayley, ed., *The Ideas of René Girard: An Anthropology of Violence and Religion* (self-pub., 2019), 45.

[392] René Girard, *Deceit, Desire, and the Novel* (Baltimore: Johns Hopkins University Press, 1966), 15–16.

[393] Cynthia L. Haven, *Evolution of Desire: A Life of René Girard* (Ann Arbor: Michigan State University, 2018), 3.

[394] James McBride, "Revisiting a Seminal Text of the Law and Literature Movement: A Girardian Reading of Herman Melville's Billy Budd, Sailor," *University of Maryland Law Journal of Race, Religion,*

in East Los Angeles and on Chicago's West Side, we need to understand Girard's theory of mimetic desire—how our envious desire and growing resentment causes us to choose a scapegoat to blame for our inability to fulfill these desires. Human societies are always in danger of uncontrolled violence. But Girard has shown that the earliest pre-Christian cultures solved the problem of mimetic violence by encouraging people to channel their violence toward sacrificial victims. Girard discovered that this "scapegoat" solution to violence—often a real goat that is sacrificed—most likely arose in the first place from a spontaneous discovery: "when everyone opposes a single victim, a social order is created that gradually develops into a cultural system, anchored in regular sacrifices." Girard calls this discovery the "foundational murder," suggesting that "culture begins with a unanimous collective murder, a turning of all against one."[395] Drawing from anthropological and sociological data, Girard concluded that the very purpose of religion is, quite simply, to control violence. In his *Violence and the Sacred*, Girard argues that "only violence can end violence." This view of religion puts Girard in opposition to several powerful currents in contemporary thought: "It offends the Romantic doctrine of original goodness. It looks askance at the contemporary nostalgia for the sacred, and it also challenges the rationalist view that religion is just self-interested priest-craft."[396]

The sociological findings on social structure and the contributors to social order promoted by Émile Durkheim, one of the earliest sociologists, prefigured Girard's definition of religion in 1915 by stressing the unifying force of religious ritual. Believing that in

Gender and Class 3, no. 2 (2003), https://digitalcommons.law.umaryland.edu/cgi/viewcontent.cgi?article=1046&context=rrgc.
[395] Cayley, *The Ideas of René Girard*, 44.
[396] Ibid., 20.

order to understand a culture, the sociologist must study its religious practices, Durkheim was the first to see religion as a unified system of beliefs and practices relative to sacred things. He pointed to the sacred as "things that are set apart and forbidden," beliefs and practices that unite in one single moral community. From the Latin *religio* (respect for what is sacred) and *religare* (to bind, or to yoke oneself to something), Durkheim was the first sociologist to analyze religion in terms of its social impact—understanding that religion was about community, binding people together to provide meaning in life.

Durkheim regarded identifying and stigmatizing deviant behavior such as violence as an indispensable process, allowing us to live by shared standards. He was especially concerned with the social controls that become internalized in individual consciousness as a result of what society defines as deviance leading to violence. This led him to believe that society must be present within the individual, and he identified religion as the force that creates within individuals a sense of obligation to adhere to society's demands. Ideology and individual devotion associated with religion did not interest Durkheim. Rather, his interest lay primarily with communal religious activities, the public sacrifices and the rituals that bind communities together and give meaning to the lives of the devout—controlling violence by exerting social control mechanisms.

Long before Girard, Durkheim pointed out that the most important social control function of religion was to provide the values, norms, and guidelines for behavior in an effort to control violence. Durkheim was the first sociologist to identify religion as the way to promote behavioral consistency and prevent the "war of all against all." From this perspective, religion is not just "socially constructed"; rather, it is something that represents the power of society. Girard believes that violence led to the development of religion because religion organizes and performs public sacrifices, and these sacrifices inoculate society against the very real threat of worse violence. Even today, when Catholics hold sacred celebrations — such as the Mass, in which the Real Presence of Christ is celebrated in the Eucharist, the ritual adoration of the cross on Good Friday, the blessing and distribution of palms on Palm Sunday, and the lighting of the Pascal candle and the Easter Fire on Easter Sunday — they are celebrating the power of their society as well as memorializing the sacred. Celebrations of the sacred involve much more than sharing food and gifts: they involve a symbolic sacrifice — a reminder of the Cross and Resurrection.

For Girard, religion is indistinguishable from culture in the earliest societies. Like Durkheim, Girard believed that religion is the "protective aspect" of culture that serves to control mimetic desire and violence through sacrifice. This is at the center of ritual and closely connected to prohibition and myth: "The violence at the heart of the traditional sacred is therefore twofold: the negative sacred of the collective violence that is associated with the dangerous aspects of the god or the other, which may become split off into a devil or demon or trickster; and the positive sacred that is associated with — as Durkheim posited first — the formation and maintenance of order."[397]

In *The Elementary Forms of Religious Life*, Durkheim pointed to the primitive totem as the earliest system of belief in which humans are said to have kinship or a mystical relationship with a spirit-being, such as an animal or plant. The totem usually involves sacrifice to that spirit being. Drawing from Australian ethnographic research, Durkheim used his analysis of the totemism practiced by these earliest humans to demonstrate the social origins of knowledge and the underlying unity of religious, philosophical, and scientific

---

[397] James G. Williams, ed., *The Girard Reader* (New York: Herder & Herder, 1996), 292.

The Politics of Envy

thought.[398] While others, like Freud, rejected the religious function
of the totem, focusing instead on its role in superstitious practices,
Durkheim believed that the totem was the essence of religion itself
because it unified the clan. For Durkheim, the totem became the
"flag" of the clan, "the concrete object on which the individual's
allegiance was projected: ultimately it was nothing other than
society's representation of itself to its members." For Durkheim,
totemism was a religion that was grounded in the "real." And the
earliest human and animal sacrifice to the totem—an act that unified the people and prevented violence—prefigured what Girard
has identified as the societal scapegoat. Girard acknowledges his
debt to Durkheim in *Violence and the Sacred*, writing that Durkheim
understood that society is of a piece and that the primary unifying
factor is religion. But Girard criticizes Durkheim for "never fully
articulating" this insight on the ways in which men are shaped
culturally by an educational process that belongs to the sphere
of religion. Girard believes that Durkheim "never realized what a
formidable obstacle violence presents and what a positive resource
it becomes when it is transfigured and reconverted through the
mediation of scapegoat effects."[399]

As we have seen throughout the preceding chapters, culture
(religion) emerges from disorder, the actual or potential violence
that is experienced when envy or mimetic desires begin to cause
chaos in society. In Girard's theory, culture came not from a single
place but from a single discovery that he thinks people must have
made many times in many places. Girard believes that violence led
to the development of religion because religion organizes and directs
the ritual sacrifice as the ritual itself inoculates society against the

[398] "Totems: Durkheim and Freud," Science Encyclopedia, https://
science.jrank.org/pages/11477/Totems-Durkheim-Freud.html.
[399] Girard, *Violence and the Sacred*, 306.

very real threat of escalating envy and mimetic violence. While the idea of the scapegoat is certainly present in the Bible, Girard was the first to discover that when mimetic desire gets out of hand, convergence upon a victim—the scapegoat—brings order to the chaos, and for a time, unity. Girard was also the first to identify the fact that mimetic desire was spontaneously resolved by the transfer of all hostility onto a single victim. He demonstrated that the sacrifice of the scapegoat brings peace for a time as all rally around the destruction of the sacrificial scapegoat.

The choosing of the scapegoat is not a conscious decision to find someone to take on the burden of the sins of the many. People do not consciously decide to find a scapegoat to sacrifice. Even today's academics whose envy of excellence continues to create victims of mobbings are not consciously creating victims to scapegoat in times of chaos or disorder on their campuses. Rather, Girard suggests that the scapegoaters do not know what they are doing. Their decision is a nonconscious one because they have convinced themselves that the victim is guilty and deserving of the persecution. In the case of the Mount St. Mary's University faculty mob, there remains a sense that they believed at the time that they were "doing their duty" in publicly destroying and removing what they viewed as a threat to the Catholic university. Every act of violence resulting from envious desire is justified similarly. Even today, three years after the mobbing, faculty members continue to believe they did what was right for their school and for academic freedom.[400]

All of this could have been predicted with Girard's theory of the scapegoat. While it may be alleged that the scapegoated president in the academic mobbing at Mount St. Mary's may have been guilty of underestimating faculty resistance to his strategic initiatives designed to address the serious problems on campus, the truth

[400] Cayley, *The Ideas of René Girard*, 54.

is that the allegations function as an alibi to justify the victim's selection as designated scapegoat. The rivalry was over who had the power to make decisions about the future of the university. In the past, a shared governance model was operative and appeared to work well. But, with the arrival of a business-oriented president who was unfamiliar with the need for shared governance, the rivalry emerged. The scapegoat in this case is chosen not for his or her transgressions but rather for the sense of "otherness" that the scapegoat brings; he needs to be "different enough" from the mimetic rivals in order to differentiate him from the other members of the community (or the faculty). In the Mount St. Mary's case, the president came from the business world, dressed in expensive suits, spoke with an accent, and made what the faculty thought were "inappropriate jokes" about student retention strategies. Newman also used profanity in front of faculty and other administrators, common in the business culture he flourished in, but a factor that marginalized him on the Catholic campus. His "guilt" was taken for granted because "everyone" on campus began to believe that Newman would destroy their school. In his two books on workplace mobbing, Kenneth Westhues concluded that those who find themselves to be the targets of a faculty mobbing are often viewed as "different" from their colleagues; many of the victims of academic mobbing he studied involved those who spoke with accents, dressed differently, and maintained an "otherness" apart from the rest.[401]

Girard believes that the most literal and precise definition of scapegoating can be found in the Gospel of Luke, when Jesus speaks

---

[401] Joan E. Friedenberg, Mark A. Schneider, and Kenneth Westhues, "Mobbing as a Factor in Faculty Work" (joint presentation to the International Conference on Globalization, Shared Governance, and Academic Freedom, Washington, DC, June 11–13, 2009), http://www.kwesthues.com/AAUP09.htm.

from the Cross: "Father, forgive them; for they know not what they do" (Luke 23:34). The Acts of the Apostles tells us that in the early days of the Church, Peter reassures the people of Jerusalem that although they have crucified the Son of God, the Messiah, they "acted in ignorance" (3:17).

Can Envy Ever Be Controlled?

Envy management is historically political. While the conservative approach is to view envy—as Hayek views it—as an evil that must be negatively sanctioned with enviers properly stigmatized and punished, progressives attempt to eradicate envy by a leveling process intended to reduce social inequality through wealth redistribution. Neither approach has worked, as politics has shown itself to be unable to restrain mass violence and prevent its tendency to escalate. In fact, in the months leading up to the impeachment of President Trump in 2019, political rhetoric—magnified by a complicit media—became so degraded that it incited an even more malign mimetic response. During the impeachment process, President Trump became a societal scapegoat bearing the burden of decades of political hostilities over policy on both sides of the aisle. Because of his perceived abrasive personality and his populist support from the historically less powerful people in the country, President Trump became the perfect scapegoat for those wanting to pull the country in a more progressive direction. As one who came from the business world, and unschooled in the ways of politics, Trump was the ultimate outsider—vulnerable to becoming the scapegoat. And although the impeachment was not successful in removing the president from office, the attempt to humiliate him has served to unify progressive politicians and their supporters as they felt a sense of satisfaction in demeaning and degrading the object of their envy and hatred. But the impeachment process also unified those on the

The Politics of Envy

political right, making them stronger and increasing their ability to gain support for formerly unpopular positions.

Still, there are no real political solutions. Girard has never put much hope in politics, believing that "politics has lost its power of containment." In *Battling to the End*, he wrote "Violence is a terrible adversary, especially since it always wins." Rather, Girard believes that we need to battle violence with a new "heroic attitude"—one that "can link violence and reconciliation and make tangible both the possibility of the end of the world and reconciliation among all members of humanity." As Eric Gans writes:

> When in 1972 René Girard formulated his generative model of the sacred in *Violence and the Sacred*, he proved himself the true successor of Durkheim in French anthropology. For Girard, the sacred is essential to the functioning of human society because it alone can protect us from self-destruction through mimetic violence.[402]

Girard attempts to bring back the sacred by linking it to envy and the violent nature of human desire. For Girard, like Durkheim, the sacred is not to be conceived as an ideology, but rather as a category connected to the ritual side of religion. Father Dwight Longenecker, a Catholic priest, connects Girard's work on sacrifice and scapegoating and the relevance and importance of the Mass:

> In primitive societies (according to Girard) the corporate tendency to violence is sacralized or made acceptable through the ritual of sacrifice—at first human sacrifice and then animal substitutes. At the cross of Christ the sacrificial system was

---

[402] Eric Gans, "The Sacred and the Social: Defining Durkheim's Anthropological Legacy," *Anthropoetics: The Journal of Generative Anthropology* 6, no. 1 (Spring/Summer 2000), http://anthropoetics. ucla.edu/ap0601/durkheim/.

ended once and for all. Christ broke it from the inside out. However, we still celebrate the 'sacrifice of the Mass'." Why? The Catholic teaching is that we represent the once for all sacrifice of Christ on the cross, and we thereby remember and participate in that action through the action of the Mass. We offer the sacrifice of the Mass not to offer a fresh sacrifice to God but to remember and give thanks for the one sacrifice that abolished that sacrificial system.[403]

For Girard, Christian charity is the only way to end the cycle of envy, violence, and revenge. Creating a community grounded in forgiveness and love—a community that identifies with the scapegoat and not the scapegoaters—Girard suggests that God cannot support a community created through violence. We know that violence is the evil legacy of Satan—the demonic gift that continues to be given and too often accepted. Girard suggests that the imitation of Christ can protect us from mimetic rivalries, and faithful Christians have always known that God has offered us an alternative to the path to the violence that emerges from envious desire. It is the path of nonviolence, the path that imitates Christ instead of envying our rivals. It is the path that is best described in biblical stories of heroic acts and in the lives of the saints. It is also the path described in some of our greatest novels, including Herman Melville's *Billy Budd*.

Billy Budd: Imitating Christ

Girard's earliest work on envy focused on the ways in which the greatest novelists reveal the imitative nature of desire. He understood that the best novels are able to portray these important themes

---

[403] Longenecker, "Rene Girard, Sacred Violence and the Mass."

The Politics of Envy

in ways that are superior to the self-reports of those who have experienced envy or the pain of being envied or scapegoated. There will always be bias in the narratives of those who have experienced directly the pain of envy. But as Girard points out, novels by Dostoyevsky, Flaubert, Proust, Stendhal, Cervantes, and others are most useful to demonstrate the terrible trauma caused by envious rivalries. We cannot know why Girard did not include Herman Melville in any of his analyses, but it would seem that Melville's mimetic masterpiece *Billy Budd* provides readers with the greatest insights on the function of the sacrificial scapegoat to suppress violence.

Some critics have interpreted *Billy Budd* as a historical novel that attempts to evaluate man's relation to the past. Other critics — such as Eve Sedgewick — have tried to portray the story as a tale of male homoerotic love and rivalry. But it is clear to anyone familiar with Girard's theory that at its core, *Billy Budd* is a story of envy, hatred, and violence. More importantly, it is a story of the sacrificial role of the innocent Christlike Billy, who is betrayed by the envious Luciferian Claggart and sacrificed as the ship's scapegoat by the dutiful Captain Vere — himself envious of the heroic careers of the great naval captains such as Horatio Nelson. And as Vere defends his actions by claiming he was just following wartime rules in trying to "keep order" on the warship, Billy's sacrifice helps him attain almost saintlike status in a now-unified crew.

All of this begins early in the novel, when Melville introduces Billy Budd as the "Handsome Sailor." Billy is described as having a "divine origin ... a form that was heroic ... a face that was lit from within, though from a different source." We learn that "the bonfire from his heart made luminous the rose-tan in his cheek."[404]

---

[404] Herman Melville, *Billy Budd and Other Tales*, based on the text edited by Frederic Barron Freeman and corrected by Elizabeth Treeman (New York: Signet Classics, 1961), 38.

Billy arrived on Captain Vere's warship, the *Indomitable*, after being transferred from the English merchant ship, the *Rights-of-Man*. The names of the ships are important, as readers are told early in the novel that the owner of the *Rights-of-Man* was an admirer of Thomas Paine, the English-American writer whose published writings influenced the American Revolution and the Declaration of Independence. And although the name of the ship, *Indomitable* (in the original manuscript, edited in 1948) was changed to the *Bellipotent* in later versions of the novel, *Indomitable* seems the more compelling name, as it derives from the Latin word *domitare*, which means "to tame." To be indomitable is to be unable to be tamed or conquered—to be uncivilized.

There was much that was uncivilized on Billy's new ship. Billy had been well liked by his previous shipmates and had been fondly called the "peacemaker" by the captain of the *Rights-of-Man*. And although his shipmates on the *Indomitable* took an instant liking to him, there was one notable exception in John Claggart, the master-at-arms, whose envious response to Billy's goodness and physical beauty is described as malign:

> Now envy and antipathy, passions irreconcilable in reason nevertheless in fact may spring conjoined like Chang and Eng in one birth. Is Envy then such a monster? Well, though many an arraigned mortal has in hopes of mitigated penalty pleaded guilty to horrible actions, did ever anybody seriously confess to envy? Something there is in it universally felt to be more shameful than even felonious crime.... But Claggart's was no vulgar form of the passion. Nor, as directed toward Billy Budd, did it partake of that streak of apprehensive jealousy that marred Saul's visage brooding on the comely young David. Claggart's envy struck deeper. If askance he eyed the good looks, cheery health and frank enjoyment of

young life in Billy Budd, it was because these went along with a nature that as Claggart magnetically felt, had in its simplicity never willed malice or experienced the reactionary bite of that serpent. To him the spirit lodged within Billy and looking out from his welkin eyes as from windows, that ineffability it was which made the dimple in his dyed cheek, suppled his joints and dancing in his yellow curls, made him preeminently the Handsome Sailor.... And the insight but intensified his passion, which assuming various secret forms within him, at times assumed that of cynic disdain—disdain of innocence—to be nothing more than innocent.[405]

Melville makes it clear that Claggart has great disdain for Billy's goodness—his innocence—which is "untouched by the bite of the serpent." Melville also makes it clear that Claggart is aware of his own evil nature but has no power to "annul the elemental evil in him, though, readily enough, he could hide it; apprehending the good, but powerless to be it." Early in the novel, readers understand the danger that Claggart's venomous nature posed to Billy, warning that "a nature like Claggart's surcharged with energy as such natures almost invariably are, what recourse is left to it but to recoil upon itself, and like the scorpion for which the Creator alone is responsible, act out to the end of the part allotted it."[406] Claggart's envious hatred of Billy moves him to lie to Captain Vere, alleging that Billy was organizing a mutiny on the ship. When Billy learns of the charges, he is stunned into silence—unable to speak in his own defense. Instead, he strikes out at Claggart with a blow that instantly kills the master-at-arms. Under the Articles of War, killing an officer while at sea during hostilities is punishable by death,

[405] Ibid., 38.
[406] Ibid., 39.

and even though Captain Vere knew that the innocent Billy did not intend to kill Claggart, the dutiful captain exerts pressure on the jury to convict Billy for Claggart's death. Billy is hanged the next morning on the main yardarm—as a "martyr to martial discipline." His final words, "God bless Captain Vere," were echoed by all of those in attendance at the execution.[407] And the wooden yardarm (the spar) from which Billy was hanged was converted into a monument by the men, and "the spar was followed from ship to dockyard and again from dockyard to ship, still pursuing it even when at last reduced to a mere dockyard boom." To those who remained devoted to the fallen sailor, "a chip of it was as a piece of the Cross."[408]

Billy's sacrificial act civilizes his shipmates, prepares them for the battles to come, and as James McBride writes in his *Maryland Law Journal Review* article on *Billy Budd*, "Revisiting a Seminal Text of the Law & Literature Movement," Melville recognizes the pivotal importance of the Protestant cultural milieu of nineteenth-century America and the Christian theological trope of sacrifice. McBride reminds readers that Melville's own religious convictions centered on the Calvinist doctrine of predestination and original sin and concludes that "Billy Budd is faced by human depravity in the form of John Claggart who assumes the 'mantle of respectability.' … Billy is a 'young Adam before the Fall … fated to be sacrificed.'"[409] McBride reminds us—as Girard does also—that although legal scholars tend to think of religion as ancillary to the law, the truth is that religion, in its violent manifestation as a

---

[407] Ibid., 80.

[408] Ibid., 87.

[409] James McBride, "Revisiting a Seminal Text of the Law & Literature Movement: A Girardian Reading of Herman Melville's *Billy Budd, Sailor*," *University of Maryland Law Journal of Race, Religion, Gender and Class* 3, no. 2 (2003): 304.

sacrificial mechanism, not only antedates law but lies in the very recesses of law. For McBride, "the implications of a Girardian reading of Billy Budd are sobering. The state and its agents, whether prosecutors, judges, juries, and even defense attorneys, indeed, even the public at large in whose name the state acts, should recognize that the cases handled by the state have a hidden dimension that eclipses the facts at hand.... The residues of sacrificial violence remain, most particularly in the death penalty.... As Girard writes, each person must ask what his relationship is to the scapegoat."[410]

Girard's theory is a constant reminder that although the Enlightenment supposedly freed us from our religious "superstitions," the sacrificial mechanism—the commitment to the violence perpetrated on the scapegoat—will continue until we are able to find an alternative way to resolve conflict. As McBride suggests in his law-review article, abolishing the death penalty may remove the state's role in the violence, but it will do little to change the current culture of violence. In some ways, it could add to the violence because there will no longer be state-sponsored sacrifices.

Ever the optimist, Girard believed that the gospel message could change hearts and minds by reminding us of the injustice of the scapegoat mechanism. Girard believed that imitating Christ or those he viewed as Christlike models could free us from the envious mimetic desire we have of our rivals. But in a culture in which the gospel message is seldom allowed outside of religious institutions and with few Christlike models to imitate, envy remains a part of our nature as we keep turning one another into rivals desiring the same shiny objects.

Still, there are indeed Christlike models in literature, and it is good to be reminded of that whenever we can. Melville understood that, as did Dostoyevsky and the other great novelists Girard has

[410] Ibid., 329.

identified. In *Billy Budd*, at the end of the novel, as Captain Vere lay dying, the Captain "was heard to murmur words inexplicable to his attendant: 'Billy Budd, Billy Budd.'" We readers are told that "these were not the accents of remorse."[411] Even on his deathbed, Captain Vere understood exactly who had been sacrificed on the *Indomitable*, as did all of the men on that ship. Billy's death on the wooden spar was what Girard might have called "a communication of love" from the peacemaker who invited others into friendship and peace.

---

[411] Melville, *Billy Budd*, 86.

About the Author

Anne Hendershott is Professor of Sociology and Director of the Veritas Center for Ethics in Public Life at Franciscan University in Steubenville, Ohio. She also serves as a Distinguished Visiting Professor at the King's College in New York City and a James Madison Faculty Fellow at Princeton University. A frequent contributor to popular press outlets, including *Crisis*, the *American Spectator*, *Catholic World Report*, and the *Wall Street Journal*, she publishes frequently on issues of importance in the Catholic Church. She is the author of six previous books: *Renewal: How a New Generation of Priests and Bishops are Revitalizing the Church* (Encounter Books, 2013), *Status Envy: The Politics of Catholic Higher Education* (Transaction, 2009), *The Politics of Deviance* (Encounter Books, 2002), *The Politics of Abortion* (Encounter Books, 2006), *The Reluctant Caregivers* (Bergin and Garvey, 2000), and *Moving for Work* (University Press of America, 1994).

CRISIS Publications

Sophia Institute Press awards the privileged title "CRISIS Publications" to a select few of our books that address contemporary issues at the intersection of politics, culture, and the Church with clarity, cogency, and force and that are also destined to become all-time classics.

CRISIS Publications are *direct*, explaining their principles briefly, simply, and clearly to Catholics in the pews, on whom the future of the Church depends. The time for ambiguity or confusion is long past.

CRISIS Publications are *contemporary*, born of our own time and circumstances and intended to become significant statements in current debates, statements that serious Catholics cannot ignore, regardless of their prior views.

CRISIS Publications are *classical*, addressing themes and enunciating principles that are valid for all ages and cultures. Readers will turn to them time and again for guidance in other days and different circumstances.

CRISIS Publications are *spirited*, entering contemporary debates with gusto to clarify issues and demonstrate how those issues can be resolved in a way that enlivens souls and the Church.

We welcome engagement with our readers on current and future CRISIS Publications. Please pray that this imprint may help to resolve the crises embroiling our Church and society today.